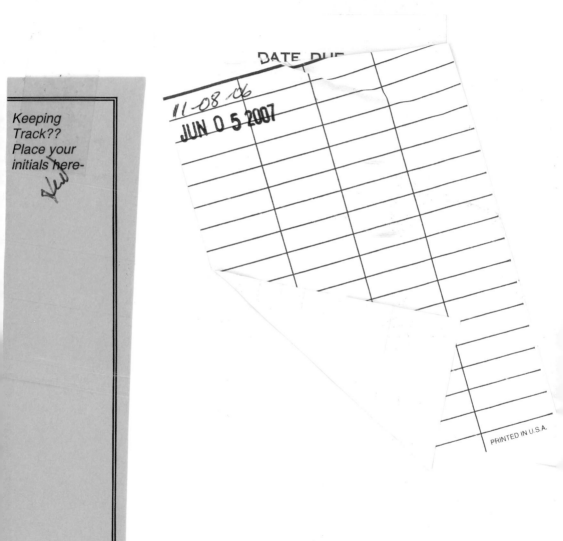

DATE DUE

11-08-06

JUN 0 5 2007

PRINTED IN U.S.A.

Democracy in Iran

Democracy in Iran

History and the Quest for Liberty

ALI GHEISSARI

VALI NASR

OXFORD
UNIVERSITY PRESS

2006

Oxford University Press, Inc., publishes works that further
Oxford University's objective of excellence
in research, scholarship, and education.

Oxford   New York
Auckland   Cape Town   Dar es Salaam   Hong Kong   Karachi
Kuala Lumpur   Madrid   Melbourne   Mexico City   Nairobi
New Delhi   Shanghai   Taipei   Toronto

With offices in
Argentina   Austria   Brazil   Chile   Czech Republic   France   Greece
Guatemala   Hungary   Italy   Japan   Poland   Portugal   Singapore
South Korea   Switzerland   Thailand   Turkey   Ukraine   Vietnam

Published by Oxford University Press, Inc.
198 Madison Avenue, New York, New York 10016

www.oup.com

Oxford is a registered trademark of Oxford University Press

Library of Congress Cataloging-in-Publication Data
Gheissari, Ali, 1954–
Democracy in Iran : history and the quest for liberty / Ali Gheissari, Vali Nasr.
    p. cm.
Includes bibliographical references and index.
ISBN-13 978-0-19-518967-4
ISBN 0-19-518967-1
1. Iran—Politics and government—20th century.   2. Democracy—Iran.
I. Nasr, Seyyed Vali Reza, 1960–   II. Title.
DS316.6.G47 2006
955.05—dc22   2005031799

9 8 7 6 5 4 3 2 1

Printed in the United States of America
on acid-free paper

Preface

In June 2005, Iranians went to the polls to elect a new president. This was the ninth presidential election and thirty-seventh national election since Iran's 1979 revolution. The intensely contested race also marked the third transition of the presidency in the post-Khomeini period and the election of the first nonclerical president since 1981. Over the course of the past twenty-five years elections have become increasingly important to distribution of power in Iranian politics. Although the most important leader of the country, the Supreme Leader, is unelected and is not subject to checks and balances of a democratic order, voting still decides the direction of popular political debates and influences policymaking. It also affects distribution of power and political offices at the national level and increasingly so at the local level as well. Elections now influence distribution of resources among various provinces on the one hand, and urban and rural areas on the other. They decide the relative power of various social groups and political forces; both reflect and determine the scope of political, cultural, and economic debates in the country.

Iran has been an improbable candidate for the flowering of democracy. The 1979 revolution created the only Islamic state to result from a successful Islamic fundamentalist drive for power. Revolutionary zeal and Islamic ideology were hostile to democracy and looked to an all-powerful state that would reflect revolutionary values as the embodiment and guarantor of an idealized Islamic order. Still, in many regards there is more progress toward democracy in Iran than in any other country in the Middle East, perhaps with the exception of Turkey. Over the course of the past two and a half decades Iranians have embraced democratic practices, participated in elections at local and national levels, and believed that their vote affects political outcomes. Iranians begin to vote at the age of fifteen, and an entire generation has now been schooled in the rudiments of voting and electioneering, in the give-and-take of promises by politicians and votes by their constituents, and above all in both the lofty ideals of democracy and the more mundane mechanics of democratic practice. The Iranian constitution vests sovereignty in God, but Iranian politicians look to the people for their mandate. All this has produced not a democratic state but a citizenry that understands the fundamental logic of democracy and the laws that govern its practice. Iranians do not live in a democracy, but their politics are increasingly informed and influenced by its foundational logic.

Democracy in Iran was not the declared goal of the Islamic Revolution but was an unintended consequence of its unfolding. As the new president, Mahmoud Ahmadinejad, said on his campaign trail, "We did not have a revolution in order to have democracy."[1] However, to be president, he had to win the election. Democracy in Iran was neither a project of the state nor imported as an ideal form of politics from the West and implemented from above, but has rather emerged as a grassroots phenomenon, so that democratic thinking and political expectations are prevalent in society and now serve as the main impetus for continued struggle toward democratic change. The challenge facing democratization in developing countries is that political reforms from above often do not grow roots because the society has not embraced democratic values and practice.

Democratic politics cannot take hold where the political culture has not internalized both the values and the practical components of democracy, and where the attitude of the people toward authority does not reflect such values and commitments. In Iran, conversely, it is the democratic attitudes in society rather than reforms from above that account for progress toward democracy. This is an important development that sets Iran apart from its Middle Eastern neighbors. Although state behavior in Iran does not normatively reflect democratic values, in many regards Iranian society has already turned the corner, passing through a more challenging threshold of democratization, by adopting the democratic ethos at the grassroots level and looking to civil society activism and elections to voice social and political demands. It is this fact that makes Iran the more likely candidate for veritable democracy in the Middle East, despite the country's theocratic edifice and authoritarian power structure. How an Islamic state in Iran has moved farther along the path of democracy than many secular states in the Middle East raises important questions.

The seeming paradox of the Iranian case has to do with the complexity of Iran's struggle with democracy, one that spans a century and that involves broad questions of state-building, social development, cultural change, and individual freedoms. Although the struggle for democracy has gained momentum in the past decade, its roots run deep in contemporary Iranian history. The 2005 presidential election elucidates this point as it encompasses not only the current struggle for political and cultural freedoms but also historical debates over state-society relations and the desired path to development. Two issues dominated the election. First, the demand for political reform and cultural opening, which means empowering the society and reducing state power. Second, the demand for the state to solve socioeconomic problems, which means strengthening state institutions and extending the purview of their decision making. The election in a way highlighted the fundamental problem of democratization, how to maintain balance in state-society relations to both foster democracy and enable the state to address social demands. This problem has been at the heart of state-building and the quest for democracy over the course of the past century. How Iran has responded to this challenge, and how it will continue to do so from this point forward is instructive for the study of democratization. The challenge facing Iran today, as it was a century ago when the country promulgated its first constitution, is how to bring together the quest for democracy and the imperatives of state-building to create a democratic state. This book chronicles how Iran has contended with this challenge, and what the legacy of that effort means for our understanding of democracy and its manifestation in the Muslim world.

This book is not a comprehensive political history of modern Iran, although it does rely on historical facts and analysis. It is conceived in consideration of Iran's struggle to become a democratic state, and therefore focuses on those themes that highlight that struggle and its outcome. The main thread that runs through the analytical narrative is how Iran has responded to the challenge of balancing state-building with democracy-building. This approach allows us to look at Iran's historical experience over the course of the past century from a very different angle, bringing new perspective to analyzing and understanding the vicissitudes of continuity and change, success and failures, and the unique path to both state-building and democracy-building that has emerged in Iran. The result is a new approach for understanding state-society relations in Iran over the expanse of the country's modern history, one that seeks to highlight overarching themes and long-term trends that will allow us to organize facts around a framework of analysis that goes beyond mere chronology of events. The idea of this book grew out of continued discussions that we have had over the nature of state and society in Iran, the role of religion in politics, and the contest between ideology and democracy in modern Iranian history.

Many of the issues raised in this book were presented at academic seminars at Tehran University, Harvard University, UCLA, Georgetown University, MIT, and Oxford University. We are grateful for comments by colleagues on those occasions. We are further grateful to Ervand Abrahamian, Kaveh Ehsani, Ali Moazzami, and Ali Rahnema for their comments. We would also like to thank Cynthia Read and Theo Calderara, our editors at Oxford University Press, for their interest in this book, Christine Dahlin, Karla Pace, and Julia TerMaat for assistance with the book's production, and Norma McLemore for copyediting the text.

We have avoided most diacritical marks and have used a more phonetic pattern closer to the current Persian pronunciation. Established words and names in English are Anglicized. All translations are by the authors unless otherwise stated. The references in this book provide sources for observations and facts but also direct the reader to other relevant works on the topic. In addition, in this book we use terms such as *fundamentalism, theocracy,* or *cleric* in the manner in which they are used commonly in both academia and the media. Although there has been extensive debate over the use of the term *fundamentalism,* it has now gained sufficient currency—especially since the literal translation of the word as *Osoulgarai* (and *Bonyadgarai*) is widely used in Persian, especially by those to whom the term actually refers. Similarly, we use the terms *cleric* and *theocracy* in the manner in which they are widely used to describe the role of the ulama in Iranian politics.

Contents

Chronology

1501–1722	Safavid dynasty and establishment of Shi'ism as the state religion of Iran.
1794–1925	Qajar dynasty.
1848–96	Reign of Naser al-Din Shah Qajar.
1891–92	Nationwide protest against the tobacco concession to a British company results in its cancellation.
1896–1907	Reign of Mozaffar al-Din Shah Qajar.
1901	William Knox D'Arcy, a British subject, acquires a sixty-year oil concession in southwestern Iran.
1906	Constitutional Revolution; Iran is granted a parliament (Majles).
1906–9	Reign of Mohammad-Ali Shah Qajar.
1907	Anglo-Russian agreement dividing Iran into spheres of influence.
1908 June 23	Bombardment of the Majles and restoration of autocracy.
1909 April	The Anglo-Persian Oil Company is founded.

July	Regaining of Tehran by the constitutionalist forces and restoration of the constitutional government.
1909–25	Reign of Ahmad Shah Qajar.
1910–11	Occupation of northern Iran by Russian forces and reversal of constitutionalists' reforms.
1914–18	First World War; Iran declares neutrality.
1919	Anglo-Persian Agreement, giving the British broad political, economic, and military control over Iran, meets with nationalist opposition and is not ratified by the Majles.
1921	Military commander Reza Khan stages a coup and overthrows the government. Reza Khan becomes Army Commander, and subsequently Minister of War.
1923	Reza Khan becomes prime minister.
1925	A constituent assembly rules to abolish the Qajar dynasty and establish the Pahlavi dynasty with Reza Khan as monarch.
1925–41	Reign of Reza Shah Pahlavi: formation of a centralized bureaucratic state, initiating broad range of civil and legal reforms and educational, industrial, and economic modernization.
1927	European dress codes imposed.
1935	Formerly known as Persia, Iran is adopted as the country's official name.
1936	Abolition of the veil.
1939–45	Second World War; Iran declares neutrality.
1941	Allied invasion and occupation of Iran leads to Reza Shah's abdication in favor of his son, Mohammad-Reza Pahlavi.
1941–79	Reign of Mohammad-Reza Shah Pahlavi.
1946	Ousting of a Soviet-backed separatist movement in Azerbaijan Province.
1951	Popular campaign in favor of the renegotiation of Anglo-Iranian oil agreement. Mohammad Mosaddeq, lead-

ing the call for nationalization of oil, becomes prime minister. Oil nationalization bill is ratified by the Majles.

1953   A military coup with British and American backing overthrows Mosaddeq and his National Front government. General Fazlollah Zahedi is appointed prime minister by the Shah.

1954   Iran signs a new oil agreement with Western oil companies.

1963   The Shah launches wide-ranging social and economic reforms known as the "White Revolution." Enfranchisement of women and land reform met with public protest led by Ayatollah Rouhollah Khomeini. Riots were suppressed and Khomeini was arrested.

1964   Khomeini exiled, first to Turkey and then to Iraq.

1964–71   Rapid industrialization of the Iranian economy: Iran achieves some of the highest manufacturing growth rates in the Third World. Modernization of state institutions and the armed forces and centralization of development planning.

1965   Prime minister Hasan-Ali Mansour assassinated; Amir-Abbas Hoveyda is appointed prime minister.

1967   Coronation of the Shah.

1971   The Shah celebrates 2,500 years of Iranian monarchy.

1973   Iran plays an instrumental role in OPEC oil price hike, leading to a substantial increase in government revenue.

1975   Foundation of Rastakhiz Party.

1977   Jamshid Amuzegar is appointed prime minister.

1978 January   U.S. President Jimmy Carter praises Iran as the "island of stability" in the region. Article critical of Ayatollah Khomeini published in *Ettela'at* newspaper leads to anti-regime riots in major cities.

August   Martial law is declared in Isfahan. Jafar Sharif-Emami is appointed prime minister.

September   Martial law is declared in Tehran. Hundreds are killed by the security forces at Jaleh Square (Black Friday).

October	Khomeini is forced to leave Iraq and goes to Paris.
November	General Gholam-Reza Azhari is appointed prime minister and forms a military government. From Paris, Khomeini promises the formation of an Islamic Republic in Iran.
December	Massive demonstrations against the Shah during the Muslim month of Muharram. Shapur Bakhtiar is appointed prime minister.
1979 January	The Shah leaves Iran.
February	Ayatollah Khomeini returns to Iran and appoints Mehdi Bazargan prime minister of the Provisional Government. Bakhtiar goes into hiding. Overthrow of the Pahlavi dynasty and the end of the monarchy.
April 1	The Islamic Republic of Iran is proclaimed following a referendum.
October	The Shah is admitted to the United States for medical treatment.
November 4	U.S. embassy in Tehran is occupied and its personnel taken hostage. Bazargan resigns.
December	Ratification of the Constitution of the Islamic Republic of Iran by national referendum.
1980 January	Abol-Hasan Bani-Sadr is elected the first president of the Islamic Republic.
May	Elections for the Islamic Republic's first Majles completed.
June	A failed coup attempt against the Islamic Republic. Cultural Revolution begins, leading to purges in educational institutions.
July	The exiled Shah dies of cancer in Egypt.
September 22	Iraq invades Iran; beginning of an eight-year war.
1981 January 20	U.S. hostages are freed during the presidential inauguration of Ronald Reagan.
June	Bani-Sadr is dismissed and flees to France.

July	Mohammad-Ali Rajai is elected president, and Mohammad-Javad Bahonar is appointed prime minister.
August	Assassinations of Rajai and Bahonar.
October	Seyyed Ali Khamenei is elected president.
1982 May	Iran recaptures occupied territory, including the port city of Khorramshahr.
1985 August	Khamenei is elected president for a second term.
1988 August	Iran and Iraq accept a UN resolution for a cease-fire.
1989 February	Iran announces that in a religious edict (fatwa) Ayatollah Khomeini has sanctioned the killing of Salman Rushdie, the author of *The Satanic Verses*, a book considered blasphemous to Islam.
June 3	Khomeini dies. On June 4 Khamenei is appointed as Supreme Leader.
July	Ali-Akbar Hashemi-Rafsanjani is elected president and is sworn in on August 17.
1989–97	Presidency of Rafsanjani: government and economic reform, postwar reconstruction and development.
1990	Iran condemns Iraq's invasion of Kuwait but declares neutrality in the Second Persian Gulf War.
September	Iran and Iraq resume diplomatic relations.
1991 August	Bakhtiar is assassinated in Paris.
1993 June	Rafsanjani is reelected president for a second term.
1995	The United States imposes oil and trade sanctions against Iran for allegedly sponsoring terrorism, seeking to acquire nuclear arms, and opposing the Middle East peace process.
1997 May	Seyyed Mohammad Khatami is elected president.
1997–2005	Presidency of Khatami: attempted political and cultural reforms, emphasis on civil society institutions and dialogue among civilizations, recurrent tension with the conservatives, conservative consolidation.

1998 September	Iran deploys troops on its border with Afghanistan after the Taliban kill eight Iranian diplomats and a journalist in Mazar-e Sharif.
1999 July	Pro-democracy students at Tehran University hold a demonstration protesting the closure of a reformist newspaper.
2000 February	Reformist supporters of Khatami win 170 of the 290 seats in the sixth Majles elections.
April	The judiciary bans the publication of several reformist newspapers.
May	Inauguration of the sixth Majles, dominated by reformists.
2001 June	Khatami is reelected president for a second term.
2002 January	U.S. President George W. Bush describes Iran as part of an "axis of evil."
September	Russian technicians begin construction of Iran's first nuclear reactor at Bushehr despite strong objections from the United States.
2003 September	UN nuclear watchdog International Atomic Energy Association (IAEA) requests Iran to prove it is not pursuing an atomic weapons program. Iran's nuclear program becomes the focus of an international crisis.
October	Lawyer and human rights campaigner Shirin Ebadi becomes Iran's first Nobel Peace Prize winner.
November	Iran signs Sa'dabad Agreement with Britain, France, and Germany, accepting to suspend its uranium enrichment program and to allow tougher UN inspection of its nuclear facilities.
2004 February and May	Thousands of reformist candidates disqualified by the conservative Guardian Council before the parliamentary elections, leading to a conservative victory in the seventh Majles.
June	IAEA rebukes Iran for failing to cooperate with inquiries into its nuclear activities.
November	Iran agrees to suspend most of its uranium enrichment as part of a deal with the European Union.

2005 June

Mahmoud Ahmadinejad, Tehran's conservative mayor, is elected president, pledging populist economic policies and a more militant foreign policy posture.

August

Tehran says it has resumed the conversion of uranium and insists the program is for peaceful purposes.

2006 February

IAEA votes to refer Iran to the UN Security Council over its nuclear program.

Democracy in Iran

Introduction

Over the course of the past two and a half decades Iran has produced a unique path to state-building—one that has attempted to incorporate Islamic values in a modern state and to place the ulama in charge of development. The paradoxes of the Islamic Republic in Iran have put into question many assumptions about the secularity of modernization, the relation of Islam to state power, and the relation of Islam and the state to democracy and development. Born of a social revolution, the theocratic edifice of the Islamic Republic has nevertheless produced a pragmatic authoritarian regime. That regime speaks in the language of Islam but rules over society and economy in ways that are familiar to political observers in developing societies.

Iran's more recent experience with state-building is the culmination of a longer political process that has spanned a century. That process has shaped the context in which contestations of power currently unfold. Iran's path to state-building fits neither the pattern of state formation in Europe nor that of the colonial/postcolonial state model.[1] In Iran, the state was not the product of war, taxation, or colonialism. Iran's case is to be understood on its own terms and in the context of sociopolitical developments that shaped it.

In the past century, Iran has produced a modernizing state as well as an Islamic one and has lived under monarchy and theocracy; the country has experimented with constitutionalism, developmentalism, revolution, and calls for democratization. It has debated the costs and benefits of order and prosperity, freedom and progress, and the need for strong institutions to achieve such goals. In the process it has had to balance democratic aspirations with requirements of development and demands of maintaining national sovereignty and territorial integrity. It has also had to contend with social turmoil, foreign occupation, imperialism, wars, and coups. Iran is the first and only country to have experienced an Islamic revolution, the first and only country to have lived under an actual Islamic fundamentalist state, and the first to have moved on to postfundamentalism.

Iran has done well with state-building and development over the course of the past century, but has not done as well with sustaining and promoting democracy. What has eluded Iranians is the Holy Grail of a democratic state—development and state-building without sacrificing democratic rights. Although achieving statehood and prosperity has been the primary goal of every developing society, achieving a democratic state marks a balanced realization of the development process. To illustrate this, Francis Fukuyama writes that "before you have democracy you must have a state, but to have a legitimate and durable state you eventually must have democracy."[2]

Grappling with this dilemma has shaped Iran's political formation. In 1906, Iranians committed themselves to promoting rule of law and holding political authority accountable to popular will, but citizens soon found out that to realize their constitutionalist dreams they first needed a viable state. By the mid-1920s they managed to build one despite overwhelming odds against them, but they failed to place restraints on the state's exercise of power. As the state became more authoritarian by the late 1930s it also became less durable: a pattern that repeated itself in the latter part of the twentieth century, culminating in the fall of the Pahlavi monarchy to the Islamic Revolution in 1979. Today Iranians seek to restrain the exercise of state power by the Islamic Republic, and to balance their democratic demands and state-building to achieve a durable state that can pursue development and provide security and order in tandem with protecting individual rights and the rule of law. How Iranians have arrived at this juncture and what prevented them from striking this balance earlier is the primary concern of this book, which also makes the Iranian case directly relevant to debates on state and democracy in the social sciences.

During the past century, the state not only grew in power and capacity, but also was able to consolidate the Iranian polity and confirm Iran's territorial integrity and its identity as a nation-state, so much so that although Iran's social and ethnic diversity resembles that of many other Middle Eastern and South Asian countries, it does not confront the same degree of challenges to its existing borders. State-building gave Iran strong institutions and development, but not democracy. That failure has tarnished state-building whether under the Pahlavis or the Islamic Republic. It has also posed challenges to the state's durability. For the Iranian state to become durable, it must be democratic. To identify those factors that matter in success or failure of creating a democratic state we must take into consideration not only the pattern of state-building, but also the trials and tribulations of democracy in the context of state-building.

The Specter of Democracy in Iran

In the May 26, 1997, presidential elections, millions of Iranians defied the wishes of the Supreme Leader of the Islamic Republic, Ayatollah Seyyed Ali Khamenei. Instead of electing his preferred candidate, Ali-Akbar Nateq-Nouri, Iranians elected a lesser known but reformist cleric with experience in public office, Seyyed Mohammad Khatami, to the presidency. For the overwhelming majority of the Iranian electorate, Khatami's promises during the presidential campaign to protect individual rights and promote democratic practices suggested a new day in Iranian politics—the beginning of the end of dogmatic theocracy and concrete steps in the direction of establishing democracy in the country, albeit under the rubric of the Islamic Republic. That the election results stood unchallenged and Khatami's first term in office brought about greater press freedoms further encouraged the expectation of change. However, Khatami's promises were not matched by his policies and less so by the room available to him to maneuver, and his presidency never managed to capitalize on its moment of triumph in 1997. The Islamic Republic's conservative leadership resisted political reform and successfully frustrated pro-democracy voices in their attempt to pry open the political system.

This meant that the presidency was not likely to serve as the vehicle for democratization, and it was futile to look to the Islamic Republic to bestow the gift of democracy on the population. The values and demands of democracy would have to be elaborated outside of the purview of the revolution's ideals as interpreted by the Constitution of the Islamic Republic.[3] Hence, it became imperative to seek not Islamic democracy, just democracy.[4]

In the years since 1997, the demand for democracy has been focused on demands for a republic, plain and simple, "without suffix or prefix."[5] This demand clearly challenges the notion of the Islamic state, which at the time of its founding was also characterized simply as the Islamic Republic. Some two and a half decades after Ayatollah Khomeini refused to dilute the idea of the Islamic Republic by adding the term "democratic" to it, pro-democracy forces refuse to obscure democracy by adding "Islamic." Iranian politics has thus come full circle, embracing the idea of democracy, which it had eschewed at the moment of enthusiasm for ideological utopias of the 1979 revolution.

In recent years Iranians have sought to alter the balance of power between state and society, subjecting state power to the rule of law while empowering civil society. Less interest has been shown in accommodating the utopian ideals and values of the Islamic Republic; instead more support has been displayed for the sober realization that democracy as an ideal and a movement cannot coexist with the kind of absolute truths and utopianism that lay at the heart of the Islamic Revolution of 1979 and the regime that it spawned. The demand for straightforward democracy was initially echoed in intellectual circles and is now permeating popular political culture. However, the absence of a functioning democracy in Iran today stands in direct contrast to the strength of the demands for it and, more important, the sophistication and maturity of the ideas that such demands have generated.

Democracy is not a new idea in modern Iranian history and politics and it is not merely a reaction to the excesses of the Islamic Republic. It is an old idea with a complex history: one that is tightly interwoven with the history of the modern state in Iran, and the main forces that have shaped Iranian society and politics, and their corresponding institutions, identities, and interests in the twentieth century. The demand for democracy first surfaced more than a century ago at the latter part of the Qajar period to help produce Iran's first constitution in 1906.[6] That constitution was notably a liberal and democratic document, one that provided lasting standards for debates on state and democracy in Iran.

The common conceptions of democracy and how Iranians have envisioned democratization—as a separate and yet interrelated concept and process—are closely tied to the central themes of Iran's history and politics since the Constitutional Revolution of 1906–1911. Most notably, the demand has evolved in reaction to the rise of the modern state in Iran and to its continuous and unabated domination over society and economy. The state has featured prominently in the development of Iranian society, politics, and economy, and in the emergence of its bureaucratic institutions, national identity, and ideologies of expressing discontent. In the crucible of state domination, democracy served as an imaginary witness to negate the state's tendency to act in arbitrary ways. Democracy encapsulated both the promise of the state and the opposition that it had spawned.

Despite the salience of the quest for democracy, democratization as a process whereby state leaders negotiate with social forces to devolve power from state institutions to democratic ones never happened in Iran. Opposition to authoritarianism precipitated conflicts that ended with suppression of prodemocracy voices and the collapse of the state to a revolution that in time strengthened state power. The failure of democracy in Iran arose out of an absence of factors—social, economic, and political—that would have necessitated negotiation and ensured the success of democracy. Thus the fact that democracy has been important in Iran but democratization has eluded the country cannot be solely explained in terms of the character and interests of individual leaders or movements; the absence of the proper context for transfer of power from state to democratic institutions must also be considered.

For much of the past century, democracy has been associated with and confused with nationalism, populism, social justice, or religious reform. It has at times been equated with the rule of law, accountability of the state, and the demand for individual rights, and at other times with the collective rights of the nation. It has embodied the demand for freedom and liberation from the state and then from imperialism. Democracy has been used as an all-encompassing slogan that has provided the veneer for the myriad of ideals and struggles that have shaped modern Iranian history and politics. It may not be possible to fully portray what democracy and democratization mean to Iranians, and how they came to occupy their current place in Iran's politics without taking note of the manner in which democracy has intertwined with other ideals and demands, and how it has both shaped and been shaped by these ideals and demands. In the Iranian political imagination, the meaning and intent of democracy have changed over the decades to encompass different values and promote different goals. Democracy, once seen as a demand for the rule of law and quest for social justice, nationalism, progress, and modernity, has come to denote cultural and intellectual freedoms, revolutionary liberation, religious reform, and individual rights.

Iran's development has unfolded in tandem with and as a consequence of the rise and empowerment of the state. A strong state in Iran denied democracy room to grow but also strengthened the demand for it. The very success of the state created a yearning for political rights but also focused attention on what must follow the triumph of the state. The story of democracy in Iran is therefore the story of Iranian politics since 1905.

Rethinking Iranian History in the Twentieth Century

Recent studies of modern Iranian history and politics have been conditioned by the Islamic Revolution of 1979. Many studies adopt the premise that the revolution occurred at a teleological moment that would make sense of all past history. Thus all evidence and analysis must necessarily point to the revolution and try to explain it, usually by taking the revolution's claims about the Pahlavi period at face value. By proceeding in this way, the discipline of Iranian studies has relied on explanations of state collapse and social mobilization from theories of revolution, on explanations of culture from Modernization Theory, or on explanations of socioeconomic imbalances, anti-imperialism, and cleavages of class and culture from neo-Marxist historiography. There is heuristic value in fitting Iran into these theoretical frameworks, but it can also detract from analyzing the intricacies of the Iran case, and if taken individually, these frameworks lead to overemphasis on those aspects of Iranian experience that best fit the corresponding theories. As such, Iran's history in the twentieth century has been depicted as being shaped by autocracy, uneven development, and imperialism, resulting in nationalist, leftist, Islamic fundamentalist, and liberal democratic opposition to the state. Although these approaches tell part of the story and have significantly contributed to the analysis of modern Iranian history, their explanatory value is limited by certain restrictions inherent in their guiding frameworks.

One such restriction arises because all political ideals and struggles tend to be viewed as manifestations of the conflict between society and state. This binary outlook does not adequately explain the complex ways in which state goals and social ideals converge in order to produce certain political outcomes, or more generally to define continuities and changes in national debates. Nor does this outlook shed light on inherent tensions that existed in the opposition to the Pahlavi regime between claims of democratic idealism and ideological posturing. The Iranian revolution marked the pinnacle of utopianism in Iranian politics. These tensions reflected the interplay of ideals with political realities and tell of a richer intellectual and political history than is obtained from narrating the conflict between the society and state. The revolution and what followed can be better understood by paying attention to the dynamics of competition between democracy and ideology in the decades before the revolution. Understanding that dynamic will also help explain the transformation of Iran since 1988.

The focus on the revolution has introduced such a degree of determinism into the study of Iranian history and politics that some have even argued that the Pahlavi regime (1925–1979) did not reflect Iranian political ideals and hence was necessarily headed for a dead end; what change the Pahlavis brought about is viewed as merely "pseudo-modernism." The assumptions on which these approaches rely have spawned formulas that, in turn, took on the quality of "open sesame," as David Blackbourn and Geoff Eley put it in describing a similar tendency in German historiography, "cropping up again and again in monographs, articles, books . . . [indicating] unreflectiveness," and leading to a hegemony of sorts.[7] The overemphasis on the negative has produced a tunnel vision that cannot acknowledge or include important nuances in assessing developments if they deviate from the established view. The result is therefore a simplified and predetermined view of events, a sort of cul de sac history in which the concatenation of events all point to the same conclusion. It is important to place the revolution of 1979 in its proper historical context: neither as end nor culmination of a historical process, but rather as an interregnum in a longer process of state-building that began in 1905 and is still unfolding.

Why Study State and Democracy in Iran?

Three decades ago, any observer of Iran would have looked to nationalism, Islam, or Marxism as the forces that mattered in Iranian society and politics. Democracy was not the focus of intellectual debates, and there was little systematic discussion of democracy in the books and articles that shaped Iranian studies or the Iranian political mind-set. Although the Lawyers Association and supporters of the National Front's old platform spoke of democracy, they never elaborated on a par with the discussion that the Left and religious activists stimulated for their own ideological tenets. As a result, vocal dissident forces, such as various groups within the student movement that could have been expected to advocate democracy, showed little concern with it.

What has changed over the past two to three decades to make the current situation noticeably different? Iran has experimented with ideologies, leftist as well as Islamist, and people are now weary of these ideologies' unending and unrealizable utopias and paucity of tangible results. Nationalism has been a widely shared political creed, but there has been little consensus as to who speaks for it, what it really means, what it can say about the country's future, and how politics can achieve it. Marxist utopianism inspired the Iranian revolution with an egalitarianism that in turn influenced the Islamic revolutionary order. However, as the revolution came of age, little survived of utopian expectations. Unlike much of the Muslim world, Iran has little confidence in the slogan "Islam is the solution." In Iran, the experience with the Islamic Republic has made Islam, from a political standpoint, part of the problem and not the solution. In fact, Iranians today shy away from adhering to utopian solutions. Iran's politics is unique in the Muslim world in that it is postrevolutionary: it has tried a revolution and has now moved past its promises. This move has been viewed by many as political maturity; they view revolutionary utopianism as akin to an adolescent idealism that is now outgrown.

In part because so many political tropes and "-isms" have fallen by the wayside, democracy as a political ideal and system of government has survived by default as the primary candidate in which to anchor state ideology. Democracy's resilience, however, is more than a matter of default. The idea of democracy in Iran was initially conceptualized and articulated at the time of the Constitutional Revolution. In subsequent decades, it was occluded by other considerations that captured Iranian political imagination. Democracy, however, never ceased to inspire Iranian political aspirations, even if it had to share the limelight with other ideals. Throughout, democracy interacted with and evolved in response to other forces that shaped society and politics. The demand for democracy that has surfaced in Iran today is deeply informed by all the other ideological and political struggles that have shaped Iran's history since 1905. It is not an idea or a movement sui generis, rather it is both a formative force in Iranian history and its product. It has been a window into the shaping of modern Iran since the first decade of the twentieth century.

In the century since the Constitutional Revolution, the Iranian society and economy have undergone profound changes. Iranians have increasingly become city dwellers and employees in the public sector. Urbanization has brought greater literacy, cultural change, and the decline of old social classes and emergence and growth of new ones. Iranian society has also become younger and more ethnically integrated, and it has witnessed greater participation by women in public life. Iran's economy has become more sophisticated, and that has deeply affected various social strata. Continuities and changes in Iranian political ideals reflect these changes. The appeal of democracy goes beyond its promise of individual freedom. Democracy also promises greater representation of Iran's social diversity in its politics, which makes it critical to the durability of the state.

What all this suggests for those who study democratization is that the way in which the ideals of democracy flourish and manifest themselves in a given society are very much a product of the specific exigencies and dynamics of politics in that society. More important, those ideals, far from being constants, change over time and interact with other ideals that are themselves products of political struggles. Although democratic aspirations and concepts in one society can inspire democratic quest in another, on the whole democracy is not a self-contained set of ideas that can be imported from the outside and implemented; it is not divorced from the historical context of a polity. By the same token, the staying power of democracy and its ability to grow roots in the consciousness of a people is a function of its arduous and at times circuitous development in the political system.

Iran and Theories of State-Building

State-building is the most important goal any society faces.[8] States provide the institutional framework for national integration, political formation, and development. They maintain order and deliver social services and public goods ranging from health care and education to security and defense. States control policymaking, regulate public and private spheres, and collect and distribute resources.[9] The socioeconomic goals that define politics in modern times cannot be achieved without a viable state. The nature of states and the scope of their powers are determined by how they perform their functions. States are, however, also loci of power and as such are defined by how they dominate society, politics, and the economy.

State power has been determined by the imperative of mobilizing resources and distributing them in society. States have risen organically out of wars and the tax collection that wars necessitate.[10] In the case of developing countries, war and taxation have not been as important as the demand for institutions that can provide order, stability, and development.[11] Here state-building has been by design, driven by the goals of national integration and development. The formation of institutions gives states the capacity to deliver on social demands, but when not checked with constitutional constraints, institutions allow states to dominate politics and exercise arbitrary power. It is the latter that accounts for the failure of development to produce democracy. The challenge is building states that can accomplish what is demanded of them without overwhelming society and while living within the normative boundaries of pluralism.

How much states can accomplish, and how much of the lives of their citizenry they control is a reflection of their power and capacity.[12] Marxist and *étatiste* theories equate state power with how much jurisdiction it has and how able it is to extract and distribute resources—in other words, with how successful it is at formulating and implementing policy while maintaining autonomy from social classes and interest groups.[13] Organizational theories have approached the issue differently, equating state power with its ability to give coherence to state institutions and to organize and manage interest groups without yielding to pluralism.[14] Other theories place emphasis on the state's ability to use force and to penetrate and dominate its society, focusing on the state's coercive abilities. However, the scope of the state's control of society, the economy, and the lives of its citizens does not reflect its ability to effectively formulate and implement policy. States can be large but get little done, or they can be small and (ideally) accomplish much.[15] The postrevolutionary state in Iran grew in size and in its control of society, but its ability to formulate coherent policies and to implement them effectively declined.

States grow in relation to their sociopolitical context. They face a multitude of imperatives that vary from one state to another. However, every state is concerned with security, hegemony, legitimacy, revenue generation, tax collection, and economic growth.[16] In Iran, too, the modern state developed out of the demand for preserving territorial sovereignty and providing order and development at a time when political decay and foreign intrigue threatened the very existence of the country. Institutional formation gave the state capacity and domination, and that allowed the state to routinely defy constitutional constraints on its exercise of power.

The struggle between state and society in Iran did not always favor the state. The unbridled rise of the state that began in 1921 was interrupted by the Islamic Revolution in 1979, and for a while the revolution both changed the dynamics of state-society relations and transformed the character of both. Revolutions are cataclysmic events that mark the failure of state institutions to contain social and political mobilization.[17] Theorists have debated the relative importance of the collapse of state authority and the concerted challenge from organized social movements.[18] Social discontent and its ability to challenge the state is a function of both the gravity of social inequities[19] and, more important, the successful channeling of discontent and opposition into social action under a defining ideology.[20] The rise and fall of the Pahlavi state provides an important case study for this discussion.[21]

Revolutions produce wide-scale social change and impart new forms of politics that redefine state-society relations.[22] Revolutionary orders are characterized by violence and purges, which empower previously disenfranchised social classes and bring about major changes to the economy, culture, and structures of power and politics. How these changes occur, which actors control them, and what factors determine their ebbs and flows have varied. Iran's Islamic fundamentalist revolution provides important insights into the flow of revolutionary politics and also provides some distinctions. The Iranian revolution's transfer of power, for example, bore certain similarities to transfers of power after Marxist revolutions in Russia, China, and Latin America, but its Islamic tenor placed greater emphasis on culture and identity as the fulcrum for change.[23]

Although the rise of the state in Iran was interrupted by war, revolution, and political change, the continued demands for institutions that would provide the preservation of territorial integrity, maintenance of order, and sustainable development came to favor state power and capacity. However, the Faustian bargain with the state did not mean that demand for democracy ceased to constitute a political ideal and potential. Democratic aspirations continued to inspire politics, just as success in state-building encouraged development and provided order and territorial sovereignty. The continuous struggle to reconcile state-building with calls for democracy accounts for much of the fluctuation of Iranian politics in the twentieth century; the study of this process in turn sheds light on the dynamics of democratization.

Iran and Theories of Democratization

Why and when democracy arises, and the politically and intellectually challenging issues that determine its success or failure have been the subject of much discussion in the social sciences. Barrington Moore saw the emergence of democracy as a product of a long historical process in which axial shifts in state-society relations change the balance of power among dominant classes, political institutions, and social forces.[24] Building on Moore's work, but also narrowing its historical focus, the New Institutionalism school and the political-economic theories of democratization have placed great importance on the balance of power between state and social institutions in determining democratic outcomes.[25] Attention has particularly focused, in these theories, on the role of state institutions and leaders in opening the political process to the civil society, negotiating constitutional frameworks, shaping the contours of democracy, and deciding whether democratic politics takes root. Here successful democratization arises from power sharing between states that cannot dominate the political process and social forces that can successfully resist their leaders' unitary exercise of authority. States become compelled to share power pursuant to economic or political crises that deeply disturb the status quo and necessitate inclusion of greater numbers in the political process. Such a process can involve intricate negotiations over power that determine the shape of the new system.[26]

Other theorists have focused on prerequisites and modalities of democratization, emphasizing socioeconomic factors in explaining the success or failure of democratization.[27] Samuel Huntington sees democratization as a function of social change—including religious reform, economic progress, and growth of a stable middle class. In this perspective, whether a democracy grows roots and what shape it takes is determined by policies that the protagonists adopt.[28] What is particularly notable in Huntington's work is his emphasis on Vatican II reforms in Catholicism and religious change in Korea in paving the way for the emergence of democracy in Latin America and East Asia, respectively.

These theories are useful in explaining the rise, fall, and rise again of democracy as a political force in Iran, and they help to identify key social, economic, and political factors that must converge to bring about a democratic movement and to consolidate a democratic system. The Iranian experience has much to offer by way of providing a test case for these theories. Social, economic, and political changes in Iran in recent years both confirm and extend the discussion about the prerequisites of democratization. However, the most direct contribution that the Iranian case can make to discussions of democratization is its emphasis on intellectual and ideological struggles that affect the fate of democracy. In Iran these struggles were instrumental in determining the extent to which democracy shaped national politics, and they decided the outcome of the competition between democracy and other political ideals. The case of Iran shows that democracy must permeate citizens' political mind-sets before it can change their political system. However, this is not a process of cultural change or an Islamic Reformation. Rather, it is one in which democracy supersedes other ideals, solutions, and priorities in determining the rules of politics, be they cultural, religious, or secular. It is therefore important to examine when and how democracy becomes an ideal and when it is likely to be superseded. Understanding these issues is key to understanding the nature and scope of political change.

The Iranian case is also instructive with regard to two other factors. First, the rise and prolonged occlusion of democratization in Iran was a consequence of the rise of the modern state in Iran. As such, the problem of democracy at the outset was not one of contending with the balance of power between state and society, but competing with the emerging state. Second, foreign interests played a central role in deciding the fortunes of democracy. Their influence on perceptions of national security and territorial integrity were instrumental in shaping attitudes toward political priorities and democracy's place among them. The Iranian case presents a new set of factors to be considered in the discussion of democratization, which are born of the country's unique historical experience.

Iran is also unique in that the challenge to democracy did not come just from the state but from competing ideas and ideologies, each claiming a better delivery plan for the promises of democracy. What happened in Iran suggests that successful democratization requires the rooting of a particular discourse of power in society and state in lieu of ideological formulations that can capture the imagination of those social strata and forces that favor democracy most. Democratization was hampered by the competition between democracy and ideology. The Iranian experience shows that prevalence of ideology (both leftist and Islamic fundamentalist), more than any other factor, accounts for the absence of democracy. The hold of ideology on the population at critical junctures, and the belief that ideology's rhetoric of liberation encompassed democracy did much to weaken the quest for democracy. Iranians confused collectivist promises of ideology with democratic ideals, and they vested their hope in ideology rather than democracy.

A number of works on democratization have focused on the role of social movements[29] and civil society institutions.[30] These works have examined the requirements for the formation and empowerment of social groups that can then spearhead reform and compel state leaders and institutions to share power. The Constitutional Revolution of 1906–1911 was one such social movement that brought together diverse groups of people who were focused on the idea of justice and good government, and that later served as the vehicle for popularizing the demand for democracy in Iran. Throughout the past century, social forces have played important roles not only in challenging state authority but in defining common conceptions of liberation and freedom, and hence determining the relative influence of democracy and those ideologies that competed with it for shaping politics. Civil society activism in Iran since 1997 has been important in sustaining the demand for democracy. This is a significant dimension of the discussion of the nature of relations between democracy and successful social movements.

Various studies of Islamic and Middle Eastern societies extensively discuss the place of democracy in the politics of these societies. Authors such as Samuel Huntington and Bernard Lewis have identified culture—and, more specifically, the Islamic faith—as responsible for the lack of successful democracies in Muslim countries.[31] Muslim thinkers have responded by going to great lengths to read democracy into Islam, and to advocate religious reform as the means of bringing to the fore those aspects of the faith that they deem compatible with democracy.[32] They are in effect suggesting that the problem is purely cultural (and therefore accidental and relative) and that democratization is both the focus and the function of religious reform. Regardless of the merits of putting so much weight on Islamic reform as a harbinger of democratization, this approach does not address the key issue because in Iran the problem has not been the incompatibility of Islam with democracy, but the prevalence of modern ideological thinking on the one hand and dominance of state institutions on the other.

A different group of scholars have challenged the cultural approach altogether as too essentialist. In this regard Dale Eickelman and James Piscatori have underscored the diversity and complexity of Muslim political expressions,[33] and John Esposito and John Voll have pointed to continuous experiments with democracy in the Muslim world.[34] Although these efforts have not yielded full-fledged democracy, they have nevertheless entrenched some of its values and practices in society and politics. The argument here is that the failure of democracy in the Muslim world is not attributable to the Islamic faith but more so to social and political constraints. These experiments have failed because they have not been able to limit the powers of state institutions and leaders and to provide a path for social forces to find a voice in the system.[35] Hence, neither the problem nor its solution lies with Islam but with the political setup.

The Iranian experience is interesting in that the origins of the quest for democracy predated the phenomenon of Islamic fundamentalism and its assault on Muslim states. Iranians first raised the demand for democracy a century ago with the support of their religious leaders, the ulama. Although the ulama placed limitations on the liberal content of the Constitution of 1906, pro-democracy forces at the time were concerned not with Islam, but with state power. In later years, democracy foundered in Iran as ideologies of the Left and the Right, secular and fundamentalist, dominated the Iranian mind-set. Thus democracy was precluded not by the domination of the Islamic faith over the people, but by the people's turn to collectivist idealism in place of pluralism as the harbinger of civil liberties and political freedom. It has been only in recent years, after the rise of the Islamic Republic, that the fate of democratization has come to depend on the relative powers of religion and secularism. Even so, the democracy debate in Iran is as much about state-society relations as it is about faith and its place in politics. Democracy today is, as it was a century ago, still dependent on altering the balance of power between state institutions and social forces to guarantee the rule of law, good government, accountability, and individual freedoms.

About This Book

This book traces both the rise of the modern state and the evolution of the idea and practice of democracy in Iran. The conclusions of this book are based on extensive fieldwork in Iran over the past seven years. The analytical narrative is informed by theoretical discussions in comparative politics and debates regarding political change in the Middle East and regarding the relationship of Islam to state power and democratic change in the larger Muslim world. This book examines how the two paths have converged and diverged to shape Iranian politics. Various actors have challenged state power and championed democratic rights, often blending their efforts with advocates of other "-isms" and political goals. What has emerged has not always echoed the demand for democracy and at times has undermined the case for it. By narrating the story of the state and trials and tribulations of democracy, this book draws a picture of Iranian history very different from the one obtained from usual treatments of the subject. Our narration does not seek to exalt or condemn ideas or actors. Rather, we seek to understand the underlying dynamics of Iranian politics and how its ideals and realities squared off against one another to determine its struggles for legitimacy and power. We seek to bring into sharp relief the centrality of the quest for democracy in Iran's historical development—to understand the past century in light of this quest. The idea of a democratic state, its values, and the power of its appeal have played an important role in defining the chasm between political expectations and realities. Democracy is the central thread that ties together the events of the past century.

Our focus in this book has been to clarify discussions of state-building and democratic change in Iran and, more important, to relate these goals and processes to the historical development of the country over the last century. As a result, although the narrative here relies on chronologies, its main focus will be to construct an analytical framework and a heuristic approach that will elucidate the nature of state-building in Iran and the nature of opposition to the state's exercise of power, including the demand for democracy and rule of law.

The book begins with the emergence of both the state and the idea of democracy as it was encapsulated in the demand for constitutional government in the first decade of the twentieth century. The confluence of demands for rule of law, individual freedoms, and efficiency in management of government affairs produced a political current that portended to alter politics in Iran. The constitutional movement's goal was not to institute democracy per se but rather was to rationalize government and bind political authority to well-defined norms— most notably accountability. It introduced new practices such as electoral and parliamentary activity, and it fused religious and liberal ideals to serve nationalism. More important, the constitutional period posed a number of political and cultural questions concerning the nature of political authority, its responsibilities, the nature of the moral foundation of politics, and the nature of the good in political life and its relation to identity. These questions remained open for decades, and subsequent Iranian history was largely shaped by efforts to answer such questions. Various actors understood and interpreted those questions in different ways and provided answers, and in the process they produced new movements and oppositions to them. The constitutional period was followed by intense debates about the direction of reform and institution-building in Iran. Those debates ultimately led to greater emphasis on developmentalism at the cost of democracy and on the reconstitution of a powerful state.

Initially the ideals that shaped the constitutional movement transfigured into other ideals and supported new trends. The demand for the rule of law and government accountability gave place to demands for order, development, and limits to autocracy. These demands were in turn replaced by populism, nationalism, and enforcement of national rights. In the 1960s and 1970s, a Marxist notion of liberation paraded as demand for freedom, a movement that defined the objective spirit of the Islamic Revolution of 1979. However, the revolution first rejected and then encompassed all that had preceded it, although it claimed to advance the cause of democracy. It refused to be defined by the political ideals that had shaped Iran until 1979. Yet the revolution first embodied the ideals of the Left, appropriating a Marxist-Leninist notion of revolutionary liberation along with populism.[36] Later it became the crucible for ideals of nationalism, developmentalism, and finally the rule of law and individual rights. In the end it was the state that prospered throughout these debates. For the needs of order, stability, and development not only favored state-building over democracy promotion but also removed constraints on exercise of state power.

The changes in the nature of the demand for democracy from that of the quest for the rule of law and constitutionalism to nationalism, populism, revolutionary liberation, and back to demand for the rule of law and constitutional and individual rights mirrored changes in the dominant ideological climate in Iran from modernization to developmentalism, nationalism, Marxism, Islamism, to liberalism. The tides of ideology in turn reflected changes in Iran's state, politics, and economy from Qajar despotism to Pahlavi autocracy and Islamic Republic theocracy. The three-way merging of political and economic realities with ideological responses and the more fundamental grappling with democracy shaped the underlying directive of Iranian history over the past century.

This book is divided into two parts. Part I will examine the rise of the state during the late-Qajar and the Pahlavi periods and the manner in which Iranians confronted the choice between state-building and democracy promotion in the context of nationalism, imperialism, war, and developmentalism between 1906 and 1979. Chapter 1 discusses the Constitutional Revolution of 1906–1911 and subsequent efforts to balance the demand for a viable state with the demand for democracy and rule of law. The chapter then traces the rise and triumph of the Iranian state under Reza Shah between 1925 and 1941. Chapter 2 discusses the ebbs and flows of state formation between 1941 and 1979. It examines key events and actors that determined balance of power between state and society, development and opposition to it, and the eventual concentration of power in the Pahlavi state between 1954 and 1979. The chapter also discusses the evolution of various ideologies and their effects on Iranian politics. Part II will examine the fate of the state after the revolution of 1979 and will explore the reemergence of the debate over state-building and democracy promotion as Iran contended with continuities and changes in the theocratic framework of the Islamic Republic. Chapter 3 will examine the unfolding of the 1979 revolution and its effects on the Iranian state, society, economy, and the context for state-building and democracy promotion. The focus here will be on the transformative effects of the revolution on conceptions of the state and also the nature of demands before it. Chapter 4 examines the shift from revolution to state-building and details how socioeconomic challenges, on the one hand, and memories of state and intellectual capital produced by the Pahlavi period, on the other, coalesced to shape the postrevolutionary state. Chapter 5 will examine the way in which state-building reignited the demand for democracy—producing a vibrant debate over balancing state-building and democracy promotion, and raising the prospects for a democratic state in Iran.

PART I

Rise of the State

1

Democracy or State-Building?
1906–1941

Modern Iranian politics has been shaped by the continuous struggle between, on the one hand, the ideals of freedom and rule of law and, on the other, the demand for stability, order, development, and the kind of state that can provide them. This struggle first surfaced in Iran at the end of the nineteenth century in response to the domestic crisis caused by Europe's attempts to dominate Iran's economy and politics. The ineffectual efforts to resist European interference underscored the debilitating effects of arbitrary rule and political decay on the country, altering the way Iranians conceived of political authority and how it should be deployed to solve the country's problems. The result was the Constitutional Revolution of 1906, which was perhaps the first movement of its kind in the Muslim world: an indigenous political reform movement directed at establishing accountable and representative government, one that would meet the demand for strong state institutions, rule of law, and individual rights.

The Constitutional Revolution produced Iran's first parliamentary system, which dominated the political scene until 1925. The 1906–1925 period marked the beginning of debates on freedom and order in Iran, when the ideals of accountable and effective government and central control of administration, functioning within clearly defined national boundaries, began to capture the language of politics and to influence the state's policy orientations. More important, the state began to rethink common conceptions of democracy, the rights of citizens and those of the government, the meaning of justice and accountability, and the place of religion in society, law, and politics and outlined a new framework for legal and political institutions. Politics during that period debated the promise and shortcomings of representative government, introducing the Iranian body politic to assumptions and expectations that continued to influence the country's historical development during the subsequent century.

Though the demand for a constitution in 1905–1906 called for democratic reforms, some proposed reforms were not democratic in nature, and in time these would justify return to undemocratic practices. The most notable of these were centralized control by the state over society, politics, and the economy. From 1905, when the constitutional movement took shape, up until 1921, when its gains were being consolidated, it may have appeared that the constitutional order could achieve all its goals. Perhaps it appeared possible to diffuse political authority by vesting it in representative institutions and to make policymaking accountable to the people while at the same time concentrating power in state institutions, enforcing the state's primacy over tribal leaders and regional rulers, and achieving rapid economic change. Perhaps Iran would build a modern state and democratize at the same time and through the same process of reform, and those changes would also address the country's security needs and protect its territorial integrity.

By 1921 it had became clear that reforms could not achieve all this at once. Providing security and protecting territorial integrity meant investing in a strong center and denying substate actors the ability to gain power through the democratic process. Similarly, economic development favored centralized policymaking rather than the give- and-take of parliamentary process. As a result, the Constitutional Revolution introduced new issues to Iranian politics, namely how to prioritize and achieve the seemingly divergent goals of the revolution. During the century that followed the Constitutional Revolution, Iranian politics has in large part been consumed by resolving this anomaly. The tug-of-war between the different impulses that were embedded in the Constitutional Revolution have worked their way through Iran's politics in tandem with changes in Iranian society, including the growing importance of the middle class, external challenges to the country's territorial integrity, and the relations between state and society.

Constitutionalism and the Demand for Justice

The Constitutional Revolution was the culmination of changes that Iran went through as a consequence of imperialism and the declining power of monarchical absolutism. Throughout the nineteenth century, the Qajar dynasty (1797–1925) had continuously declined in power.[1] Unable to defend Iran's territorial integrity and economic interests, it had succumbed to British and Russian pressure, and by the latter part of the nineteenth century had become a prisoner of imperial interests. The weakening of the Iranian state had created tensions among the monarchy, the merchants in the bazaar, and the ulama, who no longer saw the shahs as capable of fulfilling their traditional role as defenders of the faith and protectors of their domain and its interests—the function that had warranted their absolute fealty to the shahs.

This trend produced a rupture during Naser al-Din Shah's rule (1848–1896),[2] which was marked by monarchical absolutism and expansion of Russian and British reach into Iran's economy and politics. It was during this period that the monarchy shed its pretense of being the hapless defender of the nation to more openly serve as the instrument of European interests. The resultant alienation of the ulama and the bazaar merchants created tensions in their relations with the monarchy, which in 1891–1892 burst into the open. In that year, the Shah's decision to grant a European company the monopoly for the production and sale of tobacco—by then a popular commodity—precipitated protests among bazaar merchants. They mobilized the ulama to openly challenge the monarchy's authority. Mirza Hasan Shirazi, a high-ranking member of the Shia ulama who resided in Iraq issued a *fatwa* (religious ruling) that forbade Iranians to consume tobacco so long as it was handled by a foreign monopoly.[3] This ruling was the first open declaration of public distrust in the monarchy as defender of Iranian interests, and it put to question the role of monarchy in Iranian politics. If the monarchy was not going to defend Iranian interests, then it was not incumbent on Iranians to accept its prerogatives, least of all its absolutism.

Thus the Tobacco Rebellion was the opening salvo in the battle for limiting monarchical power in order to defend national interest. It was an economic reaction that had broad implications for political authority, and the bazaar merchants and the ulama were key forces in the unfolding debate.[4] The debate over reform began as an effort by economic and religious institutions that had hitherto been among the main pillars of the monarchy to look beyond that institution to defend national interest. The demand for reform was therefore intertwined with and helped shaped nationalism in Iran.

The Tobacco Rebellion ended after Naser al-Din Shah rescinded the tobacco monopoly in 1892. That the monarchy was forced to back down only encouraged further challenges to its authority. Four years after the Tobacco Rebellion, Mirza Reza Kermani, a disgruntled small merchant, assassinated Naser al-Din Shah. Mirza Reza had been brutalized by the local governor in his native Kerman. The monarchy at the time either supported arbitrary and ruthless exercise of power by local authorities or was incapable of preventing it. In either case, Iranians like Mirza Reza had developed disdain for the shahs, whose absolutist prerogatives had traditionally included the provision of protection and justice to their subjects.

Mirza Reza's misfortune turned into political dissent at the hands of the charismatic Seyyed Jamal al-Din Asadabadi (al-Afghani) (d. 1897), who met Mirza Reza in Istanbul.[5] Al-Afghani convinced Mirza Reza that the calamity that had befallen him was a manifestation of the monarchy's ineptitude and corruption. Mirza Reza then decided to address the roots of the problem by killing the monarch. Regicide thus became the manifestation of a more deep-seated disgruntlement with the institution of the monarchy and served as a direct challenge to its authority. Hence, assassination supplanted *fatwa* as the instrument of resistance to monarchical absolutism.

The assassination of Naser al-Din Shah in effect placed monarchical absolutism on trial. Mirza Reza had eliminated one shah, but the problems that Iranians now associated with the monarchy—foreign domination of Iran and arbitrary rule—continued unabated. Thus began a debate on the nature of political authority at a more fundamental level. It soon became clear that so long as monarchy dominated Iranian politics, the problems that had instigated the Tobacco Rebellion and the assassination of Naser al-Din Shah would persist. This realization fueled further debates that intensified during the reign of Naser al-Din Shah's successor, Mozaffar al-Din Shah (1896–1907), culminating in the Constitutional Revolution of 1906.

The challenge to monarchical absolutism was rooted in variegated social groups and institutions that emerged in the last decade of the nineteenth century in response to crises facing state and society.[6] Among the most important of these were secret societies and intellectual circles. The historian Mehdi Malekzadeh credited secret societies for the development and propagation of the foundational ideas of the Constitutional Revolution.[7] Fereydoun Adamiyat identified Iranian intellectuals as the source for the idea of constitutionalism.[8] In his view it was thinkers such as Mirza Malkom Khan (d. 1908),[9] Mirza Aqa Khan Kermani (d. 1896), and Abd al-Rahim Talebof (d. 1911) and newspapers and periodicals such as *Qanoun*, *Mosavat*, *Sour Esrafil*, and *Habl al-Matin* that conceptualized the political frustrations that developed during the latter part of Naser al-Din Shah's rule. These authors and publications articulated ideas of change, disseminated them among a broader cross-section of the population, convincing their audience of the prospects for reform. However, as the historian Ahmad Kasravi has noted, a sociopolitical movement of the depth and breadth of the Constitutional Revolution could not have emerged without broad support among ordinary people.[10] The ideals of the Constitutional Revolution were first developed by intellectuals, but it was through social networks that they were connected to the dissentient forces that were organizing in society. The political views that emerged from the secret societies became a social movement only after they gained popularity among ordinary people in cities.

The transition from the intellectualized dissent of the elite to a mass movement was made through the intermediary of those ulama who favored change and supported the quest for a constitution.[11] These ulama related the demands of the constitutionalist forces to the broader masses and legitimated opposition to monarchical rule by providing religious support for constitutionalism.[12] The synthesis of religion and constitutionalism was an important dimension of Iran's experience with reform—one that was altogether different from the European experience, wherein political reform was always secular and was developed to confront the alliance between church and state.

The central idea of the Constitutional Revolution was the demand for a "House of Justice" (*Edalat Khaneh*). The ideal of justice captured the demand for an end to arbitrary rule, for stability and order, and for protection of national interests from predatory foreign forces. Justice was seen as synonymous with curbing monarchical power, for the monarchy had become associated with arbitrary rule and injustice, which the people viewed as evident in the preferences that foreign interests received in economic matters. Thus the term constitutionalism was translated as *mashroutiyat* (setting conditions), which implied placing conditions on monarchical absolutism.[13] In later years, Iranians reflected this concern with justice and rule of law in how they referred to the constitution: as the Fundamental Law (*Qanoun-e Asasi*). The Constitutional Revolution was therefore not an antimonarchist movement, but an antiabsolutist one. It was a movement not only of protecting civil rights, but also of protecting the rights of the nation. It was concerned not with empowering the individual, but with placing limits on arbitrary exercise of state authority. It was concerned not only with freedom, but also with national liberation, good government, economic progress, and protection of the country's territorial integrity. It therefore enmeshed the idea of political freedom with goals that were expressed in the language of nationalism, providing a theme that would resurface in the 1950s during the Mosaddeq period and would continue to condition discourses of nationalism and democracy during the late Pahlavi era. The Constitutional Revolution therefore provided a systematic change in the structure and exercise of political authority, one that would ideally be an alternative to *fatwas* and assassinations as the means of contending with absolutism.

The ulama had consistently supported monarchical absolutism since 1501 when the Safavid dynasty (1501–1722) established the Shia monarchy in Iran.[14] The ulama had viewed monarchy as the protector of the Shia domain and propagator of the faith. During the Constitutional Revolution, some ulama, such as Sheikh Fazlollah Nouri (d. 1909), continued to defend monarchical absolutism on those lines.[15] Nouri viewed constitutionalism as a Western idea that would ultimately subvert Shi'ism and the insular sanctity of the Shia realm. On the other hand, other ulama, such as Mohammad-Hossein Naini (d. 1936), saw no tension between the requirements of Shia piety and the imperatives of Shia authority and constitutionalism. After all, the ulama had supported monarchical absolutism insofar as it was capable of protecting the interests of the people and the nation—which they had equated with the Shia realm. If the powers vested in the monarchy were manipulated by foreign interests to the detriment of the nation and if arbitrary rule alienated the masses and caused instability, then curbing those powers under a constitution was necessary. Therefore constitutionalism was not a threat to the integrity of the Shia realm, but in fact was necessary to protecting it. Political reform was sanctioned by the imperative of both preserving the faith and the nation that embodied it.

That at the dawn of the twentieth century the guardians of Shi'ism saw no threat to their religion in constitutionalism is significant. Equally important is the fact that political reformers and advocates of the constitution did not unconditionally view religion and its guardians as a threat. The constitutionalist demand for justice was focused on placing limits—setting conditions or *mashroutiyat*—on the monarchy's powers. As such, constitutionalism did not see itself as exclusively concerned with religious law or the *shariah*. Constitutionalists were primarily concerned with democracy and justice, not with secularism. In fact, they viewed the ulama as a bulwark against monarchical absolutism and instrumental in popularizing the movement, and as such an important ally in the quest for a constitution. The *shariah* was used to protest injustice and to demand accountability of the monarchy. Moreover, the *shariah* was viewed as primarily concerned with personal law, not public law. Constitutionalism mainly focused on public law (i.e., regulating the relationship between the state and its citizens, and defining their fundamental rights and responsibilities). Thus the *shariah* was not viewed as an automatic obstacle to political reform and innovations in public law, and it was expected to coexist with a new constitution. Constitutionalism was clearly not a secular ideal, and it was not expected to cut off the individual from the hold of religious law. It was neither anticlerical nor an expression of Muslim "enlightenment." In fact, to the extent that constitutionalism was a demand for the rule of law, it reinforced the writ of the *shariah*, whose stance vis-à-vis the monarchy reinforced the demands of the constitutionalists.

Constitutionalism also emerged as a response to foreign manipulation of Iran's economy, which mobilized important social classes in opposition to the colonial powers and their instruments in Iran. When the people realized that the authority that had been vested in the monarchy to protect the Shia realm was being exploited by foreign powers to undermine the realm's interests, some of the ulama were motivated to relate the ideals of freedom, justice, and accountability that had been developed by intellectuals and the political societies to the larger masses.

The demand for reform culminated in a successful social movement that changed the foundation of Iranian politics. The tensions that were produced during the Naser al-Din Shah period were further aggravated during the reign of his successor, Mozaffar al-Din Shah. When the new shah took some expensive European excursions that coincided with new taxes proposed by his Belgian adviser, and granted a new oil concession to British interests, dissident forces—who viewed the Shah as weak—were emboldened in their dissent. The monarchy responded to growing opposition to its failed policies by publicly flogging merchants in the bazaar in 1905, which further alienated the dissidents. Such actions shaped the constitutionalist movement by consolidating relations between intellectuals, the ulama—led by figures such as Seyyed Mohammad Tabatabai and Seyyed Abdollah Behbahani—and merchants. Amorphous demands for the rule of law—inspired by ideas gleaned from Abdol-Hossein Mirza Qajar's translations of Montesquieu's *De L'espirit Des Lois* (On the Spirit of the Law) and Adam Smith's *The Wealth of Nations* or Malkom Khan's conceptions of constitutionalism as expressed in his periodical *Qanoun*—gave place to concrete demands for a parliament (Majles).

Not all demands for reform had liberal intent. An important strand of the reform movement was concerned with the monarchy's ineptitude and its ability to get things done. These reformers were interested in creating efficiency to bring order to the economy, society, and politics. They favored centralization and were frustrated by the absence of effective exercise of power. Their complaint with the Qajar monarchy was not that it had too much power, but that it exercised power so ineffectively. This element in the reform movement would balance the demand for curbs on the monarchy with the desire to concentrate power in institutions that would make governance more effective. It would also confound the democratic intent of the constitutional movement, a development that would be important in determining the path that Iranian politics would follow after 1906.

The monarchy was fighting a losing battle. It was unable to present an argument for monarchical absolutism, given its abuses of power. When in 1905 Japan defeated Russia, the voices of dissent found added encouragement, believing that the monarchy's powerful European backers were vulnerable and could be defeated by natives. Eventually, powerful members of the elite such as Mirza Nasrollah Khan Moshir al-Dawlah understood the inevitability of political reform and persuaded the Shah to compromise and agree to grant the constitution.

The new constitution was promulgated in 1906, and a parliament was convened for the first time in October of that year.[16] It effectively transferred some
of the powers of the monarchy to the legislature, and it provided the people with
a forum through which to influence politics. As a result, the monarchy would
be subservient to a representative government that would be produced by the
parliament. The Constitution was less certain in delineating the relations between religion and politics. Viewing control of the monarchy rather than the
ulama as the objective of the constitutional effort, the architects of the new
document succumbed to providing broad powers of oversight in the new constitution for the ulama. It was expected that the ulama would reinforce the
Constitution's goals rather than attempt to combine religion with politics.

The Constitutional Revolution therefore did not draw boundary lines between religion and politics. It saw religion as compatible with the demand for
rule of law and curbing monarchical absolutism. Regardless of the long-term
implications of this omission, its immediate significance was that it included
religion in the emerging Iranian conception of democracy. The reform effort was
directed at creating a Shia democracy as much as it was at creating an Iranian
one.

The ideal of democracy therefore emerged with a strong religious component and emphasis on rule of law rather than demand for liberty. It was concerned with reforming the old order rather than liberating the masses from its
control. It was a movement that sought to bring balance to the structure of
political authority rather than celebrate individual freedoms. Still, it was an important step in producing an indigenous democratic movement that radically
changed popular conceptions of political authority, the rights and responsibilities of rulers, and the role that the people play in it. Above all, it turned Iranians
from subjects into citizens, and that in itself was a significant legal revolution.

Democratic Consolidation and Authoritarian Reversal, 1907–1909

Iranians got their constitution fairly quickly. Consolidating those early gains,
however, proved far more difficult. Although the constitution was popular in
Iran, the society that had produced that constitution lacked many key ingredients
of sustainable democracy: a middle class, a prosperous economy, and political
stability and order. Democracy also faced more immediate challenges. The weak
monarchy did not put up a stiff resistance before the popular alliance of ulama
and constitutionalists, and it folded quickly. Having won the call for reform, its
champions now had to build a constitutional political system. This proved a
daunting task, given the social, economic, and political problems that faced the

country. Iran had got its framework for a democracy, now it had to turn Iranians into democrats.

The constitutional period introduced new political practices, language, and attitudes to Iran. The Constitution, which was modeled after the Belgian Constitution of 1831, introduced Western legal and political concepts to Iran. The parliamentary practices introduced new conceptions of procedure, alliance making, and consensus building. The language of politics changed as deputies adopted new public postures, spoke to constituencies, and used the parliament as the forum for floating and debating ideas. Factions and parties took shape, and both their formation and their participation required new political skills and imposed their own discipline on politicians. Policymaking became a matter of debate and consensus rather than royal decree.[17] As such, Iranians learned about practicing democracy, its rules and the assumptions and logic that govern its mode of politics. All this did much to entrench common conceptions of democracy and to change past understandings of politics—sources of its legitimacy and authority as well as its mode of operation.

Democratic consolidation was far from a halcyon affair. To begin with, the various factions that had supported the constitution disagreed about the extent of democratic rights that it would provide. In February 1907, the draft constitution that was prepared by the more secular forces was put to debate. The ulama were not happy with a number of its clauses. Notably, they objected to viewing all Iranians equal before the law regardless of their religion, and they favored a privileged status for Muslims. The ulama also strongly objected to Article 20, which provided for freedom of the press; they viewed unregulated freedom of speech as a threat to the religious underpinnings of society. The draft constitution was changed to exempt speech deemed offensive to religious sensitivities from protection of freedom of expression; it also came to require permission for the publication of books on Islam and to mandate punishment for publication of anti-Islamic material. The ulama included in the final Constitution the provision for an ulama supervisory body to ensure that all legislation was in accordance with Islamic law.

The ulama who had helped end monarchical absolutism and to bring about political reform made sure that reform would not threaten the primacy of religion in society and popular culture. Their aim remained the protection of the Shia realm. The changes introduced to the draft of the constitution were directed at limiting the scope of secularism, and they did not affect the Constitution's demands for rule of law, accountability, and inclusion of the masses in the political process. The final draft reflected a compromise between the ulama and constitutionalist forces, one that tempered the liberal tendencies of the secular constitutionalists. It had the effect of including a broad cross-section of Iranian society and politics into the new constitutional order. It articulated common conceptions of democracy in Iran, its legal and moral moorings, values, ideals, and sources.

However, the problem posed by this compromise had broader ramifications for the Iranian political mind-set and common conceptions of democracy. First, the liberalism that is at the core of the ideal of democracy creates a "society of citizens." The ulama's conception was that Iran would continue to be a "society of believers" (an *ummah* in Islamic terms). They held that the prerogatives of the faith supersede those of the citizen. As such, the aim of politics and law would be to protect the faith and the society of believers, not to empower citizens. The compromises with the ulama therefore limited the scope of democratic thinking as the Constitution would not change the mind-set of the people about foundations of politics. By confirming the prerogatives of religion and the ulama, the event of the Constitution would not serve as the fountainhead of a broader revolution in political thinking.

Second, foreign pressure and Iran's precarious independence confounded the consolidation process. In 1907, the Anglo-Russian agreement that emerged from an entente between the previously competing powers divided Iran into spheres of influence. Just as the parliament was trying to build an open political order, the country's continued existence came into question. With national security at stake, finer debates regarding political rights and responsibilities had to share center stage with concerns for defending sovereignty and national integrity. The new parliament had little to offer in that regard, and the new constitution did not provide a blueprint for investing power in the state and protecting it from foreign intrigue.

Third, the old order was defeated, but it was far from reconciled to the turn of events. Mozaffar al-Din's Shah's son, Mohammad-Ali Shah, responded to the loss of monarchical power by turning to Russia and the Cossack Brigade at home to assert the monarchy's claim to power and undo the Constitution. He also sought the support of a minority group among the ulama that was led by Sheikh Fazlollah Nouri, who had earlier appeared moderately supportive of reform but, because of his objections to the Constitution's Western ideas, returned to his defense of monarchical absolutism. In June 1908, Mohammad-Ali Shah arrested many constitutionalist leaders and ordered the Cossack Brigade to bombard the parliament. The coup precipitated broader conflict after constitutionalist forces took over the government of Iran's second most important city, Tabriz. The Cossacks mounted an attack on the city, and it was occupied by Russian forces in April 1909 before it surrendered to the monarchy. Because pro-reform forces had not fully institutionalized their gains and because forces loyal to the old order wielded considerable power, democratization was effectively stalled; less than two years after the first parliament had convened in Tehran, the absolutist monarchy made a comeback. Mohammad-Ali Shah's autocratic reign came to be known as the period of Lesser Autocracy (*Estebdad-e Saghir*).

The constitutional movement, however, was not vanquished so easily. In July 1909, pro-constitution militias, together with tribesmen and peasants led by their leaders from the countryside, took over Tehran and deposed Mohammad-Ali Shah, replacing him with his nine-year-old son, Ahmad. Monarchical absolutism was thus roundly defeated, confirming the strong roots that the constitutional movement had developed in Iranian politics. Though the fall of Mohammad-Ali Shah did not end monarchy in Iran, it did confirm the monarchy's subordination to the constitution. That the parliament ensured a transition of titular power to a new monarch, and provided for a pension for the deposed Mohammad-Ali Shah, in itself was a confirmation of the commitment to the Constitution, whose rules regarding the rights and responsibilities of constitutional monarchy were used to settle the crisis.

The period of Lesser Autocracy also focused the constitutionalists on nationalism—which as an idea had been taking form during the preceding two decades[18]—and the institutional embodiment of their movement, the parliament, was now depicted as *Khaneh-ye Mellat* (The Nation's House). The demand for curbing monarchical absolutism thus matured into a concerted effort to consolidate democracy and protect the institution of the parliament.

However, the restored parliament was more strongly influenced by secular reformers. The role of Sheikh Fazlollah Nouri during the period of the Lesser Autocracy had alerted constitutionalists to the potential threat of the ulama. Hence the earlier insouciant attitudes toward the role of religion that had led reformers to accede to many of the ulama's demands in changing the first draft of the constitution were replaced with greater insistence on secular ideals. This in turn led the ulama to distance themselves from the new parliament.

The Post-Constitutional Era, 1911–1921

The defeat of the Lesser Autocracy came at a cost to Iranian politics. The tribal and provincial insurgence that restored the Constitution also gravely weakened central authority and empowered regional actors. The result was a crisis of governability that would tarnish the image of the constitutional order in the mind of Iranians as stability and democracy became dissociated from one another and increasingly were viewed as mutually exclusive.[19]

The 1911–1921 period witnessed the emergence of new insurgencies among

Qashqai tribes in southwestern Iran and Arab tribesmen led by Sheikh Khaz'al in Khouzestan. These developments were at times supported by foreign interests, suggesting that after the demise of monarchical absolutism, local leaders were likely to serve as the new clients of imperialism. So although the constitutional movement had emerged to limit foreign domination of Iran by reforming its main lever, the monarchy, the constitution's success simply led foreign interests to explore new paths for exerting their influence. The constitutional order would not be able to reverse this trend. For the circumstances of its victory in 1909 hampered its ability to produce a strong government and to effectively address law-and-order issues.

Central government became characterized by factional conflict, weakness, and paralysis as it was also undermined by continuous foreign intervention. For instance, the Russian occupation of Tabriz in 1911 undermined the credibility of the parliament because it had been helpless to remedy the situation. Efforts to assert Iran's independence, as was the case with the provisional government of Nezam al-Saltaneh Mafi (in 1916), came to naught, reflecting the plight of the constitutional order. Mafi was compelled by unrest and foreign threats to move from Tehran to Qom, on to Kermanshah in western Iran and eventually to Istanbul. The weakness at the center further encouraged foreign powers to increasingly turn away from the central government and to look to regional leaders to protect their interests, which in turn promoted division of Iran into spheres of influence. The Sykes-Picot agreement of 1916 further aggravated the problem as division of the entire region between Britain and France also weakened Iran's claim to its territorial integrity and sovereignty.

Iran was saved from the fate of the Ottoman Empire by the 1917 revolution in Russia. In its moment of revolutionary enthusiasm, Russia reneged on its earlier "imperialist" agreement with Britain to divide Iran, abrogated tzarist Russia's onerous treaties with Tehran, and ceased to interfere in Iran's domestic affairs. In time, communist Russia would resume that country's long-standing meddlesome policies in Iran. However, in the short run, the Russian Revolution arrested the rapid slide of Iran into disintegration.

The central government that was based in the parliament understood the imperative of consolidating power in the center and engaging in state formation if it were to avoid the kind of decay and collapse of authority that had almost sealed the fate of Iran in 1916. This meant shifting attention from reform, liberalism, and democracy to institution building and enabling the state to exercise authority. The problem facing the government and the parliament was that they lacked the resources and power to engage in serious institution building— to protect the country from renewed disintegrative challenges, political decay, and chaos.

The Prime Minister Hasan Vosouq al-Dawleh (1918–1920) sought to address this problem by using British interest in Iran to shore up state authority.[20] Vosouq argued that Iran had not received the kind of investment in infrastructure and institutions that the British had made in their colonies and protectorates elsewhere in the Middle East or South Asia. If it was to benefit from that kind of investment—which appeared to him to be Iran's only option—it had to more closely tie British interests in the country and the region with the central government in Tehran. Iran had to openly embrace the very dependence on a foreign power that it had shunned for three decades and that had animated its constitutional movement.

Vosouq was seen as a pro-British politician.[21] However, he was not a mouthpiece for British interests; rather, he saw Iran's national interest as lying in closer ties with Britain. He did not see nationalism as requiring rejection of foreign interests to assert national independence; rather, he thought that Iran could use foreign interests to empower and enrich itself. This view of nationalism would reemerge in the late-Pahlavi period in Mohammad-Reza Shah Pahlavi's view of Iran's national interests, and it would distinguish the Shah's view from that of Premier Mohammad Mosaddeq, who saw nationalism as requiring rejection of all foreign interests and assertion of national independence. But much as Mohammad-Reza Shah would discover for himself in the 1960s, Vosouq found that he was hard-pressed to convince Iranians of the wisdom of his approach. The Anglo-Iranian Agreement of 1919, which Vosouq hoped would lead to the large-scale British infrastructure and economic investments in Iran that the country desperately needed, was viewed by many as unpatriotic and beneficial only to Britain. It was viewed as a reversal of gains made in asserting Iran's national interests in the 1892–1919 period. Iranians were in no mood to think creatively about using imperialism to their advantage, and they were more readily swayed by the emotional appeal of rejecting British influence. The ulama, led by Seyyed Hasan Modarres, were particularly vocal in this regard. The ulama presented no alternative for constructing a strong state in Iran, but they objected to using British patronage to do so.

As mentioned earlier, the ulama had since 1892 been at the forefront of resisting foreign interests in Iran. This position had led them to support the Constitutional Revolution and its program of reform. Vosouq's gambit therefore drew a clear wedge between the government and the ulama. The former was now driven by the imperatives of consolidating and exercising power, and the latter was driven by anti-imperialism. This division would continue to define relations between the state and the ulama until the advent of the Iranian Revolution of 1979. Both Vosouq and the ulama looked to the parliament for support, and both saw it as the arena where the debate over Iran's future would be resolved. This prevented Vosouq from turning the office of the Prime Minister into a strong executive body and vesting power in it. As the specter of renewed political decay and chaos became the national preoccupation, the British—who hoped a stronger Iranian government could better withstand Bolshevik influences—and many Iranians began to look beyond the parliament and the options that it presented for alternatives.

Reza Shah and State-Building, 1921–1941

The alternative to the stalemate of the Vosouq period came from the Cossack Brigade and its coup of 1921, led by Brigadier Reza Khan (later Reza Shah Pahlavi).[22] The coup introduced a new actor to the Iranian political scene, the military.[23] At the time, there was no armed forces as such. The Cossack Brigade and South Persia Rifles were the only regimented military units, but they were not fully under the command of the central government and did not act as national armed forces.[24] These forces had up to then been led by foreign commanding officers and, as was the case during the period of Lesser Autocracy, had acted as agents of foreign powers; the Cossack Brigade was organized and patronized by Russia, and the South Persia Rifles by Britain. They had never participated in the domestic political arena with commitment to national interests. The coup of 1921 changed all that. The Cossack Brigade stepped into the political vacuum that was emerging at the center of Iranian politics and quickly became a major force in determining its destiny.

The coup underscored the imperative of restoring power at the center, and the inability of the parliament and its civilian governments to achieve that goal. Though building a strong state had been a goal of the Vosouq government, Vosouq had not been able to mobilize resources domestically to change the fortunes of the central government, which is what had brought him to seek an alliance with Britain. The coup was not a rejection of Vosouq's objectives, but it pointed to another path to realizing that goal. Reza Khan, too, wanted to end the paralysis at the center and to shore up state authority. Unlike Vosouq, Reza Khan believed that this process could be supported by mobilizing internal resources, and the Cossack Brigade had the means to go beyond the limitations that had confounded Vosouq. The scope of opposition to the Anglo-Iranian Agreement of 1919 had made such a path a necessity; the coup made it a distinct possibility.

Reza Khan's program combined opposition to tribal monarchy with desire to modernize and develop Iran. It was one of building institutions and vesting greater powers in the executive than in parliament. He saw Iran's experiment with parliamentary democracy as having failed to solve the real issues before the country. Only by concentrating power in the executive office could Iran achieve effective governance and policymaking, resource mobilization, constraints on the powers of regional power brokers and tribal leaders, and national independence. In many ways Reza Khan's rise to power rested on his ability to question the assumption that the constitutional order could achieve all of its goals, and in fact to argue that those goals were mutually exclusive. Reza Khan was also able to convince important social and political groups that the priority before the country was not pluralism, but rather was defending national integrity and homogeneity and achieving economic development.[25] This meant favoring executive powers over legislative powers and centralizing control over representative government. However, Reza Khan sought to empower executive authority within the constitutional framework. The Constitution of 1906 would be reinterpreted to achieve that end. Unlike the coup that had initiated the period of Lesser Autocracy, this coup sought not to abrogate the constitution but to shift the balance of power within it from the legislative to the executive. The "institution building through the constitution" therefore did not immediately mobilize an opposition to autocracy as the period of Lesser Autocracy had. In fact, it found much support among certain constituencies of the constitutional movement, those who, having won the battle for reform, were now keen to secure a viable state and nation.

It is important to note that Reza Khan's emphasis on institution-building was able to gain support because it evoked memories of the state among the Iranian people. The legacy of monarchical rule in Iran dating back to the Safavid period (1501–1722) had given Iranians a keen sense of the rights and duties of central authority, as well as the style and language of government. Reza Khan's promise of a modern state would resonate with a broad segment of the Iranian population through this memory. The ability to convey the promise of the new in terms of memories of the old largely accounts for the speed with which Iranians embraced Reza Khan; it also helped define the manner in which the modern state would evolve and interact with society in the years to come.

The promise of the new state particularly resonated with reformers whose views were best articulated by the statesman and scholar Mohammad-Ali Foroughi (d. 1942). Foroughi, who was influenced by modern French political thought, believed in strong state institutions. He believed that a strong state would not only guarantee territorial integrity and aid progress, it would also promote liberty. For Foroughi, institutions produced liberty and made men free. This line of thinking promoted the notion of benevolent state tutelage and helped legitimate institution formation through the constitution.

As discussed earlier, the Constitutional Revolution was supported not only by those who favored democracy but also by those who were frustrated by the inability of the Qajar monarchy to modernize Iran and solve its social, economic, and international crises. The Constitutional Revolution had promised to change Iran's fortunes by limiting the power of the monarchy, which was seen as responsible for Iran's political decay. However, when the revolution failed to reverse Iran's decline, it became evident to many that democracy by itself had no solutions and would not empower Iran. Ideas such as those put forward by Foroughi helped create a nexus between the demand for order and progress and the ideal of democracy by ascribing a sequence to them: first order and progress, and then democracy; democracy would come only after progress. For democracy was a product not of individual volition but of institutional deliverance.

Reza Khan's program appealed to those who accepted the need for a new institutional solution to Iran's problems. These people did not want to reverse the gains of the constitutional movement. Rather, they thought that the goals could be accomplished by adjusting the constitutional order so as to make it subservient to Iran's developmental needs. Reza Khan, building on Vosouq's position, successfully argued that the constitutional movement had to evolve in order to support national development. In so doing, Reza Khan, with the backing of reformers such as Foroughi, successfully associated liberation and freedom not with democracy but with development and institution-building. He subsumed the desire for democracy under his drive for national development. Glossing over inherent anomalies between the concentration of power in state institutions and the rights of individuals and civil society institutions, he conflated the ideal of democracy with national independence and individual empowerment with that of the nation. This allowed the Pahlavi state, at least during its early years, to resolve tensions inherent in the constitutional movement between liberals and centralizers. This was, however, only a temporary resolution, one that gave centralizers time and space to ensure the primacy of state in Iranian politics. That achievement would in turn aggravate and bring into the open those tensions.

Reza Khan also found support for his project among the ulama, who were more concerned with chaos and disorder than democracy, and who also had grown distant from the secular constitutionalists and reformers. It was the ulama who also would persuade Reza Khan to become a monarch (Reza Shah)—thus looking to store power in monarchy some three decades after they started stripping it of power.[26] During the postconstitutional period, some groups, most notably the Social Democrats (Ejtema'iyoun-Amiyoun), had advocated a republic (jomhouri) for Iran. For democracy demands undividable constitutional rights, which can best be articulated in a republic. As such, a "republic" is the objective spirit of democracy. However, the idea of a republic had been inchoate at the time, and it fell by the wayside after the Constitutional Revolution formally accepted monarchy as the form of government. Thenceforth, talk of a republic was later construed as sedition, and after a number of separatist regional forces proclaimed republics, it was also associated with foreign intrigue. Reza Shah's drive for a strong executive branch, his interest in Kemalism, and his abrogation of the Qajar dynasty—which followed a public campaign lamenting the shortcomings of monarchy—opened the door to discussion of a republic. Once Reza Khan became monarch, all talk of a republic was shelved. As a result, the notion of democracy as the natural fulfillment of the promise of the Constitutional Revolution remained unresolved.

Though Reza Shah became a monarch, he was not interested in the institution. Rather, he was interested in a strong executive branch. Hence, what the ulama saw in the restoration of monarchy was not what Reza Shah had in mind. Under Reza Shah, it was Kemalism—with its state domination of economy, society, politics, and cultural change—rather than constitutional monarchy that became Iran's model of government. Thus the Pahlavi monarchy was very different from its predecessor. It was for all practical purposes a "Kemalist" monarchy. Establishment of the Pahlavi monarchy ended talk of a republic, but it did not erase the interest in it, especially among those who were keen to quickly build state institutions and pursue economic and social development.

Reza Shah reduced the powers of the aristocracy, distanced monarchy from religion and the ulama, and viewed the monarchy not as a traditional institution but as an agent of modernization. He looked to the middle class—the class that was the base of support for the Constitution of 1906—to bolster the monarchy. His promise was particularly attractive to prominent merchants such as Amin al-Zarb, who were anxious about stability and development. In this, Reza Shah combined two discrete elements of the preceding regime to forge a new political institution. After the Constitutional Revolution, the monarchy had remained in the political scene as a symbol, and the parliament had become the embodiment of popular sovereignty. As argued above, the Constitutional Revolution had turned Iranians from subjects into citizens. The Pahlavi monarchy sought to fuse the moribund institution of the monarchy with the republican core of the Constitutional Revolution to produce a strong modernizing executive authority, which would embody the popular will in lieu of the parliament. However, that the monarchy, unlike a presidency, received no direct popular mandate ultimately made Reza Shah's gambit untenable.

It is important to remember that Reza Shah was made king by the ulama and the merchant class (especially its upper crust), not by parliament. After the coup, he became minister of war (1921), then prime minister (1923), and finally king (1925). His rise in stature reflected his success in concentrating power in the executive branch. It was a process that was supported by the ulama and was eventually accepted by the parliament as a fait accompli.[27] Thus Reza Shah's rise to power was a culmination of struggle for power at the center of Iranian politics within the framework of the constitution. This process was aided by Reza Shah's ability to provide a strong critique of the parliamentary order and to influence common conceptions of reform, constitution, and democracy; he was able to separate pluralism from development and national unity, and to associate the latter ideals with a strong executive branch. He also separated pluralism from religion by associating the former with secularism. As such, Reza Shah was able to force democracy to compete both with national ideals and with religion. It was his ability to manipulate that competition that accounts for his successful rise to power.

Reza Shah also identified Iranian nationalism with development rather than democracy, and he focused Iranian politics on developmentalism—creating a modern bureaucratic state and industrial economy[28]—in lieu of the rule of law and democracy. It is important to note that Reza Shah was able to deliver on his promises. He proved that, first, development was possible, and, second, that it would work best under a strong executive authority freed from parliamentary political wrangling. His success allowed him to initially co-opt larger numbers of Iranians—especially from among the ranks of pro-constitution forces—to support the new order. That support was the key to ensuring his rise to power and domination of the political process.

Reza Shah's success transformed Iran's economy and society. A modern middle class tied to the new bureaucracy emerged to assert its control over urban space and national politics. Reza Shah sent students abroad, reformed the public education system, and established the first modern university in Iran. His administration revamped the bureaucracy, introducing modern administrative procedures to it, and he created a modern judiciary. Iran developed its first industries. Reza Shah built a modern military force that effectively established Tehran's control over the country. Notably, government forces were able to defeat serious regional and tribal forces that had begun before he became king such as those of the rebellion of Mirza Kouchak Khan in Gilan and that of Sheikh Khaz'al in Khouzestan—which the British intended to use to create another Kuwait out of Iran's oil province. Reza Shah proved particularly capable of facing down foreign powers in asserting Iran's prerogatives.[29] Iran thus went from a "failed state" to a functioning one.

He also was able to rely on resources from the population to achieve his goals. For instance, a tax on major consumer items such as sugar and tea, in good measure financed the first railway line that connected the Caspian Sea to the Persian Gulf. Until then the population had paid tithes to landlords and local governors, who often acted as tax farmers, giving a portion of their proceeds to the central authorities. The central government had never before taxed the population as citizens, asserting the rights of the government to collect resources in order to provide services to those citizens. The kinds of ties between the population and the central government that emerged during this period helped build a modern state in Iran with contractual ties to the people.[30] This was a development that was made possible by notions of a national good, citizen rights, and government accountability that came from the Constitutional Revolution.

The changes that the Reza Shah period brought about in Iran were nothing short of revolutionary. Iran was able to ward off the threat of disintegration, to arrest administrative and institutional decay, and to chart a path forward toward development. All this was made possible by concentration of power in the executive authority. However, the unbridled empowerment of the executive office was not free of problems. It produced authoritarianism, which in turn revived the yearning for democracy and rekindled the debate that Reza Shah had won during the 1921–1926 period. The Reza Shah period addressed Iran's development problem, but it brought to the fore the problems of concentrating power in the executive office—that it leads to authoritarianism, and that the imperative of developmentalism comes at a cost.

In order to promote rapid development and to remove obstacles to change, Reza Shah increasingly relied on strong-arm tactics, which stood in violation of the Constitution—which he increasingly sidelined—and suggested that rather than a constitutional government, his regime was based on arbitrary rule. In effect he resurrected an absolutism of sorts, but his, unlike that of the period of Lesser Autocracy, was sanctioned by a subservient parliament and was getting much done in the country. Nonetheless, the Pahlavi state's degeneration into arbitrary rule posed moral and political problems to the people.

Reza Shah's methods eventually brought the ideal of democracy back into the political limelight as the demand for curbs on the powers of the autocracy grew. Some three decades after the Constitutional Revolution set out to limit monarchical absolutism, a new call for reform and democracy was looking to curb the power of another monarchical power structure. The difference this time was that whereas the Qajar monarchy combined political decay with arbitrary rule, the Pahlavi monarchy was a modernizing force. Hence, whereas reformists in the late nineteenth century associated constitutionalism with greater modernization, this time it was autocracy and centralism that was associated with that process. The questions facing Iranian politics were the same: how to manage monarchical power and still attend to the need for modernization and development. What was different this time was the alignments of the main actors. All this showed that democracy was not an ideal sui generis, but rather a product of a fundamental disjuncture between demand for good government and progress in Iranian politics.

The Reza Shah period was also a time of growing secularism. Reza Shah promoted a secular vision of Iranian nationalism that looked to pre-Islamic history as the source of national identity. Taking his cue from Mustafa Kemal Ataturk of Turkey, Reza Shah aggressively followed secular policies. He limited the power of the ulama, did not give an exemption to seminary students from serving in the military, nationalized most of the private religious endowments, introduced a European dress code, and forced women to abandon their traditional veils.[31] The result was that the Pahlavi monarchy weakened the ulama's influence. They were hard-pressed to resist Reza Shah's policies, given that the middle class supported his program and that it was producing tangible results. More important, the middle class had accepted the Kemalist linkage between Westernization and progress, and it was more concerned with development than with religion. As a measure of how deeply the ulama were affected by the assault on their social position, during the Reza Shah period many of the sons of leading ulama abandoned seminary education and the career path of ulama to pursue modern education and join the burgeoning bureaucracy. The Pahlavi monarchy therefore alienated the ulama, who in 1925 had viewed the monarchy as more amenable to their interests than the parliament.

By the end of the first Pahlavi era the ulama viewed the executive office and the monarchy as direct threats to the ideal of the Shia realm.[32] As a result, the notion of Shia realm found a different connotation. Since a secular monarchy was now protecting the territorial integrity of Iran, giving nationalism a priority over the country's religious mooring, the notion of Shia realm became divorced from Iran the nation-state. It was clear that protection of territorial integrity of Iran did not mean protection of Shi'ism. On the other hand, the threat to Shi'ism was no longer an external threat to Iran's territorial integrity. That threat was now internal. It was now conceivable that Iran could be secure while Shi'ism was threatened—and by the Iranian state itself. This marked an end to the age-old conceptions of Shia realm that was built on an alliance between the shahs and the ulama.

The Reza Shah period therefore showed that the empowerment of the executive branch, despite its economic, bureaucratic, and military achievements, was not able to completely change the rules of the political game and common conceptions of politics. In fact, its effect on Iranian politics was to revive the debates over democracy that it had supposedly put to rest in 1921–1926. This paradox would prove important in defining Iranian history in the years to come.

That the Reza Shah period aggravated rather than solved the very debates that had paved its way to power had to do with idiosyncrasies of the early Pahlavi period. The problem lay not in that Reza Shah did not serve national aspirations, because he did; it did not lie in that his years in power did not get much done, because they genuinely transformed Iran in fundamental ways, giving the country a new lease on life. The problem rather lay in that he was not able to achieve what he did by also remaining true to the democratic and constitutionalist ideals that continued to be important to Iranians. He sought legitimacy in serving only one dimension of the Constitutional Revolution—the demand for stability and progress—and in ignoring the other, which was the demand for justice and democracy.

In the 1921–1926 period, Iranians were persuaded that progress, modernization, stability, and strong government were priorities. That did not mean that they wished to turn their backs on their democratic ideals. As the Pahlavi state became increasingly characterized by arbitrary rule, Iranians found themselves facing a Faustian choice between developmentalism and democracy, an end that would not benefit Iran and the Pahlavi regime. Reza Shah's failure was in how he achieved his success, and in forcing Iranians to choose between the ideals of development and democracy rather than creating an institutional framework that could fuse the quest for both. At the end of the Reza Shah period, the ideals of pluralism and popular sovereignty emerged as a vibrant force with roots in the Constitution. It would now easily supersede the demand for a strong executive authority and developmentalism. Interestingly, the main beneficiary of the renewed political debate were not only the pro-democracy forces or the ulama, but also, as will be discussed more fully in the next chapter, the new ideas that were emerging on the Iranian political scene: popular nationalism, socialism, and Islamic militancy. These ideas were all rooted in the middle classes. Though these were, by and large, the products of the Reza Shah era, these ideas represented the arrival of ideological politics, which would further complicate the conceptualization of democracy in the years to come.

2

The Triumph of the State, 1941–1979

The pattern of state-building that began in Iran in the mid-1920s was interrupted with the onset of the Second World War. Foreign intervention abruptly ended the Reza Shah period and ushered in a new era in Iran, one that was characterized by greater openness in domestic politics and new possibilities for relations between state and society.[1] Reza Shah's rule fell victim to changes in the global context, which once again proved to be a decisive force in determining ruptures and continuities in Iranian politics. The Second World War allied Britain and the Soviet Union against Germany. The Allies were determined to use Iranian territory for supplying the Soviet army on the eastern front, and for this it was imperative that they maintain control over Iran; they viewed Iran as a strategic asset in their war efforts against Germany. The British were particularly interested in removing Reza Shah from the scene. His continued dispute with British oil interests, combined with Iran's reliance on Germany for a number of industrial and public projects, had made the British wary of him. The Allies were not satisfied with Iran's mere declarations of neutrality; they demanded that Iran should expel all German nationals and that Reza Shah should abdicate.[2] In 1941, Reza Shah bowed to the pressure and was replaced on the throne by his son, Mohammad-Reza Pahlavi (r. 1941–1979, hereinafter referred to as "the Shah").

Whereas elsewhere in the Third World, European colonial powers had initiated state-building, in Iran they interfered with the state-building that Iranians had done on their own. Many Iranians, especially in urban areas, welcomed the political freedoms that followed Reza Shah's abdication, but since the Allies avoided entanglements in domestic politics, the disruption in state-building was not followed by attempts to proactively reshape Iranian politics—to rearrange its institutions and alter the balance of power among them—in the manner that the United States would impose in Germany and Japan after the war. The British did not change the country's constitution, and it retained the monarchy, agreeing to allow Reza Shah's son to assume the throne. The Allies did not initiate any social, political, or economic reforms. Any change in social, political, and economic relations that followed the occupation was not by design and found no reflection in the normative and institutional basis of the state, which means it failed to grow lasting roots. The fact that in later years the Iranian state would regain its power and position of dominance is therefore not all that surprising.

Still, Reza Shah's departure and weakening of the political center opened the political process and created possibilities for alternative trajectories of development. During the war, political groups that were earlier suppressed by Reza Shah—liberals, communists, and religious activists—organized and established a place for themselves in the political arena, and merchants who had lost ground to state interventions in the preceding decade thrived on the back of the war economy. The parliament, which had since 1921 steadily lost ground to the monarchy, was empowered and once again occupied center stage in Iranian politics. The political opening suggested that Iran might develop along democratic lines and that power could permanently shift from the monarchy to the parliament and devolve from state institutions to a broader spectrum of social and political actors. By the summer of 1953, however, the democratic interregnum had ended. That the Allies did not change the rules of the game and institutional structure of Iranian politics was important, but so were the domestic problems confronting democracy and, once again, changes in the global context.

The Democratic Interlude, 1941–1953

The 1941–1953 period witnessed an intense struggle over defining political identity in Iran. The outcome of that struggle would be important for the fate of democracy. This struggle unfolded among people in the cities, who, although more diversified in terms of class and occupation, still constituted no more than a small portion of Iran's population. As a result, the effect of this struggle on Iran's immediate political makeup remained less pronounced than its mark on Iranian intellectual life and imagination. Some of the political forces that became dominant during the 1941–1953 period were illiberal. Communist, fascist, and religious groups and parties operated in the open political process but were not committed to democracy. In fact, their activities led many Iranians look to the state—and some to the institution of the monarchy—to provide stability and order.

The Main Political Forces

An important political force in the 1941–1953 period was the communist Tudeh (Masses) Party.[3] Closely tied with the Soviet Union, the Tudeh Party posed a strong challenge to the ruling order and to Western interests in Iran. Leftist activism had gained momentum during the Reza Shah period as an intellectual movement that reflected the influence of European ideological trends and of the Soviet Union on Iranian politics. The Tudeh Party formed soon after Reza Shah's abdication. For the duration of the Second World War and during the Allied occupation of Iran the party was largely an anti-fascist and pro-peace forum. After the war ended it adopted a more openly communist posture—advocating class struggle and revolution and strong support for Stalin and the Soviet Union.

In the 1940s and early 1950s, the Tudeh Party proved effective in recruiting members from the middle classes, workers, intellectuals, and students, and in mobilizing these social groups in defense of social justice. However, its adherence to Stalin's cult of personality did not favor democracy, and it left Iranian politics with a "totalitarian addiction" that later, as leftists joined government and infused policymaking with their ideas, would contribute to restoring monarchical autocracy.[4] The Tudeh Party's ambiguous stance on the Soviet Union's attempt to separate Iran's northern province of Azerbaijan after the Second World War helped create both popular and Western support for strengthening the political center, which ultimately weakened the Tudeh Party and, in the process, the budding democracy.[5] The tensions that were inherent in Tudeh's pro-Soviet posture soon led a group of party activists to break away and form the Third Force (Nirou-ye Sevvom) under Khalil Maleki (d. 1969). Maleki's followers in later years formed the core of left-of-center and social democratic nationalism in Iran.[6]

The weakening of the state also encouraged greater political activism among liberal nationalists and democrats. The opening of the political system, greater freedoms of the press and association, a more prominent parliament, and a growing private sector and bazaar all strengthened the impetus for political debates, party politics, and competition for power. Politicians who had resisted concentration of power under Reza Shah, most notably Mosaddeq, emerged as spokesmen for democracy, advocating consolidation of power in the parliament and subservience of the monarchy to popular will.[7] Mosaddeq's political views had been formed during the constitutional movement, and, like many veteran constitutionalists, he understood democracy as the rule of law enshrined in a parliamentary system. He did not advocate individual rights and liberal democracy as those terms are understood today, although later historical accounts have attributed such advocacy to him. More accurately, Mosaddeq looked to the parliament rather than the strong arm of the state to bring about rule of law and guarantee social order. Still, insofar as he sought to empower the parliament, his views came to symbolize the demand for democracy in the face of state power.[8]

The pro-democracy forces were not represented by a single political party. In fact, even when Mosaddeq's National Front came to represent this political trend, it remained an umbrella organization comprising diverse sociopolitical forces that mainly shared a commitment to wrest control over Iran's oil industry from the British. There existed little consensus on the meaning and scope of democracy, only a vague hope that national freedom would somehow protect and promote political freedoms. Mosaddeq did little to clarify the ambiguity. He never put forward a clear program for democracy and instead stood for oppositional politics. There were socialists and social democrats such as those in the Iran Toilers Party, constitutionalists such as Gholam-Hossein Sadiqi (d. 1991), liberal nationalist forces such as those who gathered in the Iran Party, and moderate Muslim modernists such as Mehdi Bazargan (Iran's provisional prime minister in 1979; d. 1992).

Islamic Voices in Politics

The Islamic modernists represented an intellectual tradition that had first surfaced in India in the works of Sir Sayyid Ahmad Khan (d. 1898), and in Egypt in the ideas of Jamal-al-Din al-Afghani and Muhammad Abduh (d. 1905) and their students.[9] Iran's Islamic modernists, too, sought to reform Islamic law and ethics so that it would reflect values and goals of modernity and would accommodate social change, progress, and political freedoms.[10] Many were influenced by the ideas of Mirza Reza-Qoli Shariat Sangelaji (d. 1944), who followed in the footsteps of Sir Sayyid and Abduh to produce a modernist approach to Shi'ism.[11] Sangelaji sought to modernize Shia religious thought and practice by purging it of its popular accretions with a view to bringing the faith into the mainstream of modernization in Iran. Others, such as those in the Society of God-Worshipping Socialists, were further influenced by leftist ideologies.

In the 1960s and the 1970s, Sangelaji's attempts to open Shi'ism to modernist interpretations found new advocates in various places: Mehdi Bazargan, Ayatollah Seyyed Mahmoud Taleqani (d. 1979), Ayatollah Morteza Motahhari (d. 1979), and Ali Shariati (d. 1977) of Iran; Ayatollah Muhammad-Baqer al-Sadr of Iraq (d. 1980); Imam Musa al-Sadr (believed to have died in 1978) and Ayatollah Muhammad Jawad Mughniyya of Lebanon; and such cliques and institutions as the Goftar-e Mah (Talk of the Month) gathering and Hosseinieh Ershad institution in Tehran.

In this regard, Bazargan's works were debates with Western liberal thought and positivist philosophy.[12] He sought to systematize Shi'i thought in scientific terms by establishing linkages between faith, science, and social action similar to those encountered in the West in the liberal and positivist philosophical circles that have existed since the Renaissance.[13] Ayatollah Motahhari began with philosophical discourses. He set out to explain and even revive the tradition of Islamic philosophy (seen mainly through the prism of Shi'ism) and Shia theology, and yet he engaged Western philosophy in a debate revolving around issues of significance to Western thought, such as epistemology and ethics.[14] He hoped to formalize and rationalize Shia thought and, at the same time, to infuse the discipline of philosophy with a sense of the sacred. In this exercise, Motahhari looked not only to the youth in religious circles but also to those among the Western-educated secularists.

Ayatollah Taleqani's approach, on the other hand, was intellectually akin to that of Bazargan, yet was not in debate with or drawn from liberalism or positivism; rather, it was influenced by Western/modern dialectical philosophy.[15] Although bent on discerning the truth of the Islamic message and the Shia perspective and hence rhetorically critical of both capitalism and Marxism, Taleqani nevertheless revealed a preference for Marxist interpretations of Islamic history, the Qur'an, and Islamic social and legal doctrines.[16]

The trend initiated by Taleqani culminated in Shariati's works and in the revolutionary teachings of the leftist-fundamentalist urban guerrilla group Mojahedin-e Khalq (People's Mojahedin). The two would represent a Marxist approach to Islamic modernism. Though the Mojahedin echoed Shariati's teachings, they also related religious modernism to armed struggle.[17] Shariati did more than any other Shia modernist thinker to fuse religion with a modern worldview, in his case Marxism. Shariati's works systematically read Marxism into Islam but not by simply comparing Islam and Marxism to find common points. Rather, he presented Marxism as Islam and Islam as Marxism. In Shariati's conception, thinking and acting Islamically would be Marxist. In effect, Shariati eviscerated Islam in general and Shi'ism in particular. He drained their intellectual and theological content—dissociating doctrines, popular beliefs, and religious rites from their philosophical and spiritual foundations—and re-molded them into a Marxian paradigm wherein the dialectics of social conflict nudge history toward its inevitably revolutionary fate.[18]

More recently, Shariati's ideas were echoed in the works of Abdol-Karim Soroush, who has advocated the modernization of Shia jurisprudence. So-roush's approach differs from approaches advocated in the 1970s in that it is in debate with Shia fundamentalism rather than with traditional Shia thought. Hence Soroush has been more concerned with promoting *fiqh-e pouya* (dynamic jurisprudence) as the means for reforming Shia fundamentalism than he has been with socioeconomic issues, which at any rate were incorporated into Shia fundamentalism by Ayatollah Khomeini.

The resurgence of religion in politics during this period was equally signif-icant. Religious forces sought to roll back the secular policies of the Pahlavi state and to institutionalize their own role in society and politics.[19] As the senior ulama, who had insisted on the quietist tradition in Shi'ism and supported the monarchy before the communist threat in the 1950s, passed from the scene, more assertive and militant ulama typified Shia leadership in Qom. Most notable in this regard was Ayatollah Seyyed Rouhollah Khomeini, who put forward a more militant resistance to state-led secularism.[20] His oppositional stance proved popular with younger clerics and seminary students, and it would evolve into an ideological resistance to Pahlavi rule.[21] To this end, the clergy became active in the political arena, but not with the aim of strengthening institutions of civil society and democracy. In fact, both the communists and religious forces, rather than effecting democratic practice, engaged in agitational politics—dem-onstrations and strikes in the case of the Tudeh Party, and political assassina-tions in the case of religious activists. By creating political uncertainty, disrup-tions, and social tensions, they hampered consolidation of a democratic movement and unintentionally drove the monarchy to rely on foreign support for its consolidation of power.

Two principal actors played prominent roles in defining religious activ-ism in politics during this time period. The first was Ayatollah Abol-Qasem Kashani (d. 1961) and the second was the Islamist fundamentalist organization Fadaiyan-e Islam (Devotees of Islam). Kashani was a midranking cleric with ties to Tehran's bazaar merchants. During the occupation of Iran by the Allied forces, he sought to mobilize religious support for regaining ground that the ulama had lost to the Pahlavi state between 1921 and 1941. Kashani was a pragmatic politician and did not espouse an ideological view. He did not put forth a theory of the Islamic state or claims to governance by the ulama. Rather he sought to restore the ulama's place in society and politics by energizing religious support. In this he would join forces with the Fadaiyan group. Kashani was able to assert religion to claim a voice in politics, but he was not able to effectively compete with liberal nationalists or communists for the hearts and minds of the middle class. It was not the ulama and religious fervor that would be the beneficiary of the decline of the Pahlavi state, but secular ideologies and political tendencies. By 1951, Kashani had reconciled to the fact that to remain relevant, he had to throw in his lot with nationalists. He therefore joined forces with Mosaddeq in supporting the nationalization of oil, although he would reverse that position when it became clear that Mosaddeq was likely to fall prey to communists or monarchists.

The Fadaiyan were perhaps one of the first expressions of militant fundamentalism, which would dominate Muslim politics after the 1980s. The group consisted of young and zealous seminary students and lower middle class youth.[22] Although the Fadaiyan never put forward a systematic ideology or a program comparable with that of Muslim Brotherhood in Egypt or Jamaat-e Islami in Pakistan, its worldview drew on similar premises. Fadaiyan drew on the pan-Islamist sentiments of Jamal al-Din al-Afghani to promote a vision of a united Muslim *ummah* (community) that would be both the repository and guarantor of Islam in society and the basis for an Islamic government that would cure society of its ills and deliver a utopian order.

Unlike Islamic fundamentalism in the Arab world or South Asia, the Fadaiyan in Iran did not create a political party or strive to organize the masses around an Islamic platform. They rather resorted to terrorist tactics that are now associated with militant Salafism, such as assassinations of leading politicians and use of violence to undermine state power. In the 1960s they joined forces with Ayatollah Khomeini's protest movement, and several of their longtime members joined Iran's revolutionary elite after 1979.

Fadaiyan's opposition to the state reflected the clergy's earlier resentments toward Reza Shah's secularism. However, the Fadaiyan did not represent Islamic institutions or all the ulama, and they did not receive the blessing of the ulama as a group. Their rise and activism in fact manifested the tensions between traditional institutions of the ulama and militant fundamentalist activism—a tension that, for example, has also been evident in Egypt between al-Azhar and Muslim Brotherhood.

Imperialism, Nationalism, and Crisis of Democracy, 1951–1953

The debates over the balance of power between state and society and the underlying values of Iranian politics unfolded in the context of a number of crises that challenged the Iranian government's sovereignty and territorial integrity.

The first of these crises came at the end of the Second World War when Britain and the United States withdrew their troops from Iran, but the Soviet army showed no signs of following suit. Stalin's intentions in Iran were the same as those he had in Eastern Europe: he intended to use the Red Army to expand Moscow's influence.[23] In 1946, the Iranian provinces of Kurdistan and Azerbaijan, with Soviet backing, formed autonomous movements and declared independence.[24]

The Azerbaijan Republic was led by Iranian communists outside the Tudeh Party. The separatist movement placed Iranian communists in other provinces in a dilemma: should they support Stalin and Azerbaijani secessionism or stand with Iranian nationalists in rejecting ethnic separatism and foreign encroachments? This dilemma weakened the Tudeh Party, prompting many to leave its ranks to join other parties; it also paved the way for the state to later suppress communism as a Trojan Horse of the Soviet Union.

The Soviet army was ultimately compelled to leave Iran by a combination of American pressure in the form of the Truman Doctrine and concerted effort by the central Iranian government at the time, led by Prime Minister Ahmad Qavam (d. 1955). Qavam successfully negotiated with Stalin, promising Moscow an oil deal in exchange for departure of Soviet troops. The deal provided Stalin with a face-saving way to withdraw his troops. The crisis also underscored Iran's need for a strong defense of Iran's territorial integrity before foreign intrigue. The success of Qavam's pragmatic diplomacy in safeguarding national interests would assert a model for pursuing nationalist goals that would be followed by Mohammad-Reza Shah, and it would confirm the state's claim to speaking for nationalism. In many regards, the events of 1946 made clear to Iranians the imperative of a strong state. This realization would play an important role in the Pahlavi monarchy's view of its own national role in the 1960s and 1970s.

More important for determining the course of state-building was the nationalization of the oil industry and the crisis of 1951–1953, and its linkage with Cold War politics. Since the 1930s Iran had unsuccessfully demanded higher royalties and more transparent accounting from the Anglo-Iranian Oil Company. The dispute had initially contributed to British distrust of Reza Shah and his removal from power. The democratic opening in the 1940s would only contribute to the intensification of the dispute, which culminated in an impasse in 1951. As the British company refused to accommodate Iran's demands for higher royalties, Iranian nationalist sentiments were aroused, and that eventually led to nationalization of the oil industry. The monarchy, the military, and some in the business community favored a low-key approach—believing that a confrontational attitude would not favor Iran. However, owing to British intransigence, the Iranian people demanded more. The popularly elected nationalist prime minister, Mohammad Mosaddeq, and his National Front coalition capitalized on the public mood and successfully campaigned for nationalization of the oil industry in 1951. The decision was widely popular within Iran, and it was supported by the Tudeh Party and religious activists as well.

Britain responded by cutting Iran out of the oil market.[25] The Iranian economy plunged into a crisis, which in turn translated into greater social tension and political ambivalence.[26] Britain even orchestrated communist demonstrations to underscore the risks involved in Mosaddeq's maverick foreign policy and to convince Iranians and the American government alike of the imminent communist threat to Iran.[27] The palpable fear of a communist takeover changed the political alignment that dominated Iranian politics. The religious establishment, worried about communism, switched sides, as did key segments of the middle classes and commercial interests, and some nationalist leaders.[28] The political realignment promoted concerted action by the alliance between the monarchy and the Iranian military in close cooperation with the United States and Britain. The result was a military coup that toppled Mosaddeq's government, ended the democratic interregnum, and restored power to the monarchy.[29]

The crisis also crystallized perceptions of nationalism and shaped debates over state-building. Mosaddeq stood for an idealistic approach to nationalism, one that argued that the British position lacked legal standing and was therefore unjust and not binding on Iran. He believed that Iran was in the right and that it should stand its ground. The opposition to Mosaddeq, led by the Shah, conservative politicians such as prime ministers Ahmad Qavam and General Ali Razmara (who was assassinated by the Fadaiyan in 1951), and commanders of the military, most notably General Fazlollah Zahedi (d. 1963), also believed that the British position was unjust and illegal. However, they thought that Mosaddeq's idealism had led to a Don Quixote foreign policy. The Shah and his allies were also resentful of Mosaddeq's insistence that Iran was a constitutional monarchy in which the writ of the parliament was supreme and that the monarchy was bound by the restrictions that were imposed on its powers in the constitution.

Regardless of the merits of Iran's position, it was unrealistic to expect that the country would be able to win its case; in "charging the windmill," Iran was more likely to jeopardize its national interests. Only five years after the Soviet attempt to separate Azerbaijan and Kurdistan from Iran, the monarchy and its allies believed that Iran's interests lay in close ties with the West to ward off the Soviet threat. Whereas Mosaddeq saw Britain as the foreign devil, they saw Britain and its imperialism as the lesser evil. They believed that Iranian nationalism was best served by realism that employed Western power to preserve Iran's territorial integrity. That Mosaddeq's passionate rhetoric did not reflect much immediate concern with territorial integrity, the imperative of state-building to realize it, or how the Cold War might affect Iran played into the hand of the monarchy and its allies.

The monarchy's position in this period was reminiscent of Vosouq's stance some two and half decades earlier, and it would continue to inform the Pahlavi monarchy's developmentalist agenda in decades to come. However, whereas Mosaddeq's idealism would capture the popular imagination, realistic nationalism would be chided for its willingness to compromise with imperialist powers. Moreover, Mosaddeq's idealism would become associated with democracy, although he was not directly concerned with consolidating democracy. Rather, the identification with democracy can be traced to the perception that Mosaddeq had been ousted by a foreign-backed military coup. Although the American CIA and the British MI6 were instrumental in the success of the coup, it would be mistaken to view the coup as entirely a foreign instigation with no support—albeit tacit—among various social and political groups in Iran. In many regards, the Iranian military was more important to the coup than was the monarchy. The military moreover manipulated British apprehensions and used CIA assets just as much as they used the Iranian military. The Iranian military realized the aim of preserving Iranian national interests before the threat it perceived in Mosaddeq's idealism. Most Iranians were sympathetic to Mosaddeq's idealism, but by the summer of 1953 they had grown wary of the wisdom of his rejectionism and the political and economic risks that it would have entailed. Although popular perceptions in later years would deny this, in the summer of 1953, the monarchy and the military's realism resonated with many Iranians, whose personal interests and perceptions of national interest had diverged from Mosaddeq's platform. Although many Iranians would later idolize Mosaddeq as a "secular saint" and lament the consolidation of power in state institutions, the threat that they perceived to Iranian sovereignty and social stability in 1953 had nudged them to acquiesce to accelerating the pace of state-building and to vesting greater powers in those institutions that could provide order and protect Iran's territorial integrity.

Finally, it is from this point forward that the demand for democracy became largely reduced to intellectual debates; it increasingly was separated from the reality of Iranian domestic and foreign policies. It is also from this point forward that any moves on the part of the state to become more autocratic were met with oppositional politics targeting state institutions. This development left Iranians with a conflicted vision of their relations with the state: they needed what the state provided, but they were deeply suspicious of its authority.

The democratic interregnum saw the possibility of alternative identities shaping state–society relations and Iranian politics developing along a different trajectory. However, by 1954, those possibilities were no longer present. The changing global context and foreign intervention first interrupted and then resumed the pattern of state formation first instituted by Reza Shah.

Resurrection of the Pahlavi State, 1954–1963

The 1954–1963 period was one of gradual consolidation of state power under the monarchy and resumption of the pattern of state-building that had been dominant between 1925 and 1941. It placed emphasis on order and development as national goals, attainment of which superseded that of the demand for democracy. It also saw state institutions declaring themselves as the embodiment of national will and responsible for realizing its aspirations. Relying on the military, and with money and technical help from the United States, the monarchy went on the offensive against its opposition. The National Front and the Tudeh Party were banned, and the military and bureaucracy were purged of their members and sympathizers.[30] The campaign also weakened institutions of civil society and ultimately the parliament, and it dimmed the prospects for democracy.

Cold War considerations led the United States to support this campaign and to help train Iranian military and intelligence agencies to protect the state, which was viewed as the bulwark against communism and the Soviet Union's southward expansion.[31] American financial aid helped buoy Iran's economy—alleviating the pressures of the preceding years—and generated support for the ruling order. The Pahlavi monarchy closely tied Iran's foreign policy to the Western position in the Cold War with the aim of both ensuring Iran's national security and rapidly developing the country.

The monarchy saw parliamentary democracy as inimical to the realization of these goals. For in the mind of the monarchy and its allies, Mosaddeq had jeopardized both Iran's economic stability and national interests. As such, democracy and development came to be viewed as mutually exclusive goals, and the former would have to be kept at bay as state-building developed and secured Iran. Opposition to the Pahlavi monarchy would from this time forward challenge both the ruling regime's assumptions about Iran's national security interests and its development goals in an attempt to undermine its claim to legitimacy.

The consolidation of power under the monarchy was also supported by the economic agencies of the state, who believed that parliamentary oversight and interference were compromising the integrity of their policymaking. Clashes between these agencies and the resurgent parliament between 1941 and 1953 had hurt economic policymaking, which was now a priority of the political leadership and its Western allies.[32] The alliance between the monarchy and the state economic agencies—and ultimately, the bureaucracy as a whole—against democratic institutions was first consecrated by Reza Shah. Just as was the case between 1925 and 1941, during this time the alliance would commit the state to a largely economic vision of development. The spirit of this posture was captured in the Shah's statement, "When the Iranians learn to behave like Swedes, I will behave like [the] King of Sweden."[33]

Single-minded pursuit of development—the public good whose provision would shape state-building—would require further streamlining organization of resources and people, the imperatives which had also propelled state formation under Reza Shah and sustained growth of state capacity. This would mean bureaucratic reforms and the replacement of political leaders with administrative managers. This trend was associated with young, Western-educated technocrats with no independent base of political support. The "Massachussetis," as this new cadre was facetiously called, represented the greater influence of the United States in Iran, but also the triumph of developmentalism over democracy in state-building. From this point forward, politics would increasingly be seen as limited to administrative affairs, and the Shah would look to managers rather than political leaders to run the affairs of the state. Competence rather than political acumen or base of support would become key to positions of power at the helm of the technocratic order. The reign of the technocrats began in 1963 with the premierships of Hasan-Ali Mansour (d. 1964) and Amir-Abbas Hoveyda (d. 1979).[34]

The focus on developmentalism produced a culture of technocracy in government.[35] The positive side of this trend was that greater emphasis was placed on bureaucratic excellence, and investment in various state institutions was increased.[36] The government also focused its attention on education—especially higher education—in order to provide development with the necessary knowhow.[37] In the process, Iran acquired a great deal of intellectual capital—educated classes that were conversant in Western ideas who also contributed to the flowering of arts and culture. That intellectual capital survived the demise of the Pahlavi regime and is largely responsible for the scientific, literary, and artistic achievements in Iran since the mid-1990s.

The culture of technocracy, however, also led to the cultural alienation of the state and the Pahlavi elite. The focus on development in the absence of competitive politics made the bureaucratic elite immune to demands from below. This also enabled them to more freely embrace Western culture and attitudes, which accentuated the divide between state and society. This eventually made it difficult for the Shah to convince Iranians of the merits and promises of his development agenda. Iranians—especially the middle class, which was supposed to benefit from development, and in significant measure did benefit— became cynical toward the Shah's vision to turn Iran into a leading industrial power by the millennium, and they saw such claims as pretentious megalomania.

This alienation became particularly problematic as the Shah followed an openly pro-American foreign policy, which, regardless of its benefits for Iranian national interests, was unpopular with Iranians who were far more inclined toward Third World causes than was their leader. That the Shah's return to the throne had been made possible by American and British intervention made his foreign policy further suspect, and Iranians saw him as a stooge of imperialist interests.[38]

The greater attention devoted to development in the 1960s also led to some social engineering. The wisdom on development at the time, reflected in the policies of international agencies and espoused in economic theory, was biased against agriculture and the rural economy and favored urbanization and industrial development. Development agencies encouraged Iran to more aggressively pursue social changes that would accommodate development. The Kennedy administration, too, pressured the Shah in the same direction after Khrushchev characterized Iran as a decaying feudal society that was ripe for a communist revolution.[39]

These pressures led the Iranian state to reformulate its relations with feudalism, which up to then had supported the monarchy; the religious establishment, with which the monarchy had only a tenuous alliance; and the bureaucracy and middle classes, which, though they were not committed to the monarchy, were the main agents and beneficiaries of development. The consequences of these reformulations would determine the course of state formation and would bring into sharper focus the ramifications of the path that the state was following on development.

Economic Growth and Authoritarianism, 1963–1979

Between 1959 and 1963, the Pahlavi state had to confront a number of challenges, the resolution of which necessitated intensifying its commitment to development and creating greater room for pursuing it. During this period, the National Front reappeared on the political scene just as unhappiness with sluggish economic and political reform led to rumblings in the military and security forces, which led to coup attempts followed by purges in the military high command.[40] The state considered the resurgence of anti-regime political opposition at a time of serious dissent among the elite as dangerous, and it viewed socio-economic reform and overhaul of the bureaucracy as necessary to its survival.

All this occurred at a time when the United States was wavering in its unconditional support of the Pahlavi state. The Kennedy administration was not willing to give the Shah total support and, moreover, viewed some form of reform in Iran as necessary to limit communist influence in the country. The change in American attitude parlayed into a momentum for wide-scale reform in Iran.[41]

In 1961–1962, an austerity package prescribed by the International Monetary Fund had led to a severe recession and a balance of payment crisis. Oil revenue, even with modest increases, would not satisfy development and other needs.[42] Subsequent government stabilization policies had failed to alleviate the problem; unemployment had remained high, and, given the general climate of political tension at the time, more widespread challenges to the regime were anticipated.[43] The perceived threat to the ruling order convinced state leaders that they could not afford prolonged economic crises. Hence reform would have to go hand in hand with economic growth. The Pahlavi state began to see development as integral to sociopolitical reform.[44] This vision culminated in the White Revolution of 1963—the term was coined to upstage the Left and its promise of red revolution.

The White Revolution was a package of sweeping reforms that aimed to change the structure of social relations in Iran and to enable more effective resource mobilization in the service of development.[45] The most important initiatives were land reform, enfranchisement of women, and provision of greater rights and share of industries to industrial labor. Through the White Revolution, the state hoped to institutionalize its hold over the middle classes and over those social groups that might serve as bases of support for an effective communist movement—the poor, the peasantry, and the industrial labor. This was especially the case since the Tudeh Party and, especially, the National Front had at one time or another advocated land reform. Paradoxically, the Shah's land reform initiative was implemented by his minister of agriculture, Hasan Arsanjani, who was a former socialist. Critiques of land reform blamed its excesses on Arsanjani's egalitarian tendencies.

The Shah also believed that these reforms were necessary for effective development. They would modernize Iranian society, changing it in ways that would help industrialization. The White Revolution expedited the pace of urbanization; the first major shift in the balance between rural and urban populations occurred in the 1960s. By the 1970s, this trend would provide a very different context for the intellectual and political struggles that had punctuated state-building since the first decades of the twentieth century.

This was a risky move. For the oligarchy and the religious establishment—the principal losers in the reforms—had in the past supported the monarchy, whereas middle-class support had at best been tenuous in modern times. The Shah was making the same mistake as his father, vesting his political fortunes in a social class whose loyalties would ultimately not rest with the monarchy. In fact, the reforms of 1963 would expand the size of that class, and though it benefited from development, it showed little support for state-building. In addition, given the Pahlavi state's pro-industry bias, it was not inclined to create a base of support among the peasantry. Industrial labor was not yet sufficiently powerful to support the monarchy, and even if it were to become a force, the monarchy would be unlikely to claim its allegiance for long. More immediately, however, the state relied on the rising power of the bureaucracy, which itself was being modernized from within.[46] The bureaucracy in general and its economic agencies in particular were committed to development, and so they strongly supported the reforms. The reforms created a ruling alliance between the monarchy and the bureaucracy. In effect, the state reformulated its linkages with society and defined the shape of its opposition. The oligarchy (which remained a force to contend with for a while longer), the religious establishment, and the Left—all of whom opposed the White Revolution, or viewed it as the means through which the state might devour their base of support—gravitated toward an antistate stance. The restoration of power to the monarchy thus reconstituted the oppositional alliance that had first surfaced during the Reza Shah period.

The first expression of this opposition was the protest movement led by Ayatollah Seyyed Rouhollah Khomeini in 1964.[47] The protest, which soon turned violent and was ultimately brutally suppressed, was strongly antistate. In 1953, the ulama had supported the monarchy, viewing the specter of communism and the political instability that was generated by the standoff over oil nationalization to be a threat to the religious establishment.[48] However, as state-building prevailed, once again the convergence of interests between the monarchy and the ulama proved short-lived. For the ulama, this was most clearly evident in the White Revolution. Ayatollah Khomeini characterized the enfranchisement of women as "un-Islamic," and he rejected land reform as a violation of Islamic protection of the right to private property. The protesters were also opposed to the proposed Status of Forces Law—the immunity from Iranian law that was afforded to American military personnel as a part of U.S.-Iranian military agreements in the early 1960s.[49]

Among those taking part in the protest movement were followers of the National Front, pro-democracy and civil liberties advocates, and socialists and communists. The first two groups opposed specific parts of the White Revolution, whereas the Left viewed the reform package as a whole a threat to its own political position. The White Revolution was promising to Iranians reforms that had traditionally been proposed by the Left. It threatened to change the social structure in opposition to which the Left had mobilized support, and to render the Left's political program obsolete.

The protest movement failed. The state's agenda of social reform and rapid economic development thus unfolded unencumbered. Still, the protest movement had the effect of committing the state to a greater use of force in contending with the opposition. This in turn led to the consolidation of the anti-Pahlavi forces into a more coherent force led by the clergy and the Left. Such thinkers as Shariati formulated a socially conscious religious perspective—something akin to Liberation Theology—that could consolidate the anti-Shah alliance.[50] This opposition would later opt for violence and, in turn, would face increased violence from the state. From this point forward, the security apparatuses of the state, most notably the secret police, SAVAK, would use repressive measures, including detentions and torture, to subdue the opposition. The opposition produced radical urban guerrilla organizations, escalating antistate activities to the level of armed conflict and acts of terror.[51] The radicalization of the opposition and the state's use of violence in suppressing it polarized Iranian politics and gradually concentrated power in a limited number of state institutions—most notably its security apparatuses—and in the monarchy.

The 1960s were a period of profound social and economic change and strong state control over society. It marked the "golden age" of the Shah's rule. The reforms of the 1960s awakened Iranians to new possibilities, and economic changes profoundly affected social relations. Political change, however, did not keep pace with the growing complexity of society and the changes that it engendered. The state's inability to adapt to the very changes that it had initiated would eventually undermine the gains that it had made in the 1960s. Although this period was the pinnacle of the Shah's rule, it also laid the foundation for political crises.

Economically, however, the 1960s were a period of relative success. Land reform, reform within the bureaucracy, and the weakening of the parliament provided opportunity for economic managers to pursue growth aggressively and with greater freedom from outside influence.[52] The result was notable industrial transformation, producing growth rates that were unmatched in Iran's history. Real gross domestic product for this period grew at an average of 9.2 percent, real gross national product at 8.8 percent per annum, and industrial growth rates averaged 15 percent.[53] These were among the highest in the Third World, and two or three times the average rates for developing countries. Moreover, during this period the central characteristics of the economy changed as it acquired medium and heavy industries, petrochemicals, pharmaceuticals, and consumer goods. There emerged a modern private sector that was closely tied to economic managers within the bureaucracy. The partnership between the two created a strong momentum for industrial planning and policy implementation. Many of the industrial projects, investments in infrastructure, and social initiatives of that time continue to be the foundation of development in Iran today.[54] Social and cultural initiatives of the government and the new institutions associated with them—even those that were unpopular at the time, such as the Women's Organization of Iran, National Iranian Radio and Television, and the Shiraz Art Festival for "its avant-garde absurdities"[55]—helped produce institutional foundations for women's activism and artistic expression that survived the revolution and fuel Iran's recent cultural vitality.[56]

The industrialization strategy had broader sociopolitical implications. Two in particular were important: the rise of a class of industrial managers and captains of industry, centered in the new private sector, and significant modernization of the bureaucracy, both of which would have lasting effects on the Iranian economy and politics. Both are, moreover, central to understanding the workings of the state and its relations with society in the later Pahlavi period and even in the Islamic Republic. The rise of the private sector and the greater efficiency, power, and autonomy of the bureaucracy for a time helped spur development and provide state leaders with social support to confront the political opposition.[57]

Economic development in Iran in the 1960s was largely based on Import Substitution Industrialization. Though import substitution produced rapid growth rates early on and helped industrialization to take off, it also resulted in political and economic challenges in the long run. Import substitution placed emphasis on capital-intensive industries and hence led to the neglect of small-scale production and the agricultural sector. It ultimately led to uneven development, rapid urbanization, and income inequality.[58] It also led to a bias in the ruling regime in favor of urbanization and industrialization, which prevented it from building a support base among the peasantry that had benefited from land reform—a support base that might have acted as a political counterweight to the boisterous middle class. Import substitution also put pressure on government finances and balance of trade just as it augmented state control of the economy.

By the late 1960s, some of these problems were evident in Iran. Some in the ruling regime argued for devoting more attention to social equity, while others favored ending autonomous decision making in the bureaucracy in favor of policy positions that would take account of the political issues that now faced the state. It was partly in response to these pressures that the Shah compromised the autonomy of the bureaucracy and limited the powers of the private sector. More important, however, the problems born of import substitution forced Iran to demand higher oil prices. Iran was able to achieve that end in 1970s when the Organization of Petroleum Exporting Countries raised the price of oil substantially.

The rise in the price of oil removed the financial pressures and allowed the state to spend more freely on various industrial initiatives, infrastructure development projects, and social programs. However, higher oil prices also put insurmountable economic and political challenges before the state. In the first place, it hurt the pattern of economic development. Whereas growth from 1963 to 1969 had been based on import substitution and the rise of the private sector and had been managed by autonomous state agencies, growth now relied more on oil income and large-scale public projects, and it was more directly controlled by the Shah. During the 1970s, the state sought to encourage industrialization by moving from assembling products to manufacturing various components, but industrial production declined in efficiency. Oil income and interference by the Shah and the political leaders with bureaucratic oversight of the economy affected the decision-making process. Whereas during the 1960s there had been significant bureaucratic autonomy in managing the growth, during the 1970s that autonomy ended in the face of different political priorities and attitudes toward the economy. Although the Iranian economy performed well in the 1970s, it veered off the path toward viable industrialization and market development, a trend that would eventually lead to serious crises.

The oil boom created bottlenecks in the economy and led to wasteful spending on grandiose projects; Iran invested heavily on infrastructure and industrial projects, but also on war materiel, nuclear power plants, and public enterprises of little economic value.[59] All this reduced public trust in the management of the economy. The rapid pace of growth also created social dislocation, cultural alienation, and new political demands that the state was both unable and unwilling to deliver.[60] In addition, the newfound wealth encouraged corruption and speculative financial activities. This hurt public morale and skewed popular perceptions of the meaning and intent of entrepreneurial activity. The oil wealth also raised expectations, so much so that the state not only gained no political support for acquiring the new wealth, but also found itself falling short of fulfilling expectations.

The Iranian state began to face political problems associated with rentier states—states in which the lion's share of national income comes not from productive activities, but from such sources as aid or revenue from the sale of oil and minerals.[61] Rentier states are generally politically weak. Since the state derives little if any of its income from the population, it does not invest in the capability to extract resources from it. As a result, the negotiation between the population and the state over rights and revenue does not feature prominently in state-building. Instead, rentier states invest in distributive mechanisms, and their relationship with the people is that of a distributor of patron and client; they do not develop strong links with society. In fact, as was the case in Iran, the dominant role of distribution in state–society relations relieves state leaders of accountability to society, renders state activity apolitical, and encourages aloofness and hyperautonomy, all of which weaken the state.

Rent, moreover, does not provide legitimacy. For the population does not credit the government for the generation of wealth, although it expects more from the government in terms of distribution of wealth. Popular support remains contingent on continued flow of rent. Rather than extraction of resources serving as the means for creating state-society ties, as was the case in early European states, here distribution of resources limits the development of those ties.

As oil income dominated the Iranian economy by the mid-1970s, the Pahlavi state faced a serious political crisis. Its developmental agenda had led to greater concentration of power in the state, with the monarchy at center stage, and to severed ties with an array of social groups.[62] All along, however, the Pahlavi state had justified its course of action in terms of provision of a public good: development. Between 1946 and 1979, the state had changed the fundamental character of the economy, shifting from agriculture to industry. Public planning, urbanization, industrialization, diversification, and infrastructural and human capital investments had produced sustained change and growth. The growth was spread across all sectors, albeit unevenly, and it increased incomes and investment rates. The oil wealth, however, denied the state the ability to claim credit for its economic achievements. It undermined the state's developmentalist claims as it depicted development as synonymous with oil revenue, rendering redundant the political apparatuses that the Pahlavi monarchs had argued were needed for realizing development. The economic and political consequences of higher oil prices therefore pushed an already narrowly based state to the brink of collapse.[63]

The Pahlavi state helped exacerbate the crisis before it by encouraging political mobilization at a time when the public mood was souring toward the regime. Yet at the same time, state institutions were increasingly unable to cope with growing political demands that the increased urbanization and social mobility had brought. This led to intense debates among the Pahlavi elite over industrialization, institutional formation, and the introduction of pluralism to the political system. These debates were informed by diverse Western intellectual trends, ranging from ideas from the Club of Rome meetings in the early 1970s that warned against the costs of industrialization to the anti-industrialization views of Ivan Illich and the institutionalism of Talcott Parsons and Samuel Huntington.[64] The debates occurred in intellectual circles close to the Queen and in such forums as the Aspen Institute conferences in 1975 and 1977, at which the Queen and a number of her senior advisors debated political change in Iran.

These debates among the elite were largely divorced from the discussions that were shaping the discourse of opposition to the Pahlavi state. Still, state leaders took these debates seriously, which led the government to experiment with new ways of contending with crises that confronted the state: the growing cost of industrialization and political participation. For instance, in the mid-1970s Majid Rahnema, a former minister of science and technology, led the Alashtar Project—named after a village in western Iran—in introducing grass-roots democracy to rural areas.[65]

More significant, a number of the Shah's advisors came to the conclusions that the only way he could stabilize his rule was to create bridges to the newly mobilized social groups through new political institutions that would give these new voices representation. Convinced that the monarchy needed to build political institutions to contend with greater political mobilization, the Shah disbanded the multiparty parliamentary system in favor of a one-party system. He formed the Rastakhiz (Resurrection) Party in 1975, hoping that it would provide greater political representation and a way to channel social demands into policymaking, thus creating new relations between state and society. Rastakhiz Party, it was hoped, would bring alienated urban Iranians into the political process in favor of monarchy.[66] One-party systems do not tolerate apathy, and Iran was no exception to this rule. The regime compelled Iranians to join the party and to vote in its internal elections and parliamentary elections. The result was that the ruling regime mobilized an alienated but apathetic urban population, which quickly turned on the regime and used the networks that were created by Rastakhiz to foment opposition. That opposition quickly linked up with ongoing leftist and religious agitation to escalate tensions.[67]

The political tensions erupted in 1977 when oil revenues dropped because of market fluctuations. The economic downturn led to cutbacks in government that proved to be politically consequential. The government cut its subsidy to the ulama in Qom, compelling many to turn to Ayatollah Khomeini for support. A state whose linkage with society had become narrowly focused on distributing wealth was in peril when that distribution was disrupted. The tensions eventually culminated in the Islamic Revolution of 1979 that toppled the Pahlavi state.

The Unraveling of the Pahlavi State

The crisis unfolded at a time of change in Iran's relations with the United States as Jimmy Carter became president in 1977. Carter was a strong advocate of political reform in Iran;[68] this new approach created confusion in the Iranian state and emboldened the opposition. The changing international context once again proved decisive in Iranian politics.

The opposition to the Pahlavi state consisted of liberal and pro-democracy forces, the Left—including social democrats, socialists, and various communist groupings[69]—and religious activists, who were increasingly militant, especially after Ayatollah Khomeini, then in exile in Iraq, assumed leadership of them. Khomeini built on the anti-Pahlavi consensus between the religious establishment and the Left that had been in place since 1964, drawing on the ideological works of thinkers like Shariati who had created a common ground between religious and leftist activism. Khomeini, however, consolidated this consensus further, and managed to successfully keep the opposition focused on the ouster of the Pahlavi regime, postponing the resolution of all ideological disagreements and cultural tensions to the postrevolutionary period.[70] His presence on the political scene, however, made the question of religious identity central to politics. Khomeini and the revolutionary forces rejected the secularism of Pahlavi state and thereby its developmentalist agenda at the ideological level. The success of the revolution in large part owed to the fact that this stance did not create tensions in the ranks of revolutionary forces, segments of which were politically at odds with the Pahlavi state but shared its secularism and were themselves products of the Pahlavi state's social engineering.

The Pahlavi state had failed to create an alliance of the secular social forces against fundamentalism. Instead, the secular liberal and leftist elements forged an agreement with Ayatollah Khomeini. Had he persuaded secular Iranians that they needed a cultural (antifundamentalist) coalition, that might have bridged divisions between the ruling regime and its secularist opposition. But instead his response was to blame the political crisis on foreign intrigue while, at the same time, trying to placate the opposition by hastily introducing reforms and negotiating with the National Front for power sharing. These negotiations did not yield any results until it was too late for the National Front to control the opposition. The basis of the dominant political alliances at the end of the Pahlavi period was distaste for the Shah; differences between fundamentalists and secular forces were glossed over to form this front. This alliance was made possible by regime policies that had, since the 1960s, prevented a secular oppositional politics to operate in the open and to produce its own leaders. In the absence

of a viable secular leader, pro-democracy elements and even some leftist elements turned to the leadership that Khomeini represented. As a result, the
revolutionary movement in Iran in 1979 was politically uniform, but it was culturally and socially eclectic in that it included both fundamentalist and secular
liberal and leftist elements. It put forward an Islamic conception of Iranian identity as a foil to the secular and pre-Islamic definition that the Shah's regime
promoted. In so doing, the revolutionary movement relied on the rich repertoire
of Shia symbolisms, which also armed it with a way to effectively relate its
message to the broader population.[71]

It is important to note that the opposition to the Shah, secular and leftist
but also Islamic, set itself not only on a higher moral ground than the Pahlavi
regime but also on a higher intellectual one. The opposition claimed intellectual
superiority over a regime that, although staffed by Western-educated technocrats, was not able to engage in the intellectualized discourse of its opposition.
It was through literary productions and in intellectual circles—"committed literature" and "committed intellectualism"[72]—that the opposition's worldview
and understanding of Iran's history, social reality, economic potential, and political and foreign policy challenges took form. It was also in these mediums
that the language of opposition was formed. Intellectuals, writers, and artists
would play a prominent role in undermining the Shah's legitimacy. On the eve
of the revolution in October 1977, ten nights of poetry readings organized by
the Writers Association at the German Cultural Center in Tehran, popularly
known as Dah Shab (Ten Nights), helped galvanize public opinion in favor of
the revolution.[73]

The intellectual dimension was also important in how various revolutionary
groupings presented their ideas and what language they adopted to relate them
to their constituencies. A great deal of debate among revolutionaries took an
intellectual tone; likewise, militant fundamentalists asserted their intellectual
credentials. Khomeini's followers emphasized his scholarly achievements, and
especially his knowledge of Islamic theology, law, philosophy, and mysticism.
However, although Shi'ism has a rich intellectual tradition, fundamentalists
would eventually feel compelled to also display their versatility with Western
intellectual sources in order to keep in step with the secular opposition to the
Shah.

The need to legitimate Islamic fundamentalism intellectually made Khomeini's movement, even at its most militant moments, deeply interested in
intellectual arguments and literature.[74] It also compelled that movement to absorb ideas from Western philosophy, Marxist thought, and the discourse of the
secular opposition to the Shah. This separates Islamic fundamentalism in Iran
from fundamentalism elsewhere in the Muslim world. In Iran, Islamic militancy

did not embrace anti-intellectual puritanism of the kind witnessed in the Muslim Brotherhood or the Jamaat-e Islami circles, as embodied in the Salafi and Wahhabi militancy since the 1980s. In Iran, fundamentalists claimed that their movement was equally as progressive as that of the Left. The intellectualism of the revolution explains why the Islamic Republic would quickly adopt all the bureaucratic and legal characteristics of a modern state. It also explains why intellectual activity continued in Iran during the revolutionary fervor of the early 1980s and why literature, culture, and arts flourished there in the 1990s.

The Nature of the Oppositional Forces

The opposition to the Pahlavi regime was centered in the middle and lower middle classes. It was strong among Iranian intellectuals and university students there and abroad, merchants in the bazaar—whose economic stature had declined as the state looked to large industries to spearhead development—and seminary students. Social change forged by the Shah's policies had created fertile ground for oppositional politics: the growth of the middle class since the 1960s, urbanization, and marked growth in the number of universities and the size of their student populations, especially abroad.[75] The legacy of 1953, the unintended consequences of rapid development, and the regime's growing authoritarianism had produced opposition in diverse social groups. This opposition was liberal democratic in tone, but more often than not it was either leftist or fundamentalist. The rump of the National Front called for political reform and greater democratization. Some of Mosaddeq's old lieutenants, such as Gholam-Hossein Sadiqi and leaders of the Lawyers Association, such as Hasan Nazih or Abdol-Karim Lahiji, demanded a return to the rule of law.[76] In the bazaar, merchants demanded economic freedoms and an end to the tariff regimes that favored import substitution industries.[77] However, the strongest voices in the modern middle class and among intellectuals and students were associated with the Left.[78] The Tudeh Party continued to be clandestinely active in Iran, but it no longer represented communism in the country. Communism was, rather, represented by diverse intellectuals and ideological thinkers, such as Bijan Jazani or the Confederation of Iranian Students in Europe and the United States[79] and guerrilla organizations such as Fadaiyan-e Khalq (Devotees of the People). The Left was not a pro-democracy force in the 1970s; its worldview was collectivist and was not primarily concerned with the rule of law, civil liberties, or individual rights. Rather, it saw the rhetoric of democracy as a means to an end. It was strongly antistate, favored class war and revolution, and promised a utopian state. The Left did not have a coherent theory of state beyond abstract promises of a Marxist utopia, but it was able to mount a strong critique of the Pahlavi state's mix of developmentalism and authoritarianism. This critique drew heavily on the Left's rejection of developmentalism, most lucidly expressed by intellectuals such as Jalal Al-e Ahmad (d. 1969) whose *Westoxication* (*Gharbzadegi*, 1962) became the symbol of this approach.

The Left was able to construct an oppositional platform, but one that did not address the fundamental issues that Iranians had debated since 1905: order, prosperity, and territorial integrity versus freedom. The Left failed to mobilize the working class, which was doing well in the import substitution industries.[80] Its greatest success was to convince the Iranian middle class of the myth of revolution—that it is a force for good and can achieve the goal of freedom and progress efficaciously.

Though the Left was able to influence the modern middle class, it was not effective in the far larger lower middle class, which was deeply tied to religious values. People of that class were more influenced by the fundamentalist ideology, which wove the Left's populist ideas with Shia mythology to produce an ideology of dissent.

After Khomeini's protest movement of 1964, religious activism became an important part of dissident politics in Iran. First, Khomeini and his followers had gained legitimacy through their direct confrontation with the ruling regime. Second, Khomeini had shown that, contrary to Marxist predictions, religion was not moribund; on the contrary, it was a strong sociopolitical force that was capable of mobilizing far larger numbers than leftist ideologies could. As a result, throughout the 1960s and 1970s, religious activism became more prominent, and secular dissident forces too began to look to Islam as a political instrument.

Islamic modernists, associated with Mehdi Bazargan and the Liberation Movement of Iran—whose early worldview had once been a part of Mosaddeq's National Front—sought to construct a reformist, politically engaged Islamic platform to lead the opposition to the Shah's regime. More important, however, were the Islamic activists who were led by Khomeini and the revolutionary ideology produced by the marriage between Marxism and Shi'ism as formulated by Shariati. These two forces would define a radical revolutionary interpretation of Shi'ism that would define opposition to the Pahlavi state, bringing together diverse secular and religious trends and those who followed them in the middle and lower middle classes.

Khomeini had gone into exile in Iraq after the 1964 protest collapsed. There his opposition to the White Revolution metamorphosed into a more systematic ideological reading of Islamic law and ethics. In a series of lectures in the 1970s, Khomeini rejected the legitimacy of monarchy as an institution of authority and put forward a theory of Islamic state.[81] The theory of *Velayat-e Faqih* (Guardianship of the Jurist) argued that supreme authority in a Muslim state rests with the ulama. Khomeini's formulation was an innovation in Shia political thought.[82] In the traditional Shia view of politics, the ulama's aim was to safeguard the interests of Shia religion; to accomplish that, they would advise and enjoin rulers, but their goal was not served by ruling directly. Aside from its not serving the goal, ruling was undesirable because it was not possible to establish just rule.[83] For according to Shi'ism's messianic doctrines, the Hidden Imam will return at the end of time to establish just rule; until that time, the ulama should seek only to protect and propagate Shia values.[84] It was this logic that had guided the ulama to accept the rule of the Qajar monarchy in the nineteenth century, support the constitutional movement of 1905–1906, and also accept Reza Shah's accession to the throne. Khomeini's reformulation of Shia political thought to assert the religious incumbency of rule by the ulama—and the necessity of just rule before the advent of the Hidden Imam—was a revolution in Shi'ism.[85]

According to Khomeini, the affairs of state must be based on the precepts of Islamic law and must therefore be managed by those who are most knowledgeable in Islamic law—the ulama. As such, Khomeini used the shared opposition to the Pahlavi regime to gloss over the tensions in secular and religious interpretations of rule of law, democracy, and state-building that had marked Iranian politics since the Constitutional Revolution of 1906–1911. What he put forward was a new theory of state that would serve as the foil to the vision of the state that had emerged in Iran since 1925. More important, but less apparent at the time, Khomeini's state was also the foil to the kind of state that secular and constitutionalist Iranians had argued for in the 1906–1925 and 1941–1954 periods, and also in liberal democratic circles throughout the 1960s and the 1970s.

Khomeini proved adept at avoiding discussion of his theory of state and focusing the dissident forces' attention on the Pahlavi regime. That the Iranian middle class and secular intellectuals and dissidents failed to realize that the competition for ideas and power was not just between the Pahlavi state and a democratic and pluralistic path to state-building, that it also involved a theocratic vision of state, accounts for Khomeini's success in dominating the revolution. Khomeini and his followers also understood the game of numbers. Though the Iranian middle class was prominent in the economy and dominated intellectual and political debates, it was far smaller than the lower middle and lower classes. The changing face of Iran's cities favored the religious forces.

The influence of Shariati, too, was invaluable in shaping the revolution. Shariati was not concerned with changing Islam to make it compatible with modernity, but with mobilizing religion for political action. In his years in Paris, he was influenced by various intellectual trends, most notably existentialism and Third Worldist trends that criticized Western imperialism and consumer culture and advocated return to nativist identity. He was in particular impressed with thinkers like Frantz Fanon and Louis Massignon. A fusion of religion with social activism was the product of these diverse intellectual influences. However, the strongest imprint on Shariati's thinking, as discussed earlier, was Marxism.[86] The modernity that informed Shariati's Islamic modernism was Marxist rather than liberal or rationalist. Shariati wanted to ignite revolutionary activism in Iran, but he understood that secular Marxism alone was not likely to excite the masses. Properly interpreted, Shi'ism could fulfill Marxist ideology's historic function and become a material force. Through his numerous lectures, articles, and books, Shariati applied Marxist methodology and analysis to Shia thought, ethics, and history, reading into Shi'ism the familiar themes of Marxism: dialectics of actuality versus potentiality, class struggle, revolution, and the utopian dictatorship of the dispossessed.

Thus Shariati reinterpreted Shia political thought. He depicted Shia history as a revolutionary struggle best captured in the paradigmatic representation of the martyrdom of the third Shia Imam, Hossein, in Karbala in 680 A.D. that would, in Shariati's own time, culminate in a revolution. Shariati saw religion as ideology, and more specifically saw Shi'ism as a creed of justice—defender of the poor—somewhat akin to how Liberation Theology interpreted Catholicism in Latin America in the 1970s. He argued that the just rule that the Hidden Imam was to bring was the same as the Marxist utopia, only better and more complete. Iranians, however, should not passively wait for the advent of just rule, but must hasten its arrival through revolutionary activism.[87] Shariati characterized his effort as attempts to recover the true essence of Shi'ism, which he described as "red" Shi'ism, in place of the quietist or "black" Shi'ism that reactionary ulama and shahs had put forth to ensure oppression of the strong over the weak.[88] "Red" Shi'ism closely paralleled Marxism—even in its color. Shariati's works suggest a modernization of Shi'ism—reducing the faith's emphasis on piety and apolitical rituals and reducing the authority of the ulama. But his main contribution was to interpret leftist dissent in Shia terms, which provided the revolutionary movement with ideological bridges between the various strands of the opposition to Pahlavi monarchy.

Shariati's ideas proved immensely popular with students and lower middle class youth who were already attracted to Marxist ideology but still had ties to Shia culture and values. In Shariati they found a vision of Shi'ism that was progressive—in promoting social resistance and political action—and revolutionary. The Shah referred to Shariati and his followers derisively as "Islamic Marxists." The characterization was more ominous than he anticipated; for, although many of Shariati's ideas do not stand up to critical scrutiny and did not amount to a new school of Islamic thought, they proved to be politically powerful. Shariati's mix of existentialism, Marxism, and a reformed and millenarian Shi'ism contributed to the popularization of a modernist and militant view of Islam that influenced the thought of a wide spectrum of Iranian youths. The political movement that best exemplified Shariati's ideology was the Mojahedin-e Khalq.[89]

Shariati died in 1977, and so he was not personally a force in the revolutionary period. However, his ideas helped mobilize many Iranians in the struggle against the Pahlavi state, and they provided the foundation for a grand alliance between the Left and fundamentalists that paved the way for Khomeini's domination of the revolution. Although traditional ulama disliked Shariati, and revolutionary religious activists who followed Khomeini viewed his ideology as a rival to that of their own, Islamic fundamentalism in Iran was nonetheless greatly influenced by Shariati's vision. For instance, the Supreme Leader of Iran, Ayatollah Ali Khamenei, was close to Shariati before the revolution and continues to express admiration for him. Although Khomeini never endorsed Shariati, and many of Khomeini's followers remained ill at ease with his views, still there is no doubt that many aspects of revolutionary activism, particularly its populism after 1979, bore the mark of Shariati's ideas. A case in point was the young clerical activist Nematollah Salehi-Najafabadi, whose biography of the Shi'i Imam, Hossein, *Shahid-i Javid* (*Immortal Martyr*) echoed Shariati's revolutionary reading of the saint's life and opened the door for the ulama to appropriate it. Salehi rejected the spirituality that is associated with Hossein's martyrdom and depicted his rebellion as a political statement. Salehi concluded that the legitimacy of the institution of Imamate is not essentially religious, but political; it is imbedded in the people rather than vested by God.[90] It was a populist and political institution closer to the Sunni view of political authority and leadership than to the traditional Shi'i one. Salehi's views were later reiterated by ayatollahs Mohammad-Hossein Beheshti (d. 1980) and Mohammad Mofatteh (d. 1979), who were instrumental in articulating Khomeini's spiritual and political authority in terms of its popular mandate.[91]

The Path to Revolution

The revolution itself unfolded over the course of a mere eighteen months.[92] It was triggered on January 8, 1978, with protests in Qom by seminary students over an article in a major newspaper criticizing Khomeini.[93] The Qom protest was brutally suppressed, but it fueled protests elsewhere that soon spread to

Tehran and gradually involved other urban areas.[94] The revolutionary process was punctuated by a set of cascading clashes between demonstrators and authorities and the casualties that they produced. The frequency and scale of the clashes eventually overwhelmed the Shah's regime, which failed to react adroitly to the challenge before it. Emboldened by the Shah's inaction and exhorted by Khomeini to take a stand against the regime, growing numbers of people in Iran's cities clamored for the Shah's removal from power. Meanwhile, the wedge between the opposition and the ruling regime deepened with events late in 1978 that included the deaths of hundreds of people in a fire at Cinema Rex in Abadan on August 20; a large public demonstration on September 4, a religious holiday marking the end of Ramadan; a bloody confrontation between protesters and the military at Jaleh Square in Tehran on September 8, dubbed Black Friday; general strikes beginning in November; and street marches by an estimated two million people in Tehran on December 10 and 11, days of Tasoua and Ashoura commemorating the martyrdom of Imam Hossein.

Throughout, Khomeini became the face of the revolution—its de facto leader and most prominent voice. In October 1978 he left Iraq for Paris, and from there he was more able to define clearly the nature of the revolution for the world media as an Islamic revolution.

The growing religious tenor of the demonstrations was aided by a network of mosques, seminaries, and religious organizations that provided a backbone to the demonstrators and helped tie their demands to Khomeini's larger ideological arguments. The popular mobilization reached a critical stage with the labor strikes. These included strikes of government employees and labor in critical industrial sectors such as oil and energy, whose walkouts constituted a daily reminder of public defiance and a drain on the economy. The demonstrations spread from the lower and lower-middle classes to the middle class and from students and activists to laborers, government employees, and eventually even the military.

After months of street clashes, the military was disillusioned with the Shah's indecisiveness. In January 1979, a mutiny by members of the military at an air force base on the outskirts of Tehran led to clashes between units loyal to the Shah and the mutineers, who were backed by Fadaiyan-e Khalq guerillas. The pro-Shah units were routed, and with that came the collapse of the last pillar of the regime. In the end, a cycle of demonstrations, religious gatherings, and labor strikes had destroyed any chance of a negotiated transfer of power, and with the collapse of the military the fate of the Shah's regime was sealed.

The Shah seemed unable to influence the course of events. His indecisiveness and aversion to politicking led him to respond too little and too late and with the wrong instruments. His initial response was to open up the political system, but he first sought to do so through a trusted senior politician, Jafar Sharif-Emami, whom he appointed prime minister in August 1978. Sharif-Emami, however, had served as the head of the senate for many years, which meant that he lacked independence from the Shah and therefore had no political legitimacy. Sharif-Emami made concessions such as granting freedom of the press and releasing some of the political prisoners, but these measures only stoked the fire of unrest. In November, when it became evident that Sharif-Emami could not contain the protests, the Shah imposed martial law and tapped a general to form the government. Again the Shah's choice foreclosed the possibility of positive results. Wary that the military might take over Iran, he chose a loyal but weak general, Gholam-Reza Azhari, whose conciliatory approach to the opposition made a mockery of martial law.[95]

Emboldened opposition, now led by Khomeini, refused to settle for anything short of the Shah's removal from power. Even the monarch's public apology and promise of accountable government failed to influence the situation. Finally the Shah agreed to leave Iran and appointed Shapur Bakhtiar, a liberal democrat and a veteran of Mosaddeq's era, as prime minister in January 1979. However, by then the momentum of the revolution was unstoppable. Bakhtiar's government lasted little more than a month before it collapsed in the face of popular pressure.[96] Khomeini emerged as the de facto ruler of Iran.

Given the Shah's actions—and inaction—throughout 1978, there were but two forces capable of dealing with the mobilization: the pro-democracy politicians who were associated with the National Front of the early 1950s, and the military. The first could have contained and managed the mobilized social force, and the second could have suppressed them. But the democratic middle failed to play its historic role, partly because it refused to reach an agreement with the Shah on the issue, and partly because it decided not to challenge Khomeini or the Left. The military was not deployed in an effective way during the early months of the uprisings, when it could have changed the outcome. It was not until the Shah left Iran in February 1979 that the military decided to flex its muscles, only to find its window of opportunity was closed.[97]

The failure of the Shah to wage a successful campaign to divide the opposition along ideological and cultural lines was symptomatic of his inability to contend with the crisis. It also precluded the possibility of negotiations between the monarchy and the pro-democracy and leftist elements over a transition of power. Elsewhere in the Muslim world, authoritarian regimes have proven adept at co-opting their opposition and manipulating divisions within the opposition to prolong authoritarian rule.[98] An alternative maneuver worked in Syria in 1982 and in Algeria in 1992: both suppressed popular mobilizations through the use of force. In Iran, the Shah proved unable to contend with the challenges to his regime either by opening up the system (through, for example, the Rastakhiz Party) or by using force.[99] As a result, the political situation continued to radicalize, and in the process it increasingly tilted in favor of the religious element in the revolutionary coalition. This did not bode well for the possibility of democratic development in Iran in 1979.[100]

In the seven decades of state-building since the Constitutional Revolution, Iran had gained much in terms of development, territorial security, and national unity. What it had failed to do was to reconcile democracy and state-building. This failure had removed all restrictions from state power and turned democracy into defiance of the state. This proved to be catastrophic for the Pahlavi state. Its power became its Achilles heel, alienating the very social classes that state power had to rely on. In the end the scope of that alienation overwhelmed the state, causing its collapse before a popular revolution. In the words of one observer: "Muhammad Reza Shah's tragedy was that he lived too long. Had he died earlier, in 1972 or 1973, he would have gone down in history as one of the greater post–World War II leaders, an autocrat who achieved much in modernizing and improving his country to a point where it was courted as never before by both West and East."[101]

Despite significant changes in how the state and the economy work in the Islamic Republic, the balance of power between state and society and the role of the state in socioeconomic change cannot be understood separately from what occurred in the Pahlavi period. Despite the change in political regimes, ideologies, and social conditions, the same conception of state-building that was accepted in the Pahlavi era continued to hold sway over subsequent development in Iran.

PART II

The Crucible of the Revolution

3

Revolution and War
Fundamentalism, 1979–1989

The ideology and force of the revolution that ended the monarchy in February 1979 transformed Iran's political landscape. What ensued was a unique period in modern Iranian history that brought about wide-scale social and political change that could be characterized, at least in its initial stages, as "state-shattering" rather than state-building. The 1979–1989 period is one in which the balance of power between state and society tilted in favor of social forces unleashed by a revolution that sought to weaken if not destroy state institutions associated with the old regime. The weakening of state institutions was not, however, a harbinger of pluralism and liberal democracy. Revolutions do not readily strengthen the foundations of democracy or assert individual rights or the rule of law; rather, they tend to assert utopian and collectivist conceptions of rights that ultimately favor state power. It is therefore not surprising that the occlusion of the state after the revolution proved to be short-lived, and, despite its claims to the contrary, the revolution did not serve as the handmaiden of democracy. Rather, it laid the foundations for expanding state power and its reach into society.

The Character of the Revolution

The revolution created a climate for aggressive and confrontational ideological posturing that imparted a particular language and mode of behavior on Iranian politics. Revolutionary politics was characterized by militant activism, political and cultural iconoclasm, millenarianism, and strong commitment to Khomeini's charismatic authority. What occurred in the years immediately after the revolution has certain parallels with the political climate created by the Bolshevik policy of "war communism" and its attitude and style in 1918–1921 Russia.[1] It was confrontational, antistate, militant in outlook, confident in its own moral superiority, disdainful of authority, and intensely political. It rejected prevailing institutions of authority, cultural norms, and social values to express itself through the medium of a counterculture that adopted a new language, dress code, social relations, and political style. In the case of Iran, this new attitude and style can perhaps best be captured by the term "war fundamentalism."

This war fundamentalism was largely based on the legacy and language of leftist activism in Iran. However, in Iran the revolution became increasingly "Islamized." So although it reproduced the kind of politics that had been evident in Bolshevik Russia, it was led by a new generation of Islamic activists, some of whom were seminarians, who drew on Islamic history and law and cloaked their message in Islamic symbols and Shia millenarianism. War fundamentalism was thus characterized by Islamic ideological values that took precedence over political considerations in defining individual, social, and even national interests, and in shaping struggles of power. This is not to say that there was no politicking during the period of war fundamentalism, but that politics had lost its autonomy and was under the sway of Islamic ideology. This tendency was reinforced by the fact that even the secular liberal and leftist politics was not driven by pragmatism or pursuit of interests but was highly idealistic and abstract.

In foreign policy, war fundamentalism perpetuated Islamic activism and an anti-Westernism that saw Iran as the vanguard of a global Islamic revolution and the bulwark against Western cultural imperialism and American hegemony. This committed Iran to a policy of exporting its revolution, which meant support for Islamic activists in Asia, Africa, and the Middle East. Iran's revolution first inspired, then organized and funded, Shia revolutionary organizations in Afghanistan, Pakistan, the Persian Gulf Emirates, Saudi Arabia, Iraq, and Lebanon—where the Hezbollah became a notable regional force.[2] Tehran ridiculed pro-Western authoritarian regimes in Islamabad, Riyadh, and Cairo, predicting their fall to revolutions similar to the one in Iran. To highlight this position, the revolutionary regime named a street after Khalid al-Istanbuli, who assassinated Egyptian President Anwar Sadat in 1980. Islamic oppositions from Morocco to Malaysia, inspired by the success of the Iranian revolution, looked to Tehran for support, and many received money and training. The global surge in Islamic activism, which quickly became a preoccupation of Western policymakers, gave Iran's revolutionary elite an aura of power and further encouraged its militancy.[3]

War fundamentalism manifested itself in such acts as the approval of the takeover of the American embassy in Tehran by radical students; the hostage crisis of 1979–1981; and the death sentence for blasphemy that was meted out to author Salman Rushdie in absentia for his book *Satanic Verses* in 1989.[4] The confrontational posturing in turn fueled war fundamentalism as they heightened enthusiasm for the revolution and mobilized public support for it.

War fundamentalism in Iran was driven by two goals: first, to destroy the old order—shatter the state and uproot its cultural and social foundations; and second, to consolidate political domination and create a new order. The two goals were interrelated, and they unfolded in tandem, although it appeared at the outset that emphasis was on destroying the Pahlavi state. War fundamentalism was also instrumental in sustaining public morale during the eight-year-long war with Iraq.

So much is typical of all major revolutions. However, in Iran, unlike Russia or China, the revolutionary struggle was not led by a well-organized and structured leadership that was equipped with a single ideology. The revolutionary movement consisted of different oppositional groups that followed different political ideas and ideological worldviews and were not organized into a single political organization—in fact, some factions of the revolution lacked organization altogether. The only formal organizations of note among the revolutionaries were the leftist guerrilla movements, Fadaiyan-e Khalq and Mojahedin-e Khalq. Each had a coherent and well-structured political and paramilitary organization, but the two movements were not tied together, did not follow the same leaders, and did not subscribe to the same ideology. The revolution in Iran was unique in that much of the organizational and ideological consolidation that precedes modern revolutions elsewhere took place only after the fall of the old regime.

Though the disparate groups that made up the revolutionary movement had been unified on the objective of ousting the Shah and restructuring Iranian polity, they did not agree on the political and social order that was to follow the revolution. And all had to contend with a disjuncture that existed between the revolution's message and the reality of the Iranian society and economy, a disjuncture created by the specific circumstances in which the revolution occurred. All these circumstances are by now familiar: The revolution was not a movement of the urban poor or the peasantry, but one of the middle and lower-middle classes. It did not occur at a time of economic hardship in the country but during a period of oil boom and relative prosperity during which Iran imported foreign labor and invested money in European countries. It did not come at a time of an international war or pursuant to a military defeat. It was, rather, a consequence of the ruling regime's loss of legitimacy and unwillingness to defend itself. This disjuncture would play an important role in the extent to which ideology would shape state and society.

Had the opposition gone through a prolonged struggle against the state—had the Shah's regime not folded so quickly—then the struggle itself might have imposed an ideological and organizational hold over its followers. As is, however, Iran produced a revolution that lacked a single dominant ideology and was not led by a well-defined revolutionary party. Thus after the revolution, a struggle for power erupted among the various factions in the revolutionary movement. First, the militant wing of the revolution—fundamentalists and leftists—purged the democratic forces. Then the Islamic revolutionaries went to war with the leftist revolutionaries. Finally, the conservative and pragmatist fundamentalists confronted the radical and Left-leaning fundamentalists. The internal war within the revolution affected the nature of the larger war on the remnants of the Pahlavi state and how revolutionaries went on to create a new sociopolitical order in Iran.

The new sociopolitical order that emerged in Iran from 1979 to 1989 was in part a product of this struggle for power among the ranks of the revolutionaries. Why and how particular factions of the revolution prevailed in this struggle, and why the revolutionary order would take the form that it did has to do with the intricate interplay of various factors that defined the context in which these struggles for power unfolded.

Ideologies of the Revolution

The ideological struggle among the main players in the revolution led them to articulate their political intent and to differentiate their political arguments. The debate over the content of their ideologies thus became more important after the revolution. Iranians had rallied to the revolution, but the revolution in fact meant different things to different people. Some saw it as a transition to democracy. Others saw it as a culmination of class struggle that would produce a Marxist egalitarian society and liberate Iran from American influence. Still others looked to an Islamic future that would end Western cultural domination. As a result, though Iranians shared the belief that the revolution was an absolute good and that it meant overthrowing the Pahlavi monarchy, there existed deep divisions among them as to where they would go once the Shah fell from power. In fact, the revolution's success owes much to the fact that the Shah failed to force his opposition to debate this issue, and to Khomeini's success in avoiding that debate.

During the period leading to the revolution, the democratic forces played a prominent role. They were led by the revived National Front leaders, such as Karim Sanjabi and Daryush Forouhar, and a new generation of intellectuals, lawyers, and political activists, such as Abdol-Karim Lahiji, Hasan Nazih, and Hedayatollah Matindaftari. The democratic forces drew on the legacy of Mosaddeq, which in 1979 most Iranians associated with democracy. These forces were for the most part secular in outlook. Some among it's the democratic ranks, such as Gholam-Hossein Sadiqi and Shapur Bakhtiar, were open to negotiating with the Shah on the basis of the Constitution of 1906. Others, with more Islamic leaning, such as Mehdi Bazargan and his Liberation Movement of Iran, joined forces with Khomeini. Still, the bulk of the democratic forces favored an end to monarchy and vesting the fortunes of democracy in a republic.

On the eve of the revolution, democratic forces were at the height of their power. Their nationalist credentials and liberal outlook were critical to swaying key social groups. The Shah failed to attract democratic forces away from the revolutionaries. At the eleventh hour he reached an agreement with Bakhtiar to appoint him prime minister, and then he left Iran. However, Sanjabi, who spoke for the main body of the National Front, had decided to follow Bazargan's lead in submitting to Khomeini's leadership,[5] and Bakhtiar could neither prevent the collapse of the monarchy nor the takeover of the revolution by pro-Khomeini forces. Subsequently, Mehdi Bazargan was appointed to be the revolution's first prime minister. Bazargan, who was religiously devout and an advocate of Islamic modernism, would try to serve as the bridge between democratic forces and Islamic forces of the revolution.

The democratic platform lacked an ideology. Its advocates called for political reform, which was not the concern of the revolution. Democracies result from negotiated transitions of power when political mobilization of the middle class compels authoritarian regimes to accept change. The mobilization is then captured in new constitutional frameworks and democratic institutions. Revolutions happen when mobilization extends to the lower classes, and its size and scope of activities overwhelms political institutions. The tidal wave of revolutionary mobilization does not favor democratic consolidation. In a social revolution, democracy falls victim to mass mobilization.

In 1978–1979, Iran's democratic forces were caught in the whirlwind of the revolution, and their opposition to the Shah and their nationalist credentials made them central to the opposition movement. However, the leaders of the liberal democratic faction were never able to separate the demand for democracy from leftist and Islamic revolutionary activism—to separate liberal values of democracy from the dogmatic utopianisms of the left and fundamentalists. As a result, democratic forces were unable to clearly define their own position, and so they could neither arrive at an agreement with the Shah nor control the flow of the revolution. Their moment of power—when they could have shaped Iran's politics—was fleeting, and before long they were devoured by the revolution. Thus Iran failed to move from authoritarianism to democracy when it had the opportunity to do so; the success of the revolution marked a distinct failure for democratic forces and their constituency in the middle class to secure power when they had the chance. Once the revolution happened, the rules of the game favored more militant actors and their power base in the lower and lower middle classes.

Ideologies of the Left—various brands of communism and socialism—represented an important pole in debates among the revolutionaries. At the juncture of the revolution there were all strands of leftist ideas extant in Iran.[6] There were Marxist-Leninists, Trotskyites, and Maoists; followers of Castro and Che Guevara; and Mojahedin-e Khalq who advocated a blend of Marxism and Islamic activism, whom the Shah called "Islamic Marxists." There were members of the Tudeh Party, many of whose leaders had lived over the years in exile in East Germany, but continued to have a networking presence in Iran. There were also members of guerrilla groups, such as Fadaiyan-e Khalq, Rah-e Kargar (Worker's Way), and Peykar (Battle),[7] some of whom had been trained in Cuba or South Yemen, and activists who were tied to European urban guerrilla groups.[8] Many more intellectuals, writers, and student activists espoused Marxist ideas without formal attachment to any organization.

After the revolution, the Left sought to move beyond its oppositional stance against the Shah to implement social and economic change. In the early phases, it successfully influenced the direction of new policies, emphasizing redistribution of wealth, confiscation of property from the rich, and, more generally, attitudes that would promote radicalism. However, the Left was never able to mobilize broad support for its programs or drive for power. It faced stiff competition from Khomeini and his followers, who had their own conceptions of what a revolution was and what the revolutionary state would look like. It is important to note that the general Marxist attitude toward religion as a reactionary force that has no place in a progressive society—and would be incapable of leading a revolution—blinded the Left to Khomeini's power and potential.[9] Khomeini proved capable of producing an Islamic ideology that could win a revolution, and the Left fell victim to the blind spots of its own ideology. Ultimately it was Khomeini's religious militants who dominated the revolution.

In the 1970s, the two different strands of Islamic activism came together to forge Islamic ideology and define its vision of state and society.[10] The first was militant fundamentalism, whose roots went back to Fadaiyan-e Islam, which had been active in the 1950s and the 1960s. The Fadaiyan had ceased to exist as an organization in the 1960s, but many of its members had joined Khomeini's 1964 protests. The Fadaiyan strand was militantly anti-Shah, advocated the use of violence, and looked to build an Islamic state in Iran. After 1964, the remnants of Fadaiyan accepted Khomeini's leadership and would later adopt his theory of *Velayat-e Faqih* (Guardianship of the Jurist) as the definition of its intended Islamic state. This strand of Islamic activism was concerned with undoing the secularism of the Pahlavi regime, promoting an Islamic state under the leadership of the ulama, and ensuring that society reflected Islamic values. It combined militant fundamentalism with the Left's antistate, antidemocratic and anticapitalist worldview that had been popularized in political discussions in the 1970s.[11] It was particularly popular among younger clerics and seminary students.

The other strand was the Islamic Left, which was associated with Ayatollah Mahmoud Taleqani, Ali Shariati, and, to a lesser extent, activists such as Abol-Hasan Bani-Sadr. In the 1960s Taleqani was a midranking member of the ulama who was known for his political activism. Although initially close to the National Front and the Islamic modernism of the Liberation Movement of Iran, by the 1970s Taleqani was mainly associated with the Left.[12] While in prison in the 1960s, he had read samples of Marxist texts and debated religion and politics with leftist political prisoners. Taleqani's works, most notably his *Islam va Malekiyat* (Islam and Ownership) argued that Islamic teachings on social justice were in line with Marxist demand for distribution of wealth and resources in lieu of right to property.[13] Taleqani's works provided for a common language and frame of reference for leftist and Islamic revolutionaries to use when speaking about the same socioeconomic issues. His ideas resonated with middle- and lower middle class youth who were looking for ways to bring leftist and Islamic worldviews into harmony. After the revolution, Taleqani would become the ayatollah of choice for the Left, and especially for Mojahedin-e Khalq.

Ali Shariati's ideas, as discussed in the previous chapter, presented a more extensive mixture of Islam and Marxism. Shariati too argued that Islam's teachings on social justice support Marxist views on egalitarianism and distribution of surplus value and private property. An unintended consequence of Shariati's ideas was to show how political bridges could be built between leftist and Islamic activists and ultimately how Islamic fundamentalism could operate as Marxism. This would provide for a very different dynamic in the competition between leftists and fundamentalists for control of the revolution. It would also promote the kind of revolutionary militancy that fueled war fundamentalism in the 1980s.

This convergence of various strands of Islamic activism to create an Islamic ideology was aided by the fact that although some militant fundamentalism was not openly leftist, it nonetheless reflected the ideological influence of the Left, especially the Stalinist creed of the Tudeh Party. What militant fundamentalism said and how it said it and even how its advocates dressed and conducted themselves resembled Leninist thinking and action as perceived in Iran, with leftist jargon replaced with Islamist jargon.

Khomeini understood that to convert his own religious and political agenda into a revolutionary movement, there had to be a single Islamic ideology that could mobilize the masses and could relate their divergent demands to the revolution's goals.[14] That ideology would have to encapsulate what each strand advocated and to weave those demands into a seamless Islamic revolutionary discourse. From 1977 to 1979 and more so after the revolution, Khomeini de-fined Islamic ideology in terms of demanding an Islamic state that would bring about social justice, empowering the poor, and freeing Iran from Western polit-ical and cultural influence. This ideology was as much based on a fundamentalist view of Islam as it was on political and economic populism.[15] It was culturally iconoclastic; it rejected the social and political authority of existing sociopolitical institutions, and it called for militant engagement by the population to tear down the edifice of the old order and to build society, economy, and polity on new arrangements. In short, it had all the elements of Marxist thought and practice, but it was couched in the symbolisms and language of Islam and pointed to an ideal order that, although Islamic in appearance and led by the ulama, bore strong resemblance to Marxist notions. Khomeini, as will be discussed later, thus appropriated the ideological appeal of the Left and then went on to mar-ginalize leftists. After the revolution, competition with the Left would lead Kho-meini to selectively sharpen and blur distinctions between Islamic and leftist ideologies. This in turn allowed him to outmaneuver and ultimately crush the Left in his drive to control the revolution.

The Revolution in Motion

The immediate aftermath of the revolution was a period of great flux. Khomeini assumed power, and informal revolutionary committees and networks laid claim to various aspects of government. Revolutionary forces purged public and pri-vate organizations, ranging from government agencies to universities to busi-nesses and factories, of alleged and real supporters of the old regime. This often became a witch-hunt that targeted the most experienced and competent, who were accused of having secured their positions through ties with the old regime and of sharing its bourgeois and secular culture. Large numbers of senior bureaucrats, managers, or academics lost their jobs; some were tried and received punishments ranging from death or imprisonment to confiscation of property. With revolutionary commitment (*ta'ahhod*) rather than professional competence (*takhassos*) as the guideline, those purged were replaced by revolutionary activists or the *san colloute*.

Revolutionary courts tried and summarily executed some senior statesmen, high-ranking military officers, and government officials, such as Amir-Abbas Hoveyda (prime minister, 1965–1977), Abbas-Ali Khal'atbari (minister of foreign affairs, 1972–1978), and Farrokhrou Parsa (minister of education, 1968–1974, and the first woman minister in Iran). The courts also executed some businessmen and leaders of the Jewish and Baha'i communities. In what exemplifies the psychology of war fundamentalism, gruesome pictures of the bullet-riddled bodies of those executed were published in newspapers.[16]

Many more people in the military and police forces were killed. Scores of generals and senior officers were summarily tried and executed. Units with potential capability of resistance were quickly disbanded, and those that were particularly close to the old regime, such as the Imperial Guard Corps, were decimated. The Left, led by the guerrilla forces, was particularly eager to see the military dismantled. They hoped that in the subsequent vacuum, their militias would have an advantage in settling struggles for power. In the months following the revolution, the military and the police were cut in size and powers, and their presence was greatly curtailed.

Another important target of the revolutionaries, especially the fundamentalists, was the judiciary. During the Pahlavi era, the judiciary was an important pillar of the state, which both manifested and perpetuated the state's secular nature. The Iranian judiciary was based on secular law after the French and Belgian legal systems. It had been designed during the Reza Shah period specifically to limit the influence of the ulama and Islamic law on the country's legal system. The image of the judiciary became that of a secular institution, although many of its leading figures were well versed in Islamic law and were now willing to craft a synthesis between traditional Islamic law and modern secular law. Moreover, the language and methodology of the new judiciary in Iran drew heavily on Islamic jurisprudence and ethics. The ulama had never reconciled themselves to the judiciary that Reza Shah had built. They were, by training, jurists, and they viewed Islamic law as the foundation of a just and moral order; thus they could not conceive of an Islamic state that did not enshrine the *shariah* in the judiciary. The revolution provided the opportunity to rebuild the judiciary and to bring it under control of the ulama. The judiciary was quickly stripped of its powers and was made subservient to new ulama-led courts and judicial institutions. Many judges and lawyers were purged from the judiciary, and the curricula for legal training were revised to more directly reflect the influence of Islamic law.

Clearly, the revolutionary elite aimed not merely to uproot the Pahlavi regime but to shatter the state. They targeted the most important institutions of the state, the military and the judiciary—institutions that define a state and enforce its authority. The revolutionary leaders would in the early years of the revolution rely on their own ad hoc procedures to fulfill the tasks of the state. The revolution's antistate attitude was best captured in a widely posted declaration that it preferred *mota'ahhed* (the ideologically committed) over *motekhasses* (the specialist). What mattered was ideology, not expertise.[17] Revolution was the end, and its ascendance would come at the expense of the state.

It is important to note that in Iran the collapse of the old regime and the rise of the revolutionary order followed a path somewhat different from that of communist revolutions. The collapse of the Pahlavi state did not completely destroy the private sector. Rather, the bazaar mercantile interests stepped into the void left by the Pahlavi state—especially after the Iran-Iraq war necessitated economic order, and state institutions were not capable of providing it. In the early years, the bazaar took over the distribution of goods, the import and export trade, and the foreign exchange market; moreover, it created a mercantile network connecting bazaars across Iran to manage the country's economic needs. This empowered mercantile interests and the bazaar as a political force and entrenched their influence in the revolutionary regime. The influence of the bazaar in turn limited the scope of war fundamentalism, and it laid the foundation for clerical-mercantile ties that would support the rise of the conservative faction in the 1980s and the revival of mercantile economy in the 1990s.

Instituting Khomeini's Authority

The antistate attitude no doubt emanated from revolutionary fervor. Still, that neither the Left nor fundamentalist revolutionaries—who had produced a number of works with the title of "Islamic government"—never put forward a coherent theory of state reinforced the antistate tendency.[18] Khomeini's views were particularly important in this respect. In Iran, Islamic fundamentalism never produced a theory of state or economics as it had in the Arab world or South Asia.[19] Khomeini (unlike, for example, an Islamist ideologue such as Mawlana Mawdudi of Pakistan) never put forward a systematic definition of the Islamic state and Islamic economics; he never described its machinery of government, instruments of control, social function, economic processes, or guiding values and principles.[20] Khomeini's focus was rather on justifying the ulama's right to rule, which he captured in the idea of *Velayat-e Faqih*.[21] Rather than a modern theory of state or even an ideology, Khomeini's approach amounted to a Shia version of Plato's *Republic* in which the Guardian Jurist would be the Philosopher King. The state that would be based on Islamic law and ruled by its interpreters, the ulama, would be the most justified state, as mandated by God.[22] Khomeini never saw the need to further justify his Islamic state in terms of how it would function or how it would deliver stability and order or manage development. What the rule of the ulama would bring about would by definition be good. He would thus dismiss subsequent concerns over the particulars of management as trivial. This attitude is captured in a famous response he once gave to a question about how the Islamic Republic would manage Iran's economy: "economics is for fools (*eqtesad mal-e khar ast*)." How a state functions and what it delivers are of secondary importance. It is the moral and ideological foundation of the state and who rules it that determine its worth.

The antistate attitude was in fact an important part of Khomeini's charismatic appeal even after he became Iran's ruler. When Khomeini became Iran's de facto ruler in 1979, he never associated himself with the state and did not deal with the details of policymaking. Revolutionary Iran was led by a ruler who symbolized the state yet simultaneously stood opposed to it.

If traditional Shia political theory had legitimated the monarchy on the grounds that the monarchy could protect the Shia realm, Khomeini argued that the pro-Western secularism and authoritarianism of the Pahlavi era showed that the monarchy was more a danger to Shi'ism than a protector of it. The Shia realm could be protected only by the true guardians of the faith, the ulama. Khomeini thus laid direct claim to political authority for the ulama and denied it to the shahs, formally ending the concordat between shahs and ulama that had lasted since Iran became a Shia kingdom in 1501.[23]

Khomeini also encouraged millenarianism and fused expectation of the return of the Hidden Imam with the rhetoric of the revolution. He would characterize the revolution as an effort to prepare the country for the advent of the Hidden Imam—evoking the notion of active expectation (*entezar*) that Shariati gave currency to in the 1970s. Khomeini himself was referred to by his followers as "Nayeb-e Imam" (Deputy to the [Hidden] Imam), and he derided the revolution's enemies with titles such as followers of *taghout* (false idol) or *mufsid fi'l-arz* (polluter[s] of the earth), which were used in the religious sources for enemies of God. By evoking Shia myths and symbolism, Khomeini's followers sought to make Khomeini's authority transcend to heights close to that of the Hidden Imam. This was the Hidden Imam's time; the leaders of the revolution were his lieutenants, the enemies of the revolution were his enemies; and battles waged were his battles. The faithful had to choose between two stark options, good and evil, and the revolutionaries correctly assumed that this would create an environment in which the masses would instinctively feel the urge to give Khomeini unwavering and unconditional support. All this imbued Khomeini's authority with spiritual and supernatural qualities and elevated his status above that of other senior ulama and any other contender for leadership.

The revolution itself was portrayed in terms of the Battle of Karbala, in which the widely popular Shia Imam Hossein (d. 682), having refused to give allegiance to an unjust caliph, rose in rebellion against him and, along with seventy-two of his companions, was killed by a large contingent of the caliph's troops on the plains of Karbala in today's Iraq.[24] The story of Hossein's sacrifice, abiding commitment to justice, and martyrdom at the hands of an unjust ruler lie at the heart of popular Shia piety.[25] No myth is more compelling for Shias than that of Karbala, and no occasion more charged with passion than that of Ashoura (the tenth day of the month of Muharram, the anniversary of Hossein's martyrdom).

In the 1970s Shariati had evoked the myth of Karbala for political purposes by portraying Hossein as the prototype of the modern revolutionary hero, and the battle of Karbala as the starting point of a revolutionary struggle that would culminate in a final revolution. Shariati's famous call, "Every day is Ashoura, and every place is Karbala," conveyed the myth of Hossein as a staple of active political struggle rather than a mere focus of personal piety. In this perspective, the Shah was depicted as Yazid (the caliph who killed Hossein) and, by implication, the Islamic revolutionary struggle as a contemporary reenactment of Karbala. For pious Shias, who every year mourn Hossein's martyrdom, a second Karbala was to be an occasion for them to take Hossein's revenge.[26]

The revolution's immersion in Shia mythology and the symbolism and power the revolution drew from it is instructive. In many regards, the fundamentalists saw revolutionary activism as directed not at institution-building but at accentuating Shia millenarian expectations and reenacting its early battles for justice. Capitalizing on Shia mythology and popular piety no doubt yielded much political benefit to Khomeini and his followers. It also had the effect of committing them to perpetual revolution, which would end only by the advent of the Hidden Imam. All this at the outset made Iran's revolutionaries eager to destroy state institutions but insouciant toward building new ones.

The revolution would nevertheless produce new institutions of its own, and for a time it would seek to replace various government agencies and the judiciary and the military. Since the revolution had not put forward a blueprint for a state, there was no clear design for the new institutions or how they would operate, relate to one another, or bolster the revolutionary regime. The new institutions surfaced in an ad hoc manner to address needs as they emerged, and they grew organically to fill the void that was left by the collapse of the old order; they interacted in a complex manner to provide the necessary functions of a state, managing the society and the economy. In time, however, this tangled web would undergo change to become more efficient in its operations, bound by new norms and procedures.

Revolution and Institution-Building

In the wake of the collapse of the Pahlavi regime in February 1979, Khomeini appointed the membership of the Revolutionary Council (RC) that was formed shortly before his return to Iran. He appointed well-trusted ulama and leading revolutionary activists, such as ayatollahs Mohammad-Hossein Beheshti and Morteza Motahhari, and a few secular activists to take charge of regime transition. The council functioned independent of the provisional government, which was led by Prime Minister Bazargan. Whereas Bazargan looked to restore power to government and establish order, the council was interested in coordinating the full potential of the revolution. Real power would lie with the ulama in the council, who controlled the streets and thrived on the popular excitement of the revolution. The council initially set out to dismantle the state, and with this aim in mind it looked to new institutions to replicate the functions of the old institutions. Some of these institutions, such as neighborhood committees, emerged on their own and then received official approval from the council; others, such as revolutionary foundations, were created from above to perform specific functions.[27] Revolutionary institution-building, however, fell short of its goal and did not amount to completely dismantling the state, but rather to old institutions coexisting, uneasily, with new ones. The result was that the revolution produced a "dual state" in which the old machinery of state, though enduring extensive screens and personnel changes, especially at top levels, remained intact. They functioned alongside parallel institutions that were loyal to the revolutionary elite, who were determined to secure for themselves the same bureaucratic turf as soon as possible.[28] Hence, revolutionary courts ran parallel to the judiciary; Revolutionary Guard to the military; revolutionary committees to the police; networks of Friday Prayer leaders and representatives of Khomeini to governors, mayors, and municipal authorities; parastatal foundations with economic and social services agencies of the state; and the Reconstruction Campaign networks (Jahad-e Sazandegi) to the Ministry of Agriculture and Rural Development. This produced complex and multilayered relations of power in the political and administrative areas, and it confounded state-building, a trend that continued for most of the 1980s. Not until 1989 would the Islamic Republic address this duality of state institutions.

A new power structure emerged much earlier, however. Young revolutionaries, especially pro-Khomeini activists, who had organized demonstrations in 1978, formed various neighborhoods committees (*Komitehs*) that served as the arm of the revolution at the local level.[29] The committees competed with leftist guerrilla groups for control. Although initially less organized, the committees had many more members and controlled large parts of the cities. In time, these committees were brought under central control of the Revolutionary Council, and later they directly contributed to the formation of the Islamic Revolutionary Guard Corps (Sepah-e Pasdaran-e Enqelab-e Eslami), which in turn assumed many functions that were traditionally associated with the police and the military.[30] The emergence of these forces was then viewed as necessary to protect the revolution from the remnants of the old regime and from the Left.

Revolutionary tribunals emerged in a similar ad hoc manner to carry out purges.[31] They claimed to be Islamic, but their summary trials and speedy judgments were meted out by vigilante judges, and their penchant for severe punishments—executions by firing squad in many cases. They were particularly motivated by revolutionary zeal, vengeance, and the desire to establish beyond any doubt the death of the old order.

Other institutions, such as Jihad for Reconstruction or the myriad of foundations (*Bonyads*) that were created, had other purposes in mind—to mobilize and organize the revolution's base of support, to secure its resources, and to provide services. Although initially inchoate and disorganized, the new revolutionary institutions were dynamic and visible and wielded considerable power. In time, their presence created a good deal of institutional confusion in the state as the purviews of the old military, police, and judiciary overlapped with those of the newly formed Revolutionary Guard, committees, and courts.

The revolutionary committees and courts undertook a broad campaign of confiscating the private property of some senior government and military officials. The redistribution of resources became the official policy as the revolution nationalized businesses in industries ranging from banking to retail, mining, and manufacturing.[32] Taking from the rich to give to the poor had been a component of Iran's revolutionary ideology. It altered the balance of power between social classes, undid the old order, and rewarded the revolution's supporters. It was further justified in terms of implementation of Khomeini's doctrine of Guardianship of the Jurist. To revolutionary leaders, nationalization of economic resources and property was the means by which to extend this "guardianship" and the Islamic state from the political to the economic arenas, and that would provide the best stewardship for the economy.[33]

In March 1979, Iranians voted in a referendum to replace the monarchy with an "Islamic Republic."[34] The nomenclature was Khomeini's, and its usage indicated the struggle between the various factions of the revolutionary alliance over identity and type of regime to rule Iran. The struggle became more pronounced throughout 1979 in the debates over the democratic nature of the new constitution and the place of Islam in it.[35] The constitution proved to be eclectic; it manifested the rising power of the religious forces but made concessions to the democrats and to the Left. The constitution envisioned the Islamic Republic to be a modern state with all the institutional and organizational features of such a state. It provided for a parliament, a judiciary, and an executive. It delineated the powers of each through a system of checks and balances.[36] Still, there existed fundamental problems. The constitution recognized Khomeini's position as that of the Supreme Leader of the revolution and the Islamic Republic—a "Caesar" and a "pope" who would remain leader for life, would not be accountable to any authority, and would have total veto power over the decisions of all the state's branches and institutions. This arrangement was to subjugate the political to the religious in state affairs and to place the state under the guardianship of the religious authority. It also made Islamic identity central to questions of state-building—above and beyond economic and social interests. The constitution also provided for a Guardian Council that would serve as a watchdog over elections and would hold veto powers over parliamentary legislations—ensuring that religious leaders would keep legislature under control. An Assembly of Experts, consisting of only the ulama, would choose Khomeini's successor and oversee the activities of the Supreme Leader. This council would ensure that political leadership remained with the ulama.

Beyond this, the constitution provided for both a strong presidency and a strong office of the prime minister. The former would be elected through popular vote, and the latter would be produced by the parliament. The constitution's vacillation between a Gaullist and a Westminster model promised to confound governance in Iran, and to strengthen the office of the Supreme Leader as the ultimate arbiter in the tussles between the president and the prime minister.

The electoral process brought new dynamics to the Iranian political system. The revolutionary forces looked at elections as a mobilization tool to keep the population actively engaged with the revolution—to gain popular legitimacy for the changes that the revolution was bringing about—and they came to be seen as a useful means for furthering ideological politics and revolutionary vigilance. For the ulama in the revolutionary leadership, elections became a suitable way of reaffirming their primacy in the revolution and, therefore, the legitimacy of their authority.

Elections also served as an important tool for fundamentalist forces to assert their control of the revolution. Because the more sizable lower and lower middle classes tended to be religious, numbers in the elections favored the fundamentalists. This led fundamentalists to take elections seriously and to create enthusiasm for elections in the lower segments of society—inculcating a culture of democratic practice, which would become important to the pro-democracy movement of the late 1990s. In the 1979 and 1981 elections, an overwhelming majority of eligible voters participated in the elections, which strengthened Khomeini's position and empowered the lower classes but also popularized electoral politics.

The outcome of the constitutional process suggested that the religious element, led by Khomeini, effectively dominated the state. This domination became more apparent as the revolutionary regime demanded greater adherence to religious strictures, especially those concerning women's dress.[37] The revolutionary committees and the Revolutionary Guard enforced these demands, subduing popular resistance to them. The religious element also continued to mobilize support among the lower middle classes—which were closely tied to the religious establishment—to marginalize the modern middle classes, who were the social base of the pro-democracy and leftist forces. The religious strictures led to an increase in middle-class emigration to the West, a brain drain that would hurt the economy.

Religious activists took over many jobs in the bureaucracy and in the state's high political offices—jobs that, soon after the revolution, pro-democracy forces and leftist activists occupied. This trend was also evident in many elected offices. With each election, the influence of the fundamentalist ulama became clearer. When, during the early months of the revolution, pro-democracy forces and leftists insisted on an elected constituent assembly to approve the draft for a new constitution, Ali-Akbar Hashemi-Rafsanjani (an active member of Khomeini's inner circle and later Iran's president) underscored the importance of numbers, remarking: "Who do you think will be elected to the constituent assembly? A fistful of ignorant and fanatic fundamentalists who will do such damage that you will regret ever having convened them."[38]

The growing influence of fundamentalists was soon reflected in the distribution of high offices. Iran's first president, Abol-Hasan Bani-Sadr (1980–1981), was a left-leaning Islamic activist. He was replaced in office by Mohammad-Ali Rajai (1981) who was a militant fundamentalist. Following Rajai's assassination, a member of the ulama, Seyyed Ali Khamenei (the Supreme Leader since 1989), became president (1981–1989). The subsequent two presidents were also from the ranks of the ulama.

The Struggle for the Control of the Revolution

The fall of the Shah had been only a prelude to larger struggles for defining the direction of the revolutionary order. Khomeini's authority was based on popular accolade and not the hierarchy of an organization. As a result, his authority over leftist and pro-democracy forces in the revolution was far from absolute. In fact, the unity in the revolutionary ranks only thinly disguised the intense conflict that was waging for defining the new order. With the triumph of the revolution, the political accord between disparate political opposition to the Shah unraveled. Democratic forces, the Left, and the Islamists each had a different vision for Iran's future and hoped to inherit the revolution. The Left believed that it was better organized and had history on its side. Leftists viewed the ulama as politically unsophisticated and incapable of operating in the modern world, and they saw religion as irrelevant to socioeconomic demands. They were also encouraged in these beliefs by Khomeini's assertions before the revolution that he would retire to Qom to pursue a life of scholarship. Leftists underestimated the ability of Islamic ideology to appropriate, and later supplant, many of the Left's ideological tools. They did not appreciate the extent to which Islamic fundamentalism had become a foil for Marxism; that it was a modern ideology with a Marxist worldview embedded in its very fabric. By the mid-1980s, Khomeini had matched or surpassed every socioeconomic promise that the Left had made to the poor, labor, peasants, and lower middle classes.[39]

Islamic fundamentalists also produced comparable intellectual, ideological, and organizational tools that had primarily distinguished the Left. For instance, the term hezbollah (literally, party of God), which would later become associated with the Lebanese Shia organization, first surfaced in Iran shortly after the revolution to describe pro-Khomeini enthusiasts and vigilantes that set out to confront secular and leftist supporters. In its modern political usage the term was used first by the Indian Muslim intellectual Abol-Kalam Azad in the 1920s, and it was introduced to the Iranian context by Shariati in the 1970s. However, it was used by militant fundamentalists after the revolution to provide a counter to the leftist notion of "party." In effect, Islamists claimed that if "party" was a mark of progressiveness, as the Left had claimed, then fundamentalism too was equipped with a party of its own distinction. The differences with the Left came to a head as Iran began to define the future shape of its state and politics.

The decisive consolidation of power in the hands of the religious faction came in 1981–1982. Although the Islamist activists had already gained the upper hand, it was the hostage crisis of 1979 and 1980 and the onset of the Iran-Iraq war in 1980 that solidified that domination. The international context helped settle the domestic struggle for power and hence the shape of the postrevolutionary state and society. The hostage crisis and the war diverted popular attention in Iran—and international attention abroad—away from the domestic power struggle. In addition, both the hostage crisis and the war created a sense of siege in Iran, which led the population to lend extraordinary support to the country's leaders to defend Iran and the revolution before American and Iraqi aggression. In this climate, pro-democracy forces, the Left, and other moderate revolutionaries were portrayed by fundamentalists as American stooges, and resistance to religion's prominence in society was depicted as a Western ploy to destabilize the revolution. Thus international conflict supplied Islamist activists with a pretext to wage a decisive campaign against pro-democracy forces and leftists. The former were purged,[40] and the latter were subdued after fierce street confrontations, bombings, assassinations, and eventually, mass executions.[41] War fundamentalism and fundamentalist ideology's hold on politics intensified.

In November 1979, a group of pro-Khomeini students led by militant clerics occupied the American Embassy in Tehran and held its personnel hostage, demanding that the United States extradite the Shah to Iran and apologize to the Iranian people for its involvement in the 1953 coup against Mosaddeq and for supporting the Pahlavi monarchy.[42] The subsequent crisis lasted for 444 days and devastated relations between Iran and the United States, but it also shaped the direction of revolutionary politics. The occupation of the embassy followed the much-publicized admission of the Shah, who was suffering from cancer, to a hospital in New York, and a less-publicized but significant meeting in Algiers between Prime Minister Mehdi Bazargan and the American national security advisor, Zbigniew Brzezinski, during the funeral of President Boumedienne of Algeria.

The militants in Tehran saw these events as the unfolding of an American plot to undo the revolution and restore the Shah to power.[43] The memory of the restoration of the Shah to the throne in 1953 that had settled the struggle of power between Mosaddeq and the Shah in favor of the latter greatly influenced how these events were interpreted. The attack on the embassy was a protest against possible American action in Iran, but, more important, it was a way to sever U.S. ties with Iran and thus reduce Washington's room to maneuver in the country.

The unfolding hostage crisis, however, also changed the tenor of domestic

Iranian politics. First, it was seen as a manifestation of war fundamentalism. Iran had openly rejected the authority of international law and had engaged in a confrontational policy with a superpower. The occupation of the embassy led to wide-scale revolutionary mobilization, with daily demonstrations around the embassy compound in favor of Iran's defiant position. The dynamics of the hostage crisis created a momentum for militancy. Khomeini sanctioned this trend, understanding that standing in the way of a tidal wave was imprudent and that his leadership position depended on successfully riding that wave.[44] As a result, although he had not ordered the embassy takeover, he refused to intercede to secure the hostages' release or to rein in the crowds in the streets. As Iranian politics became radicalized, favoring militants with popular support on the streets, the moderate elements were pushed out.

In late November, a few weeks into the crisis, Bazargan resigned as prime minister.[45] The resignation confirmed the fact that Iranian domestic politics had become too inhospitable for moderate Islamic activists and secular democratic forces. Democracy's moment had passed, and with rising revolutionary fervor on the streets, the militants saw pro-democracy forces—whom the Left derided as "bourgeois" and "liberal," and whom fundamentalists called "pro-Western"— as dispensable. The Left, exemplified by the Tudeh Party, refused to support pro-democracy forces and endorsed the militant fundamentalists' platform on the grounds that it was "anti-imperialist." They both characterized Bazargan's government as pro-American. With pro-democracy forces out of the way and the possibility of foreign intervention on their behalf diminished, the Left believed that it could successfully contend with fundamentalists.

But on that point, the Left had seriously miscalculated. Fundamentalists began to constrict the Left's room to maneuver, purging their members from positions of power, attacking their offices, gatherings, and demonstrations, and intimidating or arresting their members and supporters. For instance, they attacked university campuses, intimidated and arrested students and faculty, and in June 1980 set in motion a "cultural revolution" to cleanse the universities of the Left.[46] Fundamentalists permanently occupied Tehran University by making its grounds the site for the official Friday Prayers.

The Left resisted, and it was then that it directly challenged Khomeini's rule and that the street clashes, assassinations, and bombings commenced. Killed in the violence were many senior revolutionary figures, including Ayatollah Beheshti, who was the influential head of the judiciary; President Rajai; Prime Minister Mohammad-Javad Bahonar; and seventy-two leaders of the Islamic Republic Party, the main organ of the fundamentalist wing of the revolution.[47]

Faced with the scope of the attacks by the Left, the revolutionary elite became willing to follow a scorched earth policy against its opponents. The Iran-

Iraq war, which began in September 1980, helped fundamentalists as the campaign to rally public support for the war effort relied on the same kind of militancy that was employed to garner support for the campaign against the Left.[48] From 1980 to 1982, scores of leftist activists and guerrilla fighters were arrested, tortured, and executed.[49] The Tudeh's leaders, despite their support for the fundamentalists, were publicly tried, forced to "recant," and then put to the sword. The confession of the party's octogenarian leader Noureddin Kianouri was broadcast on television, confirming the end of a political force that had enjoyed the support of the Soviet Union and defied the Shah's regime for close to four decades.[50] The Tudeh recantations were followed by mass execution of leftists in 1988, many of whom had already been tried and sentenced to prison terms—a purge that was designed to eliminate the Left altogether.[51] With this, the party effectively ceased to exist—a feat that the Shah had never been able to achieve. The Fadaiyan-e Khalq too were routed. Only the Mojahedin, after sustaining heavy casualties, managed to survive by choosing exile.

Throughout the struggle for power, the fundamentalists tightened their hold on levers of power. Abol-Hasan Bani-Sadr who, following Khomeini's initial endorsement, had become president in January 1980 in the first presidential elections, was forced out of office in March 1981, and in July his administration was succeeded by hard-line fundamentalist leaders associated with the Islamic Republic Party, Mohammad-Ali Rajai as president and the clerical activist Mohammad-Javad Bahonar as prime minister. When Rajai and Bahonar were assassinated by the Mojahedin in August, the path was cleared for further consolidation of clerical control of power. In October 1981, Seyyed Ali Khamenei became president. Each time a president was removed from office or killed, a provisional presidential council was formed that consisted mostly of clerical leaders of the revolution. Hence, within the span of eighteen months, fundamentalists gained control of the top offices in the country, and among them the clerical leaders assumed a more prominent role. All Iran's presidents between 1981 and 2005 were clerics.

The struggle for power between fundamentalists and leftists would also push the former to more openly appropriate the ideology of the Left and to match and exceed its claims and promises. In the world of revolutionaries, fundamentalists were determined to be more revolutionary than the Left, to compete with the Left in its own court and win. So although fundamentalists set out to destroy the Left, in the process they became more Left-leaning, more radical, themselves. Moreover, the scope of the bloodletting in the 1980–1982 period deeply scarred Iranian society and nudged the budding revolutionary state toward totalitarianism. The fundamentalists had survived the challenge by the Left, but only by embracing militancy and stoking the flames of war fundamentalism.

The Consolidation of Fundamentalist Rule

With the purge of the democratic forces and the Left, the revolution assumed a wholly religious identity. The Islamic Republic was now defined on the basis of a revolutionary quest for political transformation and a Jacobin ethic that together fulfilled the collectivist demands of Islamic ideology through a theocratic populist regime. Revolutionary fervor, fueled by war and the hostage crisis, more closely reflected Islamic ideology. That ideology would in turn define the pattern of state-building and how government would relate to society. In fact, it is the ascendance of Islamic ideology at this stage that marks the end of state-shattering and the resumption of state-building—giving form to the Islamic Republic. To protect what the revolution had achieved, it became imperative to go beyond social mobilization to create political domination. The revolution led to powerful new relationships between the political leaders and society. These ties had to be formalized to channel street power into political control. The institutional consolidation occurred gradually to confirm the revolution's spread over society. As a result, the state that emerged from this consolidation had a tighter hold on society than its predecessor, necessary if it was to control larger parts of the economy and regulate more of public and private life. The leadership of the Islamic Republic would aim to expand state power and capacity to regulate and rule. The new "Islamic leviathan" fit the model of postrevolutionary states in Russia and China.

As was the case with the rise of the state under Reza Shah, the Islamic Republic justified consolidation of power in terms of providing a public good. In this Islamic Republic, this public good was seen as greater Islamization of society and politics rather than development. Given its deeper ideological mobilization and presence within society, and the power vacuum that the revolutionary change had precipitated, the Islamic Republic found considerable room to maneuver. It built on the pattern of state formation during the Pahlavi era, vesting even greater powers in the state to subdue social forces as a prerequisite for the realization of its public policy agenda. The Islamic Republic, as was also the case with the early Pahlavi state, became directly concerned with the people's dress, music, personal relations, and cultural outlook. It regulated clothing and individual conduct in public, restricted women's and minority rights, imposed controls on the news and entertainment media, changed education curricula

and introduced ideological indoctrination, and even sought to Islamize intellectual activities. It anchored state formation in tight control of the public and
private arenas, and it viewed a transformation of social values and behavior to
be central to successful policy formulation and implementation. The state's outlook on its function and powers showed great continuity with the Pahlavi period.

The centrality of Islamization to state policy made Islamic ideology the dominant factor in deciding the flow of politics and the relations between state and
society. The emphasis on Islamic ideology served the interests of the rising
fundamentalist elements; for it allowed them to mobilize the population around
values and political conflicts that would favor them in consolidating power.
Hence, ideology served the interests of one faction in the revolutionary movement, whose triumph in turn made Islamic ideology central to state and conduct
of politics.

The Significance of the Iran–Iraq War

Islamic ideology also anchored Iran's politics in even stronger allegiance to
Khomeini. This was particularly important as revolutionary fervor continued to
unfold in the Iran–Iraq war.[52] The war began in September 1980, when Iraqi
troops occupied Iran's oil province of Khouzestan, and continued until 1988.
During the early phase of the war, Iran was on the defensive, but it was eventually
able to expel Iraqi troops from Iranian territories and launch an offensive to
oust Saddam Hussein. The war ended after Iran's siege of Basra collapsed, and
it became evident that the war was unwinnable without commitment of vast
resources. Iran accepted a cease-fire with Iraq after its forces failed to prevent
a major Iraqi offensive.

The war was one of the most costly and devastating wars of the second half
of the twentieth century. In the eight years of war, almost one million Iranians
were maimed or killed. Iran lost control of parts of its oil-rich province for some
time, and it incurred tremendous damage to its cities and rural areas, and with
them its industrial and agricultural infrastructure. Iraq used banned chemical
weapons against Iranian troops, and Iranian cities were attacked incessantly
with SCUD missiles.

The war became an important determinant of the ebbs and flows of revolutionary politics, and the pattern of state-building. It has been generally accepted that the rise of states is directly correlated with "war-making"[53] and that
societies that experience wars or significant social dislocation are more prone
to producing strong states.[54] As Charles Tilly has put it, "war made the state
and the state made war."[55] It is not possible to understand the trajectory of the

Islamic Republic's development without understanding how the Iran–Iraq war affected political priorities, attitudes, and power struggles in Iran.

War management in the 1980s further embedded the state in society as Iranians rallied to the cause of the war and provided it with resources. However, resource mobilization did not produce a new social contract between state and society, because resource mobilization for the war occurred in the name of Islamic ideology; as such, the people's contributions to the war effort did not impose social demands on the state in return for those contributions. Throughout the war years, the Islamic Republic mobilized resources by using the same Shia myths and symbols and ideological arguments that had mobilized the masses during the revolution. Even nationalism was initially subsumed under revolutionary zeal and the language of jihad and martyrdom. Soldiers ran onto Iraqi positions without adequate arms and protection as part of human wave attacks, knowing that they probably would be killed. In effect they were willing martyrs who viewed their voluntarism to be in the cause of Islam and the revolution, and a way to salvation.[56] The Islamic Republic encouraged this level of commitment by promoting a culture of martyrdom steeped in Shia symbolism. These included such acts as construction of a fountain filled with red water, symbolizing blood, at the Martyr's Cemetery in Tehran, or enactment before troops on the battlefront of dramatic scenes associated with the messianic return of the Hidden Imam. The attitudes promoted by the war were later carried into Iranian society and politics by war veterans, Revolutionary Guard members and their families, and the foundations and social service agencies associated with the war, all of which constituted a powerful political constituency that continued to identify with war fundamentalism.

The need to mobilize support and resources for the war pushed the revolutionary regime to emphasize ideology and the revolutionary values that are associated with it. Consequently, throughout the 1980–1989 period, Iran's politics was defined by revolutionary zeal, and state formation remained closely tied to the pursuit of Islamization.[57] This in turn committed Iran to a confrontational foreign policy and shifted power to the more radical elements in the state leadership. Ayatollah Khomeini supported this trend, for it bolstered his position of power in Iran and served his ambitions to influence regional and international politics.

The Iran–Iraq war was important in determining the shape of the state and national politics, and it extended the life span of ideological politics by diverting attention from socioeconomic concerns and interests. It allowed the more militant faction of the revolutionary leadership to consolidate power and vested greater powers in the more radical wing of that faction.

The Emergence of Factional Politics

The ultimate power in the Islamic Republic was centralized in the person of the Supreme Leader. However, when Khomeini was at the helm, power was distributed among the leadership of the Islamic Republic. This leadership was well-knit, and it was also tied closely to religious leaders in the mosques, faculty and students in the seminaries, preachers and prayer leaders, bazaar merchants, neighborhood committee members, and activists in the society.[58] Khomeini was instrumental early on in inculcating group interests in the politically active ulama, tying their political ambitions and social position to the fortunes of the Islamic Republic. The religious leadership ruled collectively, acting as a dominant class, and they were distinguished from the general population by dress and education; the revolution transformed the ulama into a political caste.[59] Commitment to the Islamic Republic and Khomeini, however, did not eliminate power struggles, differences over policy, and disagreements over ideological interpretation among religious activists and the ulama.

The revolution did not produce a unified way of managing these political debates and conflicts. Because there had existed no dominant revolutionary party before the revolution, the Islamic Republic Party, formed after the revolution to serve as the organizational vehicle for the revolution's religious leadership, had little experience or expertise to call on in political organizing.[60] As a result, the party was not very successful in meeting its original objectives. It did not develop a cadre of following, and its role in mobilization of the population and enforcement of revolutionary values remained limited and quaint. Many of these functions were performed by militant groups, who enforce the regime's policies on the streets, by preachers in local mosques, and by the ulama during Friday prayer sermons. In fact, from 1984 onward, mosque preachers had the official tasks of mobilizing the public for demonstrations, election campaigns, and in policy support. In 1987, the Islamic Republic Party was officially discontinued.[61] Thenceforth, the revolutionary leadership relied extensively on the network of preachers and mosques for assistance. That network would later become the basis for patronage ties that galvanized support for the state through the intermediary of clerical leaders at various levels of society. Relationships of patronage in time became economically important as they created vested interests that resisted or bypassed economic reform.

In the absence of a political organization to manage struggles of power and debates over policy among state leaders, factional politics came into the open. In the 1980s, three main factions emerged within the Islamic Republic.[62] The first favored a relaxation of revolutionary vigilance and stabilization of economic relations; its members came to be known as the "moderates" or "pragmatists." Those identified with the second faction favored continued commitment to Islamic ideology, but they wished to promote a mercantile economy and the right to private property; they came to be known as the "conservatives." They were interested in deepening the Islamic rather than the populist dimension of the revolution. They had strong support within the bazaar, among the lower middle classes, and among the lower ranking preachers. The third faction favored a strong anti-Western policy, export of the revolution, state control of the economy, and nationalization of large-scale enterprises. It came to be known as the "radical" or "hard-line" faction, and it was responsible for many of the Islamic Republic's excesses in foreign policy and the expropriation of private property. This faction represented the revolutionary Left and the Jacobin dimension of the revolution.

The revolutionary fervor espoused by this faction mobilized popular support for the revolution, the Iran-Iraq war, and Iran's radical foreign policy, and for this work the radical faction received considerable power in the government and Ayatollah Khomeini's support from 1980 to 1989. That power worked to protect and expand the scope of populism, state domination of the economy, and centralized economic planning. The radicals drew on the populist and leftist dimensions of Islamic ideology that had taken shape in the early years of the revolution and on the intellectual legacy of radical Islamic modernists, most notably the ideas of Shariati. Members of this faction oversaw Iran's support for revolutionary activism in Lebanon, the Persian Gulf monarchies, and the Arab Middle East.[63]

The three factions existed only informally. There was no actual organization, charter, rules, or platforms to define membership; nor were there any grassroots movements or party structures. The factions functioned as informal circles within the revolutionary elite, with ill-defined and often changing boundaries. The factions became proto-party structures, however, especially because they shaped electoral results directly. Parallel and related to the factional divisions were two clerical groups, the conservative Association of Militant Clergy (Jame'eh-ye Rowhaniyat-e Mobarez) and the Left-leaning Society of Militant Clerics (Majma'-e Rowhaniyoun-e Mobarez), which broke away from the former in 1988 to underscore the populist message of the revolution. The two were not parties, but they had a more formal structure and more clearly delineated boundaries than other factions. They served as organizational bases for these factions to operate. The Jame'eh became dominant in the Guardian Council and the Majma' in the parliament. The latter would lose power in the post-Khomeini era and gravitate toward reformism in the late 1990s.[64]

The revolutionary regime had no institutional means of distributing power among its various elements and factions outside of the traditional mosque and seminary networks. Thus the function that ordinarily would be performed by internal party elections has been performed by general elections for parliament since 1979, so that the Islamic Republic itself functioned as a party with regular and free elections within itself, but not in the political arena at large. In effect, voters became party members—mobilized through mosque networks and ideological propagation—and the parliament they elected functioned very much as a Central Committee or Politburo of sorts. However, the regularity of general elections helped institutionalize the place of the parliament—the Islamic Consultative Assembly—in the Islamic Republic. Hence the need to decide distribution of power within the ruling regime, and the absence of institutional mechanisms to do so outside the public arena, in effect introduced electoral politics and parliamentary behavior to Iran.[65]

Struggles for power between these factions occurred not only in the parliament, but also in various consultative forums, in government agencies, in Friday Prayer sermons, and in the print media. Though debates over foreign policy were restrained, and the various contenders did not propose radically different policies, in economic matters the differences were pronounced, and the debates were intense. Most notably, the radicals clashed severely with the other two factions over the right to private property. Whereas the former favored greater populism and broader state control of the economy, the other factions favored protection of the right to property and limits to populism in favor of mercantile activities and private investments. Despite Khomeini's tacit support for the radicals, in the end the other two factions managed to compel the revolutionary government to accept the right to property, provide legal protection to mercantile activities, and to limit the scope of populism.[66]

Factionalism dominated politics in Iran throughout the 1980s.[67] It was clearly reflected in the composition of key institutions, such as the Guardian Council, and it influenced the distribution of power between the president and the prime minister, and the president and the parliament. It also influenced the state's relations with society, and, more important, the workings of the economy.

The Revolution and the Economy

The revolution significantly changed the immediate course of economic development in Iran.[68] For more than a decade, the rate of growth was retarded by political and social turmoil caused by a number of factors: the revolution itself (1978–1979); subsequent domestic political crises; legal uncertainties following the collapse of the old order; revolutionary justice; debates over the right to property; the brain drain; the war with Iraq; and international isolation after the hostage crisis.[69] Equally important was the incompetence and inexperience of the new leaders of economic agencies, who had risen to the top following purges and brain drain. The effect of bureaucratic decay was evident in such decisions as severely cutting Iran's oil production at the height of the market in the early 1980s, which denied Iran billions of dollars in oil revenue.

More important, the state now adhered to new perceptions of socioeconomic interest and the nature of development. The leftist elements in the revolution viewed economic development under the Pahlavi state as misguided, uneven in its emphasis on industry and the private sector, capitalistic, and hence, doomed to failure. The religious element was uninterested in development per se and favored replacing it as a national goal with Islamization. Khomeini set the tone when he dismissed economic concerns as "foolish" and emphasized Islamization instead.

Thus, after 1979, economic development occupied a much less prominent place in the state's priorities; moreover, it changed in nature. The influence of the Left and of the radical faction among the clerical activists, especially during the premiership of Mir-Hossein Mousavi (1981–1989), anchored Iran's economic development in centralized planning and socialist-inspired models that had been tried in Third World countries.[70] Hence the revolutionary government nationalized banks, insurance companies, and major industries and expropriated smaller industrial and business ventures of those who had been close to the Pahlavi state. By 1989, the state accounted for 80 percent of the Iranian economy, relegating the private sector to small-scale economic activities.[71]

The expansion of the state's control of the economy in time served the revolution's political needs as distribution of jobs forged patronage ties. The revolutionary government sought to establish control over labor by integrating industrial workers into the ruling political order through "corporatism"—whereby the state receives support of organized interest groups by recognizing their corporate interests and granting them monopoly of representing its interests.[72] The growth of the public sector also produced new avenues for corruption among bureaucrats and political leaders. This corruption, combined with the challenges cited earlier, reduced efficiency significantly. Between 1978 and 1988, the gross domestic product fell by 1.5 percent a year on average—in 1988, it stood at 1974 levels.[73] Industry experienced six years of negative growth. Real output and private per capita consumption fell and, in 1990, were below those of 1977.

The social demands that the revolution brought also drained state resources. By mobilizing diverse social groups, the revolution increased demands on the state to deliver more social services. The revolution also both encouraged population growth and increased the pace of urbanization, which became particularly intense during the Iraqi occupation of southwestern Iran, which led to a large exodus of people to other areas in Iran. The rapid population growth and urbanization produced high levels of unemployment, which in 1988 stood at 30 percent.[74] The relatively weak private sector was unable to create enough jobs to absorb the surplus labor. The government throughout the 1980s addressed the problem by providing employment in the public sector, which by 1988 accounted for one third of all jobs.[75] In the meantime, oil income fell—oil's share of the gross domestic product fell from 30 to 40 percent in the 1970s to 9 to 17 percent in the 1980s as production levels fell from 5.6 million barrels per day to as low as 2.2 million barrels at a time when the price of oil also declined sharply.[76] Though the government increased the rate and scope of taxation, the economy continued to depend on oil revenues, which accounted for 85 percent of Iran's hard-currency earnings.[77]

By 1989, the effects of the war, international isolation, economic sanctions, population growth, and production declines had plunged the Iranian economy into a serious crisis.[78] The economy suffered from inflation averaging 23 percent,[79] high unemployment, stagnant growth, and weak industrial output. The shortages in consumer goods produced a thriving black market, which skewed economic interests and distribution of resources and reduced efficiency. In addition, the growth of the public sector did not eradicate poverty. By weakening the private sector, it reduced income inequality, but standards of living, especially of the urban poor, did not improve substantially. Inflation and unemployment had effectively undermined populist policies.

During the 1980–1989 period, economic hardship could be blamed on the Iran–Iraq war; the end of the war denied the state that excuse. The scope of the economic crisis facing the state now posed serious political challenges. Socio-economic interests could no longer be easily made subordinate to ideological concerns, rhetoric of Islamic ideology, and allegiance to the goals of the revolution. Economic realities changed public expectations of the government. As the Islamic Republic felt the pressure of popular demand, revolutionary politics was compelled to embrace greater pragmatism and to confront the imperative of development and efficiency in state-building.

In 1988, the war with Iraq ended. After eight years of sacrifices, Iran had no victory. In July 1988, Khomeini endorsed the cease-fire agreement that ended the war, and almost a year later, in June 1989, he died. The two events marked a turning point in the revolution. War fundamentalism was now on the wane, and with the loss of Khomeini as the symbol of revolutionary fervor and the war that kept stoking it, attentions turned to mounting socioeconomic demands—to state-building.

4

An Islamic Developmental State? 1989–1997

Ali-Akbar Hashemi-Rafsanjani's two terms as president (1989–1997) was one of the more significant periods of state-building in postrevolutionary Iran. It is a period both of continuity with and change from the revolutionary past, during which new economic, social, and political developments pushed the state and society in new directions. It is during this period that preoccupation with revolution and war fundamentalism gradually gave place to state-building as the revolution entered its "Thermidor" phase.[1] Pursuit of economic growth, stability, and prosperity came to rival the preoccupation with ideology, austerity, self-sufficiency, export of revolution, and war against imperialism. This "second Islamic Republic" continued to bear the distinct mark of the revolution's ideology but was also shaped by developmentalist objectives.[2]

State-building in the Rafsanjani period was both informed by the ideological values of the revolution and its fidelity to Islamic ideology. The revolution had increased the size of the Iranian state. It now controlled a larger portion of the economy and society, and different aspects of personal and public life were now controlled. Yet the revolutionary state was a lame leviathan, for despite its size, it accomplished little in terms of delivering on socioeconomic demands. The Rafsanjani period sought to increase the capacity of the state to do more, and to do more with greater efficiency. The state would now have to view development as a part of its ideological mandate.

This turn to developmentalism was anchored in state-building concerns that had certain similarities with those that had shaped the Pahlavi state.[3] This did not mean that Rafsanjani's government was inspired by the example of the 1970s or that it credited the Shah's policies—although many bureaucratic managers began looking to the details of planning and decision making of the Pahlavi period as they sought to address socioeconomic issues. But the goal and process of development would inevitably lead the Islamic Republic back to the policies that the revolution had either rejected or at least interrupted in 1979. Many of the development plans of the Pahlavi period regarding industrial development, energy, urban planning, and infrastructure investment were revived and ultimately implemented, but, more important, many of managerial procedures and planning doctrines—such as five-year economic planning—were also put back in place. The reflection of the Pahlavi era developmentalism in fashioning state-building during this period as well as Rafsanjani's own style led many Iranians to facetiously refer to him as "Akbar Shah."

The goal of development was tied to postwar reconstruction (*baz-sazi*) and to the ambition to build the country (*sazandegi*) as it had been promised by the revolution when it rejected the Shah's developmentalist agenda. Achieving the latter goal would validate the message of the revolution. The turn to development sought to address socioeconomic demands, but also to reinterpret the meaning of the revolution and its promise: it would achieve "true" progress; that, rather than class war or the Islamization of society, would be its goal. The notion of an "Islamic developmental state," as incongruous as it may seem at face value, was the driving force during Rafsanjani's presidency. It is also of heuristic value in analyzing changes during this period, and it may explain many of the paradoxes of the Islamic Republic since 1989.

Khomeini's successors looked to build a modern state on the foundations of the Islamic revolution but never managed to reconcile the inconsistencies of pursuing development while remaining true to the revolution's ideology. However, in trying to do so, they shaped state and society in new ways and precipitated debates over ideology, state-building, and democracy. The Rafsanjani period is worthy of particular attention not because it produced a viable model of state, but for what its grappling with the conflicting impulses of revolutionary politics and developmentalism, fidelity to Islamic ideology while pursuing efficiency in government and economy, reveals about the vicissitudes of state-building. The Rafsanjani period was also one in which mercantile capitalism made a comeback to overshadow the Jacobin ethos and war fundamentalism. Economic reforms empowered the private sector and the middle class and expanded the space for them grow in, and in the process they changed the character of Iranian society in a fundamental way.[4]

The effort to streamline government was limited, however, by the fact that the political structure of the country remained anchored in the fundamentalist ideology of the revolution. Policymaking was driven by the imperative of pragmatism but was constrained by the demands of Islamic ideology and its militant advocates. Thus the Rafsanjani period did not provide a break with the revolutionary past but rather ensured institutional and ideological continuities with the Khomeini period that sustained the edifice of the Islamic Republic just as it introduced limited changes to it. As such, Rafsanjani's presidency failed to resolve the dilemmas facing state-building, but it went some distance in presenting a new context for doing so. An unintended consequence of this was to create an impetus for fundamental political changes that would manifest themselves in renewed interest in democracy.

Successors to Khomeini

After Khomeini's death, leadership was passed to Seyyed Ali Khamenei (then the president), who became the Supreme Leader. In his place Rafsanjani (then the speaker of the parliament) became president. The two were not particularly noted for their religious scholarly credentials and did not rank high in Shia ulama hierarchy. They had gained their stature during the revolutionary struggle and as a result of their close ties to Khomeini and the experience that they had gathered managing government affairs between 1979 and 1989. With the rise of these two, the foundational principle of the Islamic Republic was turned on its head. Khomeini had believed that Islam alone would ensure the virtue of the state. Hence religious knowledge defined the worth of political leadership. The theory of *Velayat-e Faqih* stipulated that the supreme religious authority should also be the supreme political authority, not the other way around. Khamenei was hard-pressed to justify his assumption of the status of *vali-e faqih* and source of emulation for the pious masses. He had been chosen to succeed Khomeini at a time of urgency and confusion in the ranks of revolutionary ulama. Shortly before his death, Khomeini had dismissed his heir apparent, Ayatollah Hossein-Ali Montazeri, leaving little time to groom a successor. With no obvious candidate, the clerical leadership compromised by appointing Khamenei. He was not the most qualified candidate, but he was the most expedient one. Because of the way he was chosen, Khamenei would have to rely on the conservative ulama who sponsored him to shore up his authority. This created a strong conservative power bloc that would exercise great influence on the new Supreme Leader and would impede reforms.

The installation of Khamenei and Rafsanjani as new leaders signaled a novel understanding of the notion of Islamic state. It would be true to the spirit of

Islamic ideology, but its leaders would be more political than religious. In a departure from war fundamentalism and Khomeini's antistate posturing, the choice of new leaders would signify that the revolution had to deliver more than ideological fervor to the masses; that knowledge in Islam alone was not sufficient to ensure the proper working of the state, and for these reasons the revolution had to take state-building seriously. In many regards, Khomeini's death separated religion and politics. The leaders of Shia religion in Iran were no longer in the halls of power. Those who ruled Iran were turbaned activists with slim authority in religious matters.[5] From this point forward, it would be Islamic ideology and not Islam that would ensure the excellence of the state. For the new leaders could muster credentials in the former but not the latter.

The rise of Khamenei and Rafsanjani to power was the product of an alliance between the conservative and pragmatic factions of the revolutionary leadership to marginalize the radical faction—most closely associated with the ideological politics and war fundamentalism of the 1980s.[6] The conservatives and the radicals each represented one aspect of Khomeini's ideology. The conservatives represented the Islamic fundamentalist dimension, and the radicals the militant leftist dimensions of that ideology and, more generally, the revolution. Once Khomeini died, the conservative fundamentalists and the leftists parted ways. The conservatives—especially senior clerics such as ayatollahs Mohammad-Reza Mahdavi-Kani or Mohammad Emami-Kashani and politicians such as Habibollah Asgarowladi, who was close to the bazaar—had close ties to the bazaar and represented interests that ran counter to the radical faction's economic outlook. Khamenei was once ideologically close to Shariati,[7] and his views on the economy and society were in tune with those of the radical faction. However, as president from 1981 to 1989, he had to compete with Prime Minister Mir-Hossein Mousavi of the radical faction for control of the executive office. That competition had pushed him closer to Rafsanjani and the conservative faction. It was in this context that Khamenei became the choice of the conservative faction for Supreme Leader and Rafsanjani for the presidency. Their alliance moved policymaking toward greater pragmatism in politics and management of the economy.

Constitutional changes in 1989 provided for changes that would end confusion over exercise of authority in government and would promote greater pragmatism. The most important change in this regard was the elimination of the office of the prime minister, which made the president the undisputed head of the executive branch and the person responsible for the management of the country's administration. The gridlock that competition for power between the president and prime minister had caused was blamed for economic crisis and growing disenchantment with the government. Constitutional changes also strengthened the Guardian Council, which had the power to veto parliamentary legislation and through which the credentials of all candidates for parliamentary or presidential elections had to be approved. The council's members were selected by the Supreme Leader, and it quickly became the bastion of conservative clerics who had selected Khamenei.[8]

The elimination of the office of prime minister weakened the radical faction. Before the constitutional change, the prime minister was chosen by the parliament, which was controlled by the radical faction. Although the radicals would stay in control of the parliament until 1992, they lost their voice in the executive branch.[9] Radical ministers such as Behzad Nabavi (minister of heavy industries) were purged, and the new managers in the bureaucracy gradually marginalized the radicals' supporters. Khameini's newly acquired powers were further used to purge members of the radical faction from the judiciary and important supervisory bodies such as the Guardian Council.[10] Influential senior clerics associated with the radicals, such as Abdol-Karim Mousavi-Ardebili and Mehdi Karroubi, lost their positions to conservative stalwarts such as Ahmad Jannati, Ali Meshkini, and Mohammad Yazdi. These new appointees in turn led a campaign to confirm the relationship of the revolution to Islamic ideology and a fundamentalist base of power. The greater emphasis on morality and ethics in place of economic populism signaled the prominence of the conservatives and the waning power of the radicals.

The radicals, led by Mehdi Karroubi, the Speaker of the parliament—who would in later years emerge as a reformist—resisted these changes until 1992, advocating socialist-inspired economic policies of centralized control and self-reliance.[11] In the parliamentary elections of 1992, the conservatives won control of the parliament, and with that victory, the radicals were all but eliminated as a main contender for power. Still, the radicals' position continued to be advocated by some clerics, such as Mohammad Mousavi-Khoiniha and Ali-Akbar Mohtashemipour, politicians such as Behzad Nabavi, and activists such as Abbas Abdi. They disseminated their message through the press and organizations affiliated with radicals, such as the Sazman-e Mojahedin-e Enqelab-e Eslami (Organization of the Mojahedin of the Islamic Revolution) and the Majma'-e Rouhaniyoun-e Mobarez (Society of Militant Clerics).

The marginalization of the radicals, however, did not pave the way for pure pragmatism in state-building. Freed from the pressures of radical revolutionaries, state-building now came under pressure from the revolution's fundamentalist guardians. Though state-building could now serve the goal of development and represent private sector interests more freely, it was restricted by the moral and ideological strictures of conservatives who were insistent that the Islamic Republic remain true to its name.

Consolidation of New Order

The immediate consequence of Khamenei's assumption of power was to both centralize power in the office of the Supreme Leader and also to streamline its functions and workings.[12] Khomeini had initially maintained informal and personal ties with various revolutionary leaders, and he did not follow a decision-making process in rendering his opinions; he simply issued rulings that would then be binding on the state. Under the new leadership, decision making became formalized in a process that involved procedures and the participation of various institutions and political leaders.

The changes in the working of the offices of the Supreme Leader did not, however, address the nature of its relations with the presidency. Khomeini had enjoyed unique powers that came from his supreme religious status and charismatic authority. Moreover, Khomeini was not interested in the micromanagement of the country but in defining the ideology of the state and the ethos of its politics. Khamenei lacked Khomeini's charisma and religious standing, and his more recent career had been shaped not in the seminary but in government. His interests did not lie in theology and Islamic law—nor did he have the credentials to take the lead in those areas—but in managing government affairs, and he was well known in bureaucratic circles for his attentiveness to details. Khamenei was thus much more likely to interfere in executive functions reserved for the presidency. This would confound distribution of power and boundaries of political and executive functions in the Islamic Republic despite efforts to bring rationality to governance through constitutional changes in 1989.

Soon after he rose to power, Khamenei took full advantage of constitutional changes that were initiated during the last months of Khomeini's life to strengthen his own powers at the expense of elected officials.[13] He curtailed the powers of the president by assuming control of the armed forces, ordinarily a presidential function, and he tightened his control over various foundations that controlled vast financial resources and managed large social services.

Khomeini had had both religious and popular legitimacy, and he served as the Supreme Leader in both religious and political arenas. However, the succession process failed to replicate Khomeini's role. What emerged was a diarchy that lacked religious legitimacy and broad popular support. This posed a challenge to the Islamic Republic. Constitutional changes had sought to address this issue by vesting greater powers in the state to compensate for the informal power that Khomeini had wielded and that Khamenei was not capable of exercising and in those offices of the state that are not representative of popular will but of the ideological and ad hoc products of the Islamic Republic. This was intended to protect the character of the Islamic Republic from expression of popular will that diverged from the leaders' interests. But this anticipation of a need for protection suggested that the Islamic Republic and its ideology no longer represented the popular will. By extending the powers of Supreme Leader, the conservative supporters of Khamenei made sure that the core values of the Islamic Republic would be preserved through the absolute powers of the unelected and unaccountable Supreme Leader.[14]

Khamenei's success in consolidating power under himself gradually constricted Rafsanjani's room to maneuver, and it reduced his ability to act pragmatically on policies. By 1991 Khamenei had asserted the Supreme Leader's primacy in the Islamic Republic, and the 1992 parliamentary elections increased the power of conservatives. This development compelled Rafsanjani to temper his push to rationalize and normalize state policymaking. This was particularly true of his second term in office, from 1994 to 1997, when he sought to more carefully balance pragmatic considerations with ideological demands.

Rafsanjani was reelected with a weak mandate. The election turnout was only 53 percent of the electorate—far below the levels seen in elections in the 1980s—and Rafsanjani received a mere 63 percent of the votes.[15] Without clear public support for his reforms, he became vulnerable to a conservative backlash. Between 1994 and 1997, the conservative parliament incessantly attacked Rafsanjani's policies and managers, forcing the removal of all reform-minded ministers—including Mohammad Khatami, the reformist and moderate minister of culture who would later become president. As Rafsanjani's presidency drew to a close, the conservative elite became more determined to assert its positions. The press began to attack him personally, accusing him of corruption, and his daughter was criticized for relaxed and unorthodox mores. The judiciary sought to intimidate bureaucratic managers associated with reforms, and in 1998 Karbaschi, who as mayor of Tehran was a major face of reconstruction and reform, was publicly tried on corruption charges. All this would compel Rafsanjani to confirm his fidelity to the core values of the Islamic revolution and to back away from the openings that his administration had created in society and politics.

In the end, although he was fashioned by his supporters as "commander of development" (Sardar-e Sazandegi), Rafsanjani's commitment to development proved to be far from steadfast.[16] He had been associated with the revolutionary agenda in the early 1980s, and he had supported war fundamentalism, the export of revolution, and continuation of the Iran-Iraq war after Iraqi troops were expelled from Iran in 1986. He was not initially an advocate of pragmatism and never put forward a clear vision of state-building and development. He rather advocated development out of expediency—to relieve pressure on the Islamic Republic—and showed limited commitment to the values or requirements of development.[17] As a result, when faced with conservative pressure, he proved willing to compromise on pragmatism and to support policies that ran counter to demands of development. Consequently, government policy unfolded in tandem with continued ideological posturing, which was reflected also in radicalism in foreign policy.

Rafsanjani's image was marred by violations of human rights, continued support for radical movements in the Muslim world, assassination of dissidents in Europe, and murders of journalists and intellectuals in Iran. Despite talk of pragmatism and greater political opening, Rafsanjani dealt with dissent in a heavy-handed manner. When, for instance, the Society for the Defense of Liberty and Sovereignty of the Iranian Nation (Jam'iyat-e Defa' az Azadi va Hakemiyat-e Mellat-e Iran) presented him in May 1990 with a letter with ninety signatories demanding political freedoms, the society and its principle voices were suppressed severely.[18] In 1994, the author Ali-Akbar Saidi-Sirjani mysteriously died in prison after he was jailed and tortured for criticizing the Supreme Leader. In 1996–1997, a concerted smear television campaign, named *Hoviyyat* (Identity), was launched against intellectuals. Afterward, dissident journalists and intellectuals disappeared or were jailed, and six dissident political activists and intellectuals were killed in 1998 in what came to be known as serial murders (*qatlha-ye zanjireh-i*). It was later revealed that the ministry of intelligence was behind the killings. Rationalizing government in the 1990s had strengthened the ministry, which was popularly believed to be tied to Rafsanjani and to the conservative faction.

Similarly, in 1991, at a time when Rafsanjani's economic managers were arguing for ending Iran's international isolation, the Shah's last prime minister, Shapur Bakhtiar, was assassinated in Paris. Bakhtiar's murder caused tensions between Iran and France and led the French president to cancel a state visit to Iran.[19] Shortly after, in 1992, the German government indicted Khamenei, Rafsanjani, and Ali Fallahian, the minister of intelligence, for their part in the "Mykonos Affair," named for a restaurant in Berlin where dissident Kurdish leaders were assassinated. The European Community reacted by asking all member countries to withdraw their ambassadors from Tehran, which left only Greece with an embassy in Iran. The Mykonos Affair—whose charges are still outstanding—damaged Rafsanjani's attempt to change the tenor of Iran's politics and cast the country's image in a new light. It was followed by the bombing of a Jewish cultural center in Buenos Aires in 1994 in which Iran was accused of having a hand. In 1995, the United States reacted to these events by tightening trade sanctions against Iran—adding a blow to the goals of development.[20] These developments further led to a debate over the core values and ideology of revolution.

Contending with Socioeconomic Challenges

As discussed in the previous chapter, the turn to state-building was motivated by growing social tensions that resulted from a decade of neglect of the economy, investment in infrastructure, and social services. In the 1980–1989 period, Iran's economy was damaged by populist economic policies and centralized planning, which had been pushed especially by the radical faction that controlled the parliament and the office of the prime minister.[21] As was the case in socialist economies of the Soviet bloc and other Third World countries, these policies proved to be economically disastrous—creating a bloated public sector, economic stagnation, inflation, shortages, and poverty.

A summary examination of economic data from the 1980s underscores the depth and breadth of the challenges that faced the country. In the first decade of the revolution, some 3.1 million people were added to the workforce, but only 1.9 million new jobs were created by the economy. In 1989, unemployment stood at 15 percent of the labor force, some 2 million people; but if underemployment were also to be counted, the figures are much higher: 41 percent of the workforce, or 6 million strong.[22] Inflation in the same year was 29 percent.[23]

During the war years, the country's rulers blamed the war for economic hardships, and they used food rationing, price control, and extensive regulations to stabilize the economy and contain socioeconomic pressures. Those policies ensured a certain degree of egalitarianism in the distribution of basic staples and protected the poor from the vagaries of price fluctuations. However, short-run benefits of such an approach were more than matched by long-run structural problems caused by extensive regulation of the economy. The controls led to growth of an underground economy, skewed production and consumption, and deepening economic inefficiencies.[24]

Once the war ended, the public demanded the much-delayed economic recovery and change. That the stagnation of Iran's economy was compared by many to its dynamism in the 1970s placed even greater pressure on the leaders to address economic expectations.[25] The growing discontent, which extended to the bazaar and the lower classes tied to the revolutionary power structure, created a consensus among Iran's revolutionary leaders that socioeconomic issues had to be addressed. This provided Rafsanjani's administration with an opportunity to initiate economic reforms and to undertake the state-building necessary to realize them.[26]

Back to State-Building

Between 1989 and 1997, the Rafsanjani administration sought to resolve the structural problems that were inherent in the Islamic Republic. The revolution had created a dual state in which revolutionary institutions operated alongside preexisting state institutions, at times duplicating their functions and interfering with their operations.[27] Beginning in 1989, many of those parallel institutions were gradually merged together. For instance, revolutionary courts and the judiciary were integrated. Others, such as parastatal foundations, Jihad for Reconstruction, and the Revolutionary Guard were made into new organs of state, and their relations with other state institutions were clarified. This did not completely resolve the duality, as intent was never matched with adequate action. Integration of parallel institutions generated resistance from those who would lose power and fringe benefits. Moreover, it proved much easier to promise integration than to implement it, as the government lacked necessary authority or know-how to fully carry it out. These shortcomings notwithstanding, the attempt to integrate revolutionary and state institutions brought some degree of rationality and functional normalization.

Rafsanjani also vested greater powers in the bureaucracy, giving it more autonomy from ideological politics. If the motto of the government in the 1980s was "we want the ideologically committed, not specialists," in the 1990s it was "we want specialists who are also ideologically committed." Emphasis on management became the credo of Rafsanjani's administration. The new breed was exemplified by Gholam-Hossein Karbaschi, who, as mayor of Isfahan and later Tehran, created effective local governance capable of mobilizing resources, delivering social services, and bringing about effective change in a relatively short period of time despite political constraints. The extent of change witnessed in Tehran in the 1989–1997 period in comparison with other Third World cities of similar size and with similar challenges is quite remarkable. In fact, given its population growth and infrastructure constraints, the projection for the city in 1988 was that it would drift into chronic poverty and mismanagement.[28] That the city avoided the fate of many other troubled metropolises of the Third World owed much to the policies of the Rafsanjani period.

The drive to reform the bureaucracy and strengthen managerial skills in various government agencies also led the Rafsanjani government to turn to many specialists and managers of the Pahlavi period who had lost their jobs during the purges of the early 1980s. Many academics who had been expelled from universities were encouraged to go back to the universities or join new institutes that were formed to conduct research, and to help with planning and policymaking. Some of these institutes, such the Institute for Studies of Theoretical Physics and Mathematics, would become internationally recognized centers of excellence. Government training centers that had atrophied in the 1980s were revived to assist bureaucrats with management.

The government also strengthened higher education in order to produce the skilled personnel it needed for development.[29] This began by deemphasizing ideological fervor on campuses. For instance, soon after Rafsanjani became president, his government demanded incoming students to sign a contract with universities that they would not challenge the authority of their professors—the "cultural revolution" was formally over. The government also invested in new institutions of higher education and encouraged the private sector to do so as well, leading to the rise of the Daneshgah-e Azad-e Eslami (Islamic Open University), whose many campuses across Iran provide private higher education. As a result, the number of university students grew rapidly. In 1977, there were 154,000 university students in Iran; in 1997, that number stood at 1.25 million.[30] The growth in the number of university students would play an important role in democracy debates in the late 1990s. University education would also help boost the ranks of the middle class, with important implications for political change in the country.

The investment in universities yielded some intended economic results. Throughout the 1990s university graduates joined the bureaucracy and private and public companies, which provided development with skilled labor.[31] By the end of the 1990s, Iran boasted a strong community skilled in the sciences, a significant portion of which was a product of domestic universities.[32] In some areas of research, especially in mathematics and theoretical physics, Iranian scientists now rank among the best in the world. This community has been instrumental in propelling development by providing it with technical know-how, skilled labor, and, equally important, a scientific-industrial culture.

The Rafsanjani government changed the economic agencies particularly and opened the door for the emergence of pockets of efficiency, most notably at the municipal level. These efforts once again made development a central concern of the state and a justification for its power and capacity. The post-Khomeini era thus saw the revival of the Pahlavi conception of the state. Memories of the Pahlavi state and the intellectual capital that it produced had survived the revolution to once again influence state-building. The marriage of the old and the new was quite clear in a meeting in New York in 1991 between a delegation of Iranian officials and some 450 expatriate Iranian academics and former captains of industry who had left Iran after the revolution and lived in the United States and Canada.[33] In the meeting, the Iranian government officials encouraged the exiles to return to Iran and participate in the economic reforms initiated by

Rafsanjani and even to resume ownership of businesses that the revolution had expropriated.

Through these initiatives, Rafsanjani was able to reduce revolutionary fervor and to give the new breed of bureaucratic managers room to develop. He even contemplated following a pragmatic foreign policy—opening Iran to the world.[34] This was not, however, a halcyon affair. Those who represented the new face of the bureaucracy continued to face pressure from revolutionary zealots, who invoked the early values of the revolution and insisted on ideological commitment above technical competence. These tensions at times took the form of open conflict with the conservative press; *Keyhan* or *Salam,* for example, would attack government managers or agencies for their policies, but more often would accuse them of failing to uphold revolutionary ideals. The Ministry of Foreign Affairs and the Central Bank were particularly criticized on grounds that their policies and management style were too relaxed. Insofar as state-building evoked memories of the Pahlavi era, it was bound to raise the ire of the revolutionary old guard. For instance, the aforementioned meeting in New York had no sooner been concluded that it was denounced in Tehran in conservative newspapers and in the pulpits in Qom by conservative clerics.

The challenge facing Rafsanjani was how to vest and pursue the fortunes of an Islamic state that took shape as the embodiment of the economic and cultural interests of the poor in the middle class. That proved to be a Herculean task that would doom Rafsanjani's experiment. What the middle class wanted in terms of political reform, economic prosperity, and cultural opening would ultimately diverge from what the Islamic Republic as the "government of the have-nots" stood for.

Ideological and Intellectual Changes

Economic reforms divorced of political or ideological change quickly reached the limit of their effectiveness. For state-building to succeed, revolutionary values and Islamic ideology had to change. The disjuncture between politics and bureaucracy became particularly significant when structural reforms involving privatization, ending black markets through currency reform, and the like threatened the political and economic privileges of vested interests with ties to the conservative faction. The reaction to reform initiatives often took on an ideological tone. For instance, in the 1980s government-owned industries had become employers of last resort. In 1990–1991, the public sector accounted for one third of the labor force.[35] Government-owned companies employed excess labor, which accounts for their inefficiency and financial troubles. Privatization reduced the number of jobs available to the labor force. That in turn increased unemployment. More important, it hurt the patronage relationship between the revolutionary institutions and leaders and those segments of the population that formed their base of support. Also, clerics and revolutionary leaders used employment in public sector to assert their own political control.

Those resistant to full-fledged privatization pressured the government by attacking it on ideological issues. For instance, renewals of the fatwa against Salman Rushdie during the Rafsanjani period had the support of critics who opposed government economic policies, including clerics such as Ayatollah Mohammad Fazel-Lankarani—an influential member of the Association of Teachers of the Seminary Center of Qom (Jame'eh-ye Modarresin-e Howzeh-ye Elmiyeh-ye Qom)—and foundations such as the Fifteenth of Khordad Foundation. As a result, the government had to routinely go on the defensive to prove its revolutionary and Islamic credentials. It was for this reason that Rafsanjani backed away from engaging the United States in a diplomatic initiative to resolve outstanding disputes between the two countries.

The crises facing the Rafsanjani administration led a group of "religious intellectuals" (rowshanfekran-e dini) and activists to formulate a critique of theocracy in the early 1990s. This group consisted of Abdol-Karim Soroush and several writers associated with the journal Kian. Soroush was the most influential voice in this group. In the early 1980s, he had been associated with the radical faction of the Islamic Republic, and he had been a member of the Council of the Cultural Revolution.[36] In the 1990s, Soroush and his colleagues at Kian captured the growing frustrations of those thinkers and activists, as well as government managers, who saw the Islamic Republic as being at an impasse.[37]

Soroush began a systematic critique of Islamic ideology and the prominence of the ulama in state affairs in 1992. He advocated an interpretive reading of Islamic law (fiqh-e pouya, literally "dynamic jurisprudence"), challenging the special position of the vali e faqih and identifying it as the cause of the inertia that beleaguered the Islamic Republic. Soroush had initially been influenced by Shariati and echoed his anti-clerical views. However, Soroush's critique parted ways with Shariati's ideological reading of Islam, which was at the core of his work and had been enshrined in the ideology of the revolution. The political implication of this approach was to undermine the clerical leadership's claim to power and the inviolability of Islamic ideology. At a more fundamental level, what Shariati suggested was that no one could claim a monopoly over the interpretation of Islam—that there was no definitive interpretation. This amounted to a "reformation" of Islam that would legitimate individual interpretation and ultimately would break down the ulama's authority.

From the outset, it was the pragmatists during the Rafsanjani period who were looking for ways to loosen the revolutionary leadership's hold on government and who were most attracted to the promise of Islamic reform. Soroush's ideas appealed to those whose ideological and political orientation was within the general framework of the Islamic Republic—those who favored reform but continued to define Iranian identity and politics in terms of Islamic ideals. As such, Soroush provided an important transition from war fundamentalism and rigid conservatism to pragmatism by providing the intellectual foundations for political changes that were occurring.

Soroush helped open up the intellectual environment in Iran by encouraging debate. More important, he provided an example for a critical approach to Islamic ideology and the role of the clerics in Iranian state and society—in effect emboldening a new generation of intellectuals to break away from the unconditional subservience to *Velyat-e Faqih* that characterized the Khomeini era. A number of intellectuals and journalists who later gained fame and visibility in the pro-reform movement after 1997, such as Mohsen Sazegara, Emaddedin Baqi, or Mashallah Shamsolvaezin, began with *Kian* and were followers of Soroush. Similarly, Soroush paved the way for younger clerics such as Mohammad Mojtahed-Shabestari, Mohsen Kadivar, and Hasan Yousefi-Eshkevari to launch their own critiques of *Velayat-e Faqih* and the inflexibility of the ulama's views on state and society.[38] In the late 1990s, as Iranian politics moved from debates over Islamic reform to demands for political reform, Soroush's works were no longer seen as directly relevant.[39]

Soroush's critique provoked angry reaction from conservatives. Conservative newspapers such as *Kayhan* and *Salam* attacked Soroush and his ideas, and vigilante groups disrupted his lectures. He was expelled from his teaching post and was eventually compelled to temporarily leave Iran. The criticism of the clerical leadership also led to a concerted effort in Qom, led by Ayatollah Mohammad-Taqi Mesbah-Yazdi and his Imam Khomeini Educational and Research Institute (Moasseseh-ye Amouzeshi va Pajouheshi-ye Emam Khomeini), to assert the conservative position and silence critics such as Soroush. This effort used strong-arm tactics, such as convening a special tribunal to try errant young clerics and intimidating pro-Soroush intellectuals. The ulama also produced a new conservative intellectual position, espoused by figures such as Hamid Parsania and Mohammad-Said Bahmanpour, that could respond to challenges to Islamic ideology.[40] These efforts would become important in contending with dissident clerics and reformist voices after 1997.

Economic Changes and Their Social Consequences

The Iranian economy underwent important structural adjustments during Rafsanjani's first term as president (1989–1993). At first the government was defined by the objectives of postwar reconstruction because its most pressing task was to address immediate socioeconomic demands.[41] Revolution and war had severely damaged the country's economy, creating stagnation, imbalance among sectors of the economy, shortages, inefficiencies, and poverty.[42] In the first decade after the revolution, population had grown, production declined, import dependency increased, but national income plummeted. Between 1977 and 1990, Iran's per capita income declined by 45 percent.[43] Population growth posed the greatest long-term challenge. In the 1980s, Iran's population had grown by 45 percent, or by more than sixteen million people, creating a youth bulge for which the economy could not provide jobs. The consequence was growing unemployment, underemployment, poverty, social problems, and political tension.

In the face of these challenges, Rafsanjani's administration contended that revolutionary rhetoric and policies could not ameliorate the problems, and thus he proposed a developmental approach within the framework of the revolution.[44] He proposed restructuring the Iranian economy and changing the policymaking environment so as to better reflect economic interests and pragmatic considerations.[45] His government also proposed an aggressive monetary policy, an increase in external debt, an increase in imports, an extensive privatization program, investment in infrastructure, introduction of free trade zones, deregulation of foreign exchange, attraction of expatriate entrepreneurial talents and investments, institutional reform, and introduction of development planning (with some similarity to planning in the 1960s and the 1970s). The government in effect hoped to generate growth through effective state management of the economy.[46] In a manner reminiscent of the 1970s, Rafsanjani's government promoted a number of grand development projects, some of which   such as Tehran's subway transit network, new international airport, and new city center— were originally conceived during the Pahlavi period. However, unlike the Pahlavi era, during the Rafsanjani period economic change went hand in hand with devolution of power to provincial and municipal authorities that had gained in power and prominence in the revolution. This made development planning more broad based, with many initiatives coming from local authorities. This trend in turn changed the balance in center-periphery relations and encouraged greater pluralism in Iranian politics as it sought to accommodate the emerging provincial and municipal power centers.[47]

The instrument through which Rafsanjani sought to bring about change was the "five-year plan," a prominent feature of development planning in the Pahlavi period. Rafsanjani's first five-year plan was introduced in 1989–1990.[48] It was ambitious in its objectives. It forecasted per annum growth rates of 8 percent between 1989 and 1994, the creation of two million jobs in five years, growth in trade—raising imports threefold between 1989 and 1993, to $25 billion—and large-scale investment in heavy industries and infrastructure. The government built new dams and oil refineries, upgraded the electric grid, and invested in irrigation projects and in heavy industries such as steel, petrochemicals, and aluminum smelting. What was different in Rafsanjani's five-year plan compared to those implemented in the 1970s was its emphasis on the private sector. Economic growth in the 1990s was supposed to follow from a combination of state planning, macroeconomic management, investment in large projects, and private sector activity in smaller markets. The combination of state planning and market forces was necessitated by the financial constraints facing the government in the 1990s, which were markedly different from those of the 1970s, when surplus government revenue made the need for capital mobilization in the private sector unnecessary.

Rafsanjani's administration borrowed heavily from international markets to support domestic growth. As a result, Iran's international debt grew from $10 billion at the end of the first decade of the revolution to $30 billion in 1995. Still, the scope of investments required the generation of capital internally. The five-year plan therefore called for private sector investment to constitute 52.8 percent of all investment by 1994, and 75 percent to 80 percent in 1994.[49] The private sector played an important role in the economy during the Iran-Iraq war by alleviating some of the problems caused by shortages. It was apparent to economic policymakers that to continue to increase domestic production to compensate for international economic sanctions, the private sector would have to be strengthened. The five-year plan also called for revival of Tehran's stock exchange,[50] monetary reform to end multiple exchange rates, regulation of currency conversion,[51] creation of trade free zones, increase in foreign ownership in Iranian companies to 49 percent from 35 percent, and removal of restrictions on imports. These reforms were designed to encourage trade and more tightly integrate Iran's isolated economy into the global economic system.[52] The government also encouraged the private sector to become more tightly integrated into the expanding economies of Persian Gulf emirates, that of Dubai in particular. The objective here was to use the private sector to provide outlets for Iran's insular economy.

Also important was Rafsanjani administration's greater emphasis on taxation. The five-year plan proposed tripling tax revenues, increasing revenues from 986 billion Rials in 1989 to 3,180 billion Rials in 1994.[53] The greater reliance on tax income had important political consequences, as it would increasingly compel the state to negotiate with society over representation and devolution of power from the center to the periphery. If authoritarianism in the Middle East can be explained in terms of the autonomy of the state from society owing to its rentier character, the Iranian state in 1989–1997 was displaying less of the autonomy that is characteristic of rentier states and was becoming more dependent on its society; to that extent, it was losing its ability to resist political participation.

The reform initiatives of the Rafsanjani administration enjoyed some success. Investment in infrastructure increased, the bureaucracy was given greater autonomy, economic management became more efficient, and, as a result, the economy began to grow.[54] However, more fundamental reforms proved difficult. First, structural adjustments hurt the lower rung of society. High inflation rates—up from 19 percent in 1989 to more than 40 percent in 1993—and cuts in populist programs such as government subsidies, price controls, and market regulations led to protests in Tehran, Mashad, and Qazvin. All were suppressed, but they served as a warning sign to the government. This compelled Rafsanjani to back away from many of his reforms. In an effort to mitigate the effects of economic changes on the poor, his administration reintroduced price controls and tightened government's hold on fiscal and monetary policies. Unbridled economic restructuring was replaced with a gradual approach that fell far short of the objectives of the first five-year plan.

Moreover, as discussed earlier, the government faced stiff resistance to privatization from the bureaucrats, the myriad of semiprivate foundations that managed state-owned enterprises, labor, and the power brokers who had used public sector jobs as patronage. The resistance expressed itself in the form of challenging the government's religious and revolutionary credentials, and in time the government was forced to adopt more hard-line positions domestically and internationally and to give up on full-fledged privatization. As a result, privatization took the form of transferring ownership of public sector industries to state-controlled foundations or cronies of the regime.[55] The state thus retained control of the industries that it had, technically, privatized.

The bureaucracy's attempt to assert its autonomy in economic policymaking also faced resistance from private sector interests who viewed state-led developmentalism as inimical to their interests—similar to what had once turned the bazaar against the Shah—and various foundations that sought to protect the dynamics of patronage. Their resistance translated into supporting the conservative faction in subsequent parliamentary elections and influencing the new government after the 1997 elections. Popular disgruntlement with widespread corruption in government circles—which also provoked criticism from conservative clerics such as Ayatollah Ahmad Jannati (head of the Guardian Council)—further constricted Rafsanjani's room to maneuver in seeking constitutional changes that would have allowed him to run for a third term.

Privatization and Private Sector Growth

One of the Rafsanjani period's most important legacies is the growth of the private sector.[56] This development has had implications for Iran's economy, society, and politics. Interest in the private sector came from both political and economic pressures on the ruling regime in 1989. The conservative faction that supported Rafsanjani in his contest with the radicals was closely tied to the bazaar. The bazaar had been a strong defender of commerce and private sector activities that were closely tied to the revolution, and so it had been instrumental in defending the private sector before the radical tendencies of the revolution in the early 1980s. As a consequence, the occlusion of the radicals and the greater influence of the conservatives in the 1990s gave a greater voice to the private sector.

As mentioned earlier, the government, looking to the private sector for capital, imposed structural reforms to encourage private investment. Important to this effort was the rise of new markets for mobilizing private capital. For instance, faced with limited funds and the gargantuan task of urban renewal in Tehran, the city's mayor, Karbaschi, resorted to "auctioning congestion" to raise money for the city—selling building permits for high-rises through a bidding process. This helped reduce pressure on the housing sector by allowing the private sector and market forces to address housing needs.[57] It also generated a partnership between the government and the private sector at the municipal level and gradually shaped the growth of a new urban political culture.[58]

The most ambitious part of private sector mobilization involved the privatization (khosusi-sazi) of government-owned companies. In 1989, public sector companies constituted 20 percent of the gross domestic product and 60 percent of government receipts and payments, and it employed about a third of the labor force.[59] In the first five-year plan, the government listed some 800 companies to be privatized. The problem was that many of the companies on the selling block were not attractive to private buyers because they were operating in the red, were dependent on scarce imports, had a small domestic market, and were not in a position to rid themselves of excess labor. This last restriction was tied to the revolution's populist claims and commitments. It was a central theme that lay at the heart of the revolution's "social contract" with its power base, which could not be altered without jeopardizing the revolutionary elite's hold on power. More attractive companies were never really privatized; they were handed over to the close associates of the regime or to various parastatal foundations. In fact, during the Rafsanjani period, privatization helped turn many social services foundations into powerful business conglomerates that were able to exercise great power through the companies they controlled and to participate in the more open economy of the 1990s.

The foundations consisted of large religious endowments, such as the old Endowment of the Shrine of Imam Reza (with approximately $25 billion in net assets), or several umbrella corporations which emerged after the revolution, such as Foundation of the Downtrodden (with approximately $15 billion in assets) or the Martyr's Foundation (with approximately $20 billion in assets), that manage vast and diverse financial holdings and own real estate, construction, manufacturing, retail and infrastructure development companies in the public and private sectors.[60] The foundations exercise extensive monopoly powers in the economy, employ large numbers of people, and serve as a source of revenue for the network associated with the regime and several of its key leaders. A distinct trait of the economy in the 1990s was capitalism based on patronage and controlled by large monopolies rather than a competitive market economy.[61]

Privatization also extended to shrinking the size of the government. The Rafsanjani administration tried to do this by encouraging all government agencies to outsource some of their activities to private contractors, who were often former government employees who had left the government.

The proliferation of contracts helped strengthen the private sector and increase both its size and scope. The outsourcing also generated new economic ties, weaving various state institutions with private sector companies that in time would cultivate ties with other private companies to secure financing, services, and supplies.

However, outsourcing also created new space for corruption and rent seeking.[62] In particular, it helped create powerful business interests with ties to senior state leaders who could influence the granting of contracts. Consequently, the contracts were dominated by relatives of prominent ulama and their associates.[63] The popular perception that economic changes benefited the ruling regime damaged government policy in the public mind and produced cynicism toward claims of development. This in turn hurt Rafsanjani's political standing, which was largely dependent on its promise to bring about positive change in the economy and society. Economic reforms and privatization also spread corruption in the top echelons of the bureaucracy, generating complex ties between political and bureaucratic decision makers and business interests. Corruption would eventually flow down into all the orifices of the bureaucracy. As inflation continued to reduce the purchasing power of government salaries, which were no longer supported by government subsidies, salaried government workers looked to corruption to supplement their wages. Rafsanjani acknowledged the institutionalization of corruption when he referred to bribes as "expeditionary fee[s]" (*haqq al-tasri'*). The problem of corruption was that it would inevitably affect the rationality of decision-making and, by implication, both state-building and development.

Social Changes

The many social changes that the revolution brought can be distilled into a few salient developments. First, the revolution changed the relations between social classes. It empowered the lower and lower middle classes at the expense of the middle class. This had implications not only for politics and culture, but also for the economy: it encouraged populist economic policies. Second, the revolution distributed power away from the center as revolutionary leaders from small towns and provinces empowered local forces. The revolution relied on local support across the country, and to achieve this it had to cede power to provincial and municipal authorities and local religious leaders. Third, the revolution produced substantial demographic effects. It led to more rapid population growth, and it encouraged migration between cities and from rural areas to cities.[64] Rafsanjani sought to address many of the economic and social problems that these changes had brought about. For instance, the loci of decision-making and the flow of investment into urban development, infrastructure, and industry shifted from large cities to smaller towns and provincial centers.

At another level, the economic policies of the Rafsanjani period benefited from the growth in the domestic labor force that had resulted from the social changes of the previous decade and presence of large numbers of Afghan refugees in Iran. The construction boom of the Rafsanjani years was fueled by cheap labor that was available in the Iranian market. In turn, the gradual absorption of the excess labor into the economy also expanded the size of the domestic market, which boosted private sector activity, especially that directed at consumer goods.

More broadly, the Rafsanjani period witnessed an economic revival of the middle class and its greater influence on society and culture. Growth in the private sector, emphasis on education, emphasis on competence and skills in management, and investment in social infrastructure all expanded the size and role of the middle class. At the same time, a greater opening in the cultural sphere resulted from the government's loosening of its grip on society—as witnessed in a relaxation of press censorship and lax enforcement of dress codes and personal behavior—and the public's access to criticism of Islamic ideology by Soroush, his followers in *Kian,* and reformist clerics. These developments coincided with a greater cultural dynamism that was associated with new sources of information made available by satellite dishes. This allowed the rising middle class to carve out its cultural space. Whereas the "first" Islamic Republic (1979–1989) empowered the lower and lower middle classes, the "second" Republic, from 1989 onward, witnessed growing political prominence of the middle class—which opened socioeconomic gaps that the revolution had sought to bridge. This in turn polarized Iranian society and politics. In the 1980s, the revolutionary elite relied on its network of mosques and their prayer leaders for political communication and control. However, those instruments could not encompass middle-class politics. As a result, the rise of the middle class placed before the state new cultural and political demands that could not be addressed through revolutionary institutions. The conservative clerical elite resisted these changes, and conservative newspapers such as *Keyhan* often attacked cultural changes as signs of an "invasion" and an "imperialist plot" against the Islamic Republic. The conservative attack was focused in particular on the Ministry of Culture and Islamic Guidance, which was then led by Khatami, and held him responsible for permitting objectionable publications and films. Attacks in print were followed by physical attacks on women and youth that displayed "moral laxity" in the streets and on intellectuals who embraced cultural change.

Nonetheless, middle-class political participation led to greater civil society dynamism, which moved the Islamic Republic toward greater openness in the late 1990s. State policies policing private behaviors as well as public action had generated much unhappiness, and with the rise of the middle class, opposition became more apparent. Responses to political repression have been more obvious and more commonplace across the Third World, and Iran was no exception. But the responses to repressive cultural policies of the state were perhaps unusual and unpredictable in Iran, and they were as important as demands for political liberalization.

As said earlier, the Pahlavi state, too, had used public policy to transform its citizens, secularizing and modernizing them as a prelude to socioeconomic progress. The collapse of the Pahlavi state in 1979 diverted attention from the extent to which that state was successful in transforming Iranian society and had produced a sizable new social stratum—a new breed of secular, Western-oriented Iranians. In 1979, the Pahlavi state was weak politically but far stronger culturally. That its secular subjects did not have the same political outlook as their rulers weakened the state. The Islamic Republic, on the other hand, enjoyed far more political appeal than cultural support among the middle classes.[65] The revolutionary movement in Iran triumphed politically in large measure because it was able to divide secular Iranians along political lines. The Pahlavi state's political failure, however, should not be read as evidence of its cultural irrelevance, for the underlying cultural effect of Pahlavi policies continued to be a major force in Iranian society after the revolution. Its continued salience is attested to by the inability of the Islamic Republic to establish uncontested cultural hegemony and by the fact that prerevolutionary cultural attitudes have increasingly served as the starting point for important political dissent. Social and cultural norms of the past may have gone out of power, but they remained potential contenders.

The Islamic Republic neither won over nor eliminated the secular social stratum. However, it asserted its political dominance over that segment of the population, suppressed it, and politically marginalized it. New laws and regulations were imposed on that segment, largely by force. For instance, mandatory styles of attire for women were introduced after a demonstration in 1979 drew a large number of women protesters into the streets.[66] The strict women's dress code was enforced throughout the 1980s by officially authorized revolutionary units. And it was during this same period that universities were "cleansed" of those who did not subscribe to the new state ideology.[67]

Though secular Iranians, among them professionals and intellectuals, were marginalized, they remained important as they shifted their activities to their private lives and to civil society. In fact, secular Iranians acted much the same way as those groups who had spearheaded the uprising, in the name of civil society, against East European communist states. Secular Iranians' refusal to abide by state ideology eventually challenged the domination of Islamic ideology and forced changes on the Islamic Republic. The cultural influence of the Pahlavi era continued and remained personally powerful among members of the middle classes.

The fact that the cultural effects of the Pahlavi period survived among a critical social group is politically significant. It has been a source of resistance, especially intellectually, to the domination of the postrevolutionary state. Its strong presence in civil society meant that it remained a challenge to the state and was likely to become more important as the political system opened up and the state's control over society lessened. In recent years, economic crisis and problems of isolation have constricted the state. Adhering to pragmatism in policymaking in lieu of ideological politics has, moreover, moved the secular middle classes and the values they espouse to the forefront of political dissent. That economic growth both needs and will empower secular Iranians has made it difficult for the Islamic Republic to successfully resist their opposition.

5

State and Limits to Democracy, 1997–2005

The Rafsanjani period was a transitory phase in postrevolutionary politics. It moved state and society away from revolutionary activism, but it did not produce a stable framework for managing state-society relations. Rather, the Rafsanjani presidency tried to graft the vision of a modern state to the body politic of the Islamic Republic, glossing over the inherent anomalies that existed between the demands of Islamic ideology and those of modern statecraft; between revolutionary attitudes and the requirements of development. In the end, this formula proved to be untenable, and Rafsanjani's conception of a modern and legal-rational state that is also rooted in and committed to the ideology of the revolution proved to be unworkable. Its attempt to bridge what the conservative ulama and revolutionary institutions wanted and what civil society and democratic forces hoped for appealed to neither. The failure of Rafsanjani's approach intensified debates over the role of the state and the extent to which ideology and efficiency ought to guide the functioning of the government.

That failure also precipitated a serious crisis of legitimacy for the Islamic Republic. By 1996, the Islamic Republic had slid back into international isolation as most European ambassadors had left Iran, and the U.S. Congress had passed the Iran-Libya Sanctions Act to further limit international trade with Iran. In the domestic scene, a pall had descended over the reformist movement as the security forces and vigilante groups were given a free reign to intimidate writers and activists, a number of whom disappeared or were murdered.[1]

Despite structural changes, the economy continued to languish, and unemployment and inflation rates remained high.

The trials and tribulations of Rafsanjani's pragmatism occurred at an important time for electoral politics in Iran. What emerged in the Rafsanjani period were efforts by both him and the Supreme Leader to consolidate their respective powers, and more intense competition in the elections and within the parliament over policymaking among various factions of the revolution. These two tendencies, toward consolidation of power and competitive contestation over power, would point to divergent paths for state-building at the end of the Rafsanjani period. This had important effects on power struggles among the political elite and on the electorate's political attitudes. The electorate had, throughout the 1980s and 1990s, become increasingly educated in the spirit and practice of electoral politics.

The presidential election of 1997 occurred in this context. That election was a significant event in modern Iranian history, with broad implications for the trajectory of the Islamic Republic's development. First, the election was an occasion for including a broader cross-section of the population in the political process. Although voter turnout in elections after the revolution had always been high, the 1997 elections expanded the size of the electorate further by capturing the votes of those who had shunned previous elections.[2] In so doing, the election did not legitimate the Islamic Republic so much as it produced a pro-democracy movement. This, however, did not spell the end of the conservative control of power. In fact, Khatami's two-term presidency (1997–2005) would be marked by intense struggles between the conservative leaders who sought to consolidate power in the clerical leadership and pro-democracy forces who sought to consolidate power in civil society institutions.

The Khatami period therefore saw two divergent trends at work in Iran, one centered in the president, who promised democratization, and the other led by the Supreme Leader, who sought to consolidate authoritarianism. The two trends pulled Iranian politics in different directions, setting in motion struggles for power that can help explain the ebbs and flows of Iranian politics since 1997.

The Presidential Election of 1997

The presidential election of 1997 was the first election after the revolution in which the public will expressed at the ballot box overturned the writ of the conservative leadership. Given the debates over the relative importance of ideology and pragmatism, clerical rule and democracy, the election was viewed as decisive. And indeed the vote itself left no mistake as to the mood of the country:

Khatami won the elections with 70 percent of the vote, some twenty million votes. The overwhelmingly democratic impulse of the election suggested that initially, at least, in the post-Rafsanjani era, reform would affect the power struggle.

The catalytic role that the elections came to play in 1997 owed to the interplay of a number of factors. Some were a product of the Rafsanjani period's socioeconomic changes, and others were particular to the political climate and the personality of the main presidential candidates. First, enthusiasm for reform that the elections generated must be understood in the context of fundamental social changes of the previous decade. The population growth of the early years of the revolution had produced a youth constituency that was coming to electoral age in the late 1990s. By 1997, these youths constituted 25 percent of the population of 67 million.[3] This generation was reared in the years of revolutionary activism and war, but it was also a principal constituency for pragmatism. Its cultural outlook and political expectations diverged from the rigid conservatism of the country's leaders, and it demanded jobs and economic prosperity. These demands echoed the call for reform in civil society, bureaucracy, and bazaar.

The decade leading to the elections of 1997 had also witnessed other profound changes in Iranian society. There had been significant gains in literacy, women's participation in the economy had increased considerably, and growing urbanization of the population along with significant changes in the rural economy had changed the face of the Iranian population. Intellectual dynamism, reflected in the scope and caliber of philosophical, literary, and political debates and in the quality and size of the scientific community, indicated that a degree of social sophistication coexisted with the conservatism of the state and its ideology.[4] By the late 1990s, society was placing demands on the political system that could not be accommodated by the Islamic Republic. It was apparent to all—even the country's conservative leaders—that Iran needed an open political environment to encompass the diversity and complexity of Iranian society. The conservative leaders hoped that small concessions would resolve the issue, but the elections of 1997 threatened to undo the Islamic Republic altogether.

Khatami was not the natural spokesman for this new political constituency. He was a moderate cleric who was seen by the conservative elite as a compromise candidate—a turbaned moderate who could assuage demands for reform. Pro-democracy forces saw him as more palatable than the hard-line cleric running against him, Ali-Akbar Nateq-Nouri. Khatami's victory and his emergence as the champion of reform was therefore a product of political conjecture—a confluence of various factors that brought an outcome that the conservatives had not anticipated.[5] Throughout his presidency, Khatami was unable to resolve the demands of his reformist mandate with the pressures to do what the conservatives had all along wanted of him: to protect the regime and to compromise for the sake of stability and order in the country.

Early on in the election campaign, the nominee of the conservative faction, Nateq-Nouri, emerged as the front-runner.[6] The faction had a strong base of support in the bazaar and in the ruling political establishment of the Islamic Republic, and it had the backing of Ayatollah Khamenei. In addition, the conservatives posed as a force for continuity and, to some extent, retrenchment of the values and norms of the Islamic Republic. They held to a conservative line on social and cultural issues, and they supported the thrust of Iran's anti-Western foreign policy.

The conservatives viewed the elections of 1997 as a routine exercise to confirm leadership transition. The conservative leadership sought to contain the growing popular discontent at the end of Rafsanjani period by allowing moderates a voice in the presidential elections. To this end, the Guardian Council approved the candidacy of Mohammad Khatami. The clerical leadership expected that Khatami's reformist background as Rafsanjani's Minister of Culture and his message of tolerance and change would placate popular discontent without threatening the ruling order. They underestimated the elections' ability to bring large numbers of Iranians into the political process and to challenge the conservative position. The elections broke the mold in that they transformed a contest among various factions of the clerical leadership into a genuine political contest. This meant that social groups that had been previously excluded from revolutionary politics could decide the leadership's factional rivalries and lay claim to defining the Islamic Republic.

Khatami's persona and message appealed to a broad cross-section of Iranians. His style in both manners and speech, which contrasted with the dour expression of many among the clerical elite, quickly gained him a following. His supporters came from all walks of society and did not constitute a cohesive movement, but they shared a demand for political reform and social change. Khatami had had limited involvement in the revolution's excesses or participation in running the state in the 1980s. He had served as director of the National Library and Minister of Culture and Islamic Guidance. He was well-versed in Western political literature and patronized secular intellectuals and artists. He claimed credit for policies at the Ministry of Culture that led to the cultural opening of the late 1990s and building bridges with the secular intelligentsia. His own writings on Islam advocated a humanistic and tolerant approach to the faith that he contrasted with the rigid conservatism of the clerical leadership.[7] His promise of relaxing the state's ideological vigilance also gained him support among women, youths, and secular voters.[8] He appealed to the pragmatic faction within the state, represented by the Kargozaran-e Sazandegi (Implementers of Development) group led by Karbaschi and its supporters in the private sector, who did not have a candidate of their own. He also was quickly endorsed by the remnants of the Radical faction that was prominent in the 1980s, who saw in him the opportunity to impede the conservatives' consolidation of power.[9]

Khatami's bid for the presidency enjoyed the support of Rafsanjani and his pragmatic followers. Rafsanjani, who, in accordance with the constitution, could not run for a third term, used the powers of his office to ensure fairness in the elections to Khatami's advantage. Similarly, Karbaschi and his Kargozaran group—consisting of Rafsanjani-era pragmatists—used the resources and especially the political machine of the mayor's office of Tehran to assist Khatami's campaign. More interesting, the burgeoning reform movement enjoyed the support of some prominent veteran revolutionaries of 1980s. Khatami's campaign was supported by radicals such as Mir-Hossein Mousavi (prime minister 1980–1988), Behzad Nabavi (a member of the radical faction and a onetime minister of heavy industries), Abbas Abdi (a student leader in the hostage crisis), Akbar Ganji (a onetime revolutionary activist turned reformist journalist), Said Hajjarian (former member of the Information Ministry and later an editor with the pro-reform newspaper *Sobh-e Emrouz* and later advisor to Khatami), and Mohsen Sazegara (a founding member of the Revolutionary Guard and later the editor of pro-reform *Tous* newspaper). These transformed revolutionaries were instrumental in setting up and managing Khatami's nationwide campaign organization. More broadly, they helped legitimate the demand for reform from within the system rather than opposed to the Islamic Republic.

The intensity of the factional rivalry guaranteed the openness of the elections and even led to greater freedom of expression in the media. In this respect, the political machine of the pragmatists and the radicals in various municipalities and urban districts within the capital and in the provinces was important to Khatami's campaign and ultimate victory.[10] The election itself, held in May 1997, proved very significant in Iranian politics. The results changed the direction of political debates and marked a major turning point in relations between state and society.[11] Most observers had expected Khatami to do well, but certainly not well enough to win. But Khatami enjoyed the support of a broad cross-section—not simply youths, women, intellectuals, and civil society forces, but also voters from the bazaar, key ethnic groups such as the Kurds, and even many within the military and Revolutionary Guard. In one estimation, some 70 percent of those in the Iranian armed forces voted for Khatami.[12]

The defeat of the conservative faction was blunt and humiliating. The electoral defeat was quickly dubbed a "second revolution," and *Do-e Khordad* (Second of Khordad—the Persian date of Khatami's election on May 23) became synonymous with the reform movement. Iranians had taken the elections seriously, and had voted overwhelmingly in favor of fundamental changes in the working of the Islamic Republic. Many saw the elections as a referendum on how the Islamic Republic's leadership ought to understand its mission and its relations with society.

Iran's election results were unique in the Middle East in that a president stepped down from power at the end of his term of office and peacefully handed over power to a successor who was elected through constitutional means. The transition of power from Rafsanjani to Khatami was itself significant. In addition, the large turnout—some thirty million, an overwhelming majority of the eligible voters—meant that Iranians of diverse political persuasions had decided to voice their views and demands within the political process, rather than outside of it. This suggested that the electoral process had become institutionalized in the Islamic Republic and had become an important means of integrating various social groups into the political system. It was not an artificial appendage to the Islamic state but was very much part of the fabric of its politics. Democratic practices had therefore opened their way into Iran's body politic—an unintended consequence of revolution and an outgrowth of its factional rivalries. The 1997 election transformed voting in Iran from merely settling factional power struggles into expressing popular political will. This generated democratic expectations and encouraged the belief that political change could come through the ballot box rather than through reform at the top.

The decision by the majority of the electorate to use the ballot box to promote change at first strengthened the Islamic Republic, as those who had opposed the status quo chose to participate in the political process rather than withdraw from it. The elections included greater numbers of Iranians in the political process in the Islamic Republic. However, to consolidate this gain, the Islamic Republic would have had to accommodate a broader set of sociopolitical demands and most notably move further away from ideological politics and the values of the revolution.

Khatami's victory also prompted the leadership of the Islamic Republic to engage in an intense debate over whether to expand its base of support by accommodating the demands of those whom Khatami brought into the political process—most notably the middle class—or to remain tied to its ideological politics and exclude those who demanded a less ideological and more open politics. In this debate, the president became the advocate of change, and the Supreme Leader the rallying point for defenders of revolutionary values. Consequently, the debate now involved the relative power of the two offices, and the resolution of the debate over greater liberalization or conservative consolidation would also resolve the ambiguity of power at the helm of the Islamic Republic.

The opportunity before Khatami was to institute state-building and democracy. The challenge here was how to transform a diverse movement that shared little other than how its members had voted into a coherent political movement, and how to harness the power of this movement to anchor the state in democracy in the face of the conservatives' drive for political domination. The elections opened Iran to democratic possibilities, but it also set the stage for strong competition between those who wanted a democratic state and those who wanted continued state monopoly of power. Khatami had put himself at the center of these opposing forces.

The Democratic Opening

Khatami's campaign speeches made ample references to "democracy," "civil society," "women's status," "rule of law," and "dialogue among civilizations."[13] He in particular emphasized *"jame'eh-ye madani"* (civil society) and advocated cultural freedoms and the legal protections to empower them.[14] He rejected coercion in religious observance and argued that a more open and tolerant Islamic Republic would receive a wider popular mandate. As such, Khatami gave new direction and energy to the demand for reform, and he sought to create a base of support for reformists inside the regime and in civil society institutions.

An important outcome of the election was the empowerment of the middle class and the institutions associated with it in the private sector and, in particular, the civil society. The political victory of the revolution in 1979 was never matched by cultural success. The Iranian middle class that had supported the leftist and liberal elements of the revolution was politically disenfranchised by Islamic Republic's theocratic populism, but it had remained important to Iran's civil society institutions. In the late 1990s, the middle-class influence became more marked as the Islamic Republic began to lose control of popular culture, and growing numbers of Iranians flaunted public behavior proscribed by the ruling regime.

It was at this juncture that the base of support for reform shifted from those within the regime to those who had resisted its ideological control.[15] This constituency was no longer satisfied with debating Islam; it wanted fundamental political reforms.

Khatami's campaign promised to address those demands and by so doing to create a bridge between reformers inside the regime—who were attached to its ideological foundations—and the larger constituency for reform. His ideal of "Islamic civil society" captured this objective. If he succeeded, he would transform the Islamic Republic while keeping the state in control of the process of change. Otherwise, he would create a rift between reformers within the Islamic Republic's ideological fold and reformers in the larger society.

The elections of 1997 therefore pushed Iran's politics beyond debates on pragmatism and the promise of Islamic reform. That the population had been able to vote for a candidate of reform against the thrust of theocratic politics in Iran—and that the results of the elections had stood—accelerated the pace of demand for change and made the presidency and elections central to that debate. This led to a short-lived "Prague Spring" in Iran, during which Iran's relations with the outside world improved significantly. Just as important, increases in freedom of the press and certain relaxations in control of social behavior gave new impetus to demands for change.

Khatami's election was followed by improvements in Iran's relations with the European Union and with Saudi Arabia. Khatami went on a number of state visits to Europe, and several European state leaders visited Iran. Foreign investment returned to Iran, and European multinational companies formed business partnerships in various sectors of the economy—including oil and gas, telecommunications, consumer electronics, and automotive—especially after a bill in 2002 eased some of the restrictions on foreign investment.

In interviews with the international media, Khatami built on his message of "dialogue among civilizations" by advocating cultural exchanges with the United States. These changes were popular with the Iranian people, who showed their enthusiasm for ending Iran's isolation in an outburst of street celebrations on November 27, 1998, after Iran qualified for the soccer World Cup. The jubilant crowd took control of the streets from security forces as men and women flouted restrictions on public conduct. Despite popular support for joining the world community, Khatami was not able to wrest full control of foreign policymaking from the clerical leadership, and as a result he was not able to build on the goodwill that his election elicited from the international community.

Allowing greater freedoms of expression to the press changed the face of the media in Iran. This change was entirely within Khatami's purview. Although he did not control all levers of power, he did exercise power over the Ministry of Culture that oversaw censorship and regulation of print media. The reformist Minister of Culture, Ataollah Mohajerani, led the charge against the strictures governing various cultural activities and publicly defended use of satellite dishes to gain access to information and programs from outside Iran.[16] By relaxing government control of newspapers, arts, and cinema, the Khatami years brought a flowering of intellectual and political discourse in Iran that rapidly reshaped the style and content of Iranian politics. Newspapers such as *Jame'eh, Hamshahri, Tous, Yas-e Naw*, or *Asr-e Azadegan* raised the standards of journalism both in form and content, thus contributing significantly to new changes in the cultural environment. These newspapers covered previously avoided subjects such as government mismanagement, corruption, and political repression. Rafsanjani did not benefit from this new opening, as his administration came under severe attack from reformists in the print media.[17] The greater openness increased the number and circulation of newspapers; among the most popular were *Hamshahri* (associated with Karbaschi's office) and *Jame'eh*, whose circulation quickly grew to 100,000. By mid-1998 there were some 740 newspapers in print in Iran.[18] In addition, the open discussion created a vibrant atmosphere of literary and political debate.[19] This discussion also generated much popular enthusiasm for reform and using the electoral process to achieve it. This led reformists to win municipal elections in 1998 and the parliament in 1999, which confirmed that reformism was a surging political trend and that elections were not likely to favor conservatives.

Reformists also enjoyed modest gains in government reform during Khatami's first year in office. Khatami was able to bring pressure on the security forces over the killing of intellectuals. He forced changes on management of prisons and on the Ministry of Intelligence and Security—at one point admonishing its staff that they should cease being the "fist of the regime" (*mosht-e nezam*) and embrace the winds of change.

Emboldened by the reformist surge, dissident clerics mounted a direct challenge to Khamenei and the dominant interpretation of *Velayat-e Faqih*. In November 1997 Ayatollah Hossein-Ali Montazeri, who had been Khomeini's heir-apparent until 1989, when he fell from favor for his criticism of the regime, broke his silence to criticize the clerical leadership's resistance to reform. He called for a liberal interpretation of *Velayat-e Faqih,* legalization of political parties, and greater pluralism in the Islamic Republic.[20] Montazeri's challenge extended to questioning Khamenei's qualifications to serve as Supreme Leader. Although the regime responded to Montazeri swiftly by putting him under house arrest, the challenge to the clerical leadership from reformist ularria continued. Montazeri's initiative was carried forth by other pro-reform clerics such as his student, Mohsen Kadivar, and by Ayatollah Jalaleddin Taheri, Mohammad Mojtahed-Sabestari, and Hasan Yousefi-Eshkevari.[21]

Khatami's reform program was primarily geared toward cultural and political change, and less so toward economic issues. Economy had dominated debates over reform during the Rafsanjani period, and continued economic problems— aggravated by a drop in price of oil in 1997—constituted an important part of popular discontent with the Rafsanjani administration. The political opening in 1997 had increased interest in economic reform and presented a possibility for the government to pursue this goal more effectively than did the Rafsanjani administration. Khatami's lack of focus on economic development was a mis-calculation; many who had voted for him had done so in hopes that he would improve economic conditions. Failure of the new government to present a clear economic plan made it more difficult for the reform movement to consolidate its hold over the coalition that had brought Khatami to power or to expand its reach into the lower classes. Moreover, the failure of the reform movement to relate its demand for political change to bread-and-butter issues made it easier for the conservative leadership to resist the push for change.

Conservative Backlash

Khatami's strong mandate at the polls did not translate into strong executive powers. The conservative leadership accepted the verdict of the elections but moved quickly to limit Khatami's room to maneuver. He was given control of certain ministries but not others. Notably, the important ministries of oil, foreign affairs and intelligence remained outside of his full control. Similarly he had very limited authority over the armed forces and the judiciary.

The conservative forces had miscalculated the potential for the reformist movement, and they construed the outcome of the 1997 election as a serious challenge to their control of power in Iran. Although on the defensive immedi-ately after the election, the conservatives quickly rallied behind the Supreme Leader to mitigate reform's effects.[22] The conservatives' response to Khatami's election unfolded at a time of relative opening of Iranian political system—of growing political consciousness of an increasingly urban and literate population, economic and cultural activism of the middle class, and assertiveness of women and the youth.[23] These were important developments over which the Supreme Leader had little control, and from which the president stood to gain. Moreover, a popular president with mandate from a population that was not committed to the Islamic Republic presented the ruling leadership with an existential chal-lenge.[24] On June 1, some two weeks after Khatami's election, the conservative parliament reelected Khatami's challenger, Nateq-Nouri, as speaker of the par-liament with a vote of 211 out of 243, forcing Khatami's choice to withdraw his candidacy.[25] In October, the parliament passed a bill to tighten segregation of men and women in public, in direct contravention to Khatami's attempts to relax public morality regulations.

The conservative leadership also moved quickly to protect its traditional bastions of power from reformist influence.[26] The leadership of the Revolution-ary Guard was changed. Although Khatami favored the dismissal of the com-mander of the Guard, Mohsen Rezai, it was clear that the change of leadership

was designed to insulate it from reformists and to use it in asserting the conservative position. The new leaders of the Guard came from a group of ideologically cohesive veterans of the Iran-Iraq war who shared a commitment to the
values of the Islamic Republic. Khamenei increased funding for the Guard's
training, new weapons systems, salaries, benefits, housing, and various services
for its rank and file, strengthening the Guard's ties to the clerical leadership.
The new commander, Yahya Rahim-Safavi, quickly became a strong critic of
Khatami.

As an important pillar of the regime, the Guard grew in power and influence
steadily during the Khatami period as it built its capabilities to defend the regime
against both domestic challenges and external threats. In that capacity, the
Guard also became prominent in politics. By the end of the Khatami period, the
commanders of the Guard had assumed additional government and security
positions in decision-making circles. In the parliamentary elections of 2004,
veteran Guard members also gained close to 30 percent of the seats in the
parliament. Not since Reza Shah's ascent to power in the 1920s had a military
force wielded so much power and influence in Iranian politics.[27]

Khamenei also tightened his hold on the leadership of various foundations:
clerical associations such as the Association of Teachers of the Seminary Center
of Qom—one of whose senior members, Ayatollah Ahmad Azari-Qomi, was
expelled from the society for his support of Montazeri; the Guardian Council
and the Expediency Council (which oversee the legislative and judicial processes); the judiciary; and key seminaries in Qom. Khamenei used these levers
of power to constrict Khatami. For instance, between 1997 and January 2004,
when reformists lost control of the parliament, the supervisory Guardian Council
vetoed 111 of his 297 legislations.[28] During the same time period, the judiciary
limited the scope of cultural changes ushered in after 1997. A Special Court for
Clergy (Dadgah-e Vijeh-ye Rowhaniyat) was set up to prosecute reformist clerics.
It began its work in 1997 and continued throughout the Khatami period, trying
other reformist ulama such as Abdollah Nouri, Kadivar, and Yousefi-Eshkevari.
All three were sentenced to prison terms, and Yousefi-Eshkevari was also de-
frocked.

The conservatives worked to strengthen the ideological underpinnings of
the Islamic Republic in the face of reform initiatives that steadily eroded their
authority. In this, Khamenei received the support of leading conservative clerics,
such as ayatollahs Mohammad-Taqi Mesbah-Yazdi, Ahmad Jannati, Ali Meshkini, Ali Taskhiri, Abol-Qasem Khaz'ali, and Mohammad Yazdi. These men dominated the Guardian Council, Assembly of Experts, and the judiciary and advocated the implementation of a narrow interpretation of Islamic law. Khamenei
and his allies saw the presidency as the seat of pragmatic politics, which they

viewed as a catalyst that would facilitate the abandonment of the revolution's goals. The task of ensuring fidelity to Islamic ideology fell on ayatollahs Jannati and Mesbah-Yazdi, who led the charge against those who criticized the Office of Supreme Leader and mobilized the militias and irregular security forces to intimidate pro-reform forces.[29] The Guardian Council and the judiciary limited the ability of the government and parliament—after it fell to reformists in 1999—to carry out reforms; they also curbed the scope of press freedoms and civil society activism that had followed the 1997 elections.

The security forces continued to intimidate intellectuals by attacking reformist gatherings and silencing prominent dissidents. The brutal murder of veteran National Front politician Daryush Forouhar and his wife in 1998 led to widescale condemnation of the rogue elements within security forces. In 1999, an attempt on the life of the reformist strategist and advisor to Khatami, Said Hajjarian, set off large student demonstrations that were suppressed by security forces. The same method was again used in handling student demonstrations in November 2002 to protest a death sentence imposed on Hashem Aghajari, a university lecturer, for alleged blasphemy, and in 2003 to demand greater political rights.[30]

Violent tactics went hand in hand with using the judiciary to cripple the Khatami government and to intimidate the executive branch specifically. This began with the arrest and trial of Tehran's mayor, Karbaschi, on corruption charges in 1998.[31] Karbaschi had supported Khatami's campaign for president, and he had mobilized the political machine of Tehran's municipal authority in the service of his campaign. Moreover, Karbaschi's much-vaunted tenure as mayor of Tehran had become the public face of pragmatism and reform. As mayor he was instrumental in launching the newspaper *Hamshahri* which was widely circulated and popular for its pro-reform tenor. Karbaschi's trial was broadcast on television and was keenly watched across the country. The ignoble end to Karbaschi's mayoralty was to serve as a warning to those who dared challenge the conservative elite.

Following Karbaschi's trial, the reformist press was further repressed. In August 1998, the popular newspaper *Jame'eh* was shut down, though its editor, Mashallah Shamsolvaezin, continued to publish it, under the name of *Tous*, with a new license from the Ministry of Culture. When *Tous* was shut down, it was replaced by *Neshat*, and finally by *Asr-e Azadegan*. The conservative leadership increased the pressure on Ataollah Mohajerani, minister of culture, who eventually faced impeachment proceedings and was forced from office. Similarly, Abdollah Nouri, the minister of interior, faced the wrath of the Special Court for the Clergy; he was removed from office and imprisoned. In May 1999, nineteen reformist papers were shut down, and a number of leading reformists were arrested. In summer 1999, the Supreme Leader vetoed an amendment passed by the new reformist parliament to soften the press law.

Faced with conservative pressure, a growing number of reformists questioned the likelihood of transforming the Islamic Republic from within and looked to Khatami to take bold steps to promote more fundamental changes. Some, like Akbar Ganji and Mohsen Sazegara, spoke of instituting limits to theocracy and advocated more aggressive pursuit of rule of law and the protection of individual rights. Student leaders, meanwhile, staged street agitations and directly challenged the Supreme Leader.

Khatami, however, shied away from openly breaking with the theocratic core of the Islamic Republic, and he always discouraged confrontational politics. He would not endorse fundamental constitutional changes, and he proved unwilling to openly oppose Khamenei's authority by encouraging a popular movement. Rather than leading the student protests of 1999, Khatami admonished the student leaders for precipitating clashes with security forces. On a number of occasions he threatened the Supreme Leader with resigning, and on one occasion he threatened not to run for reelection in 2001, but each time he backed away from an open breach with Khamanei.[32] More important, Khatami continued to declare fealty to the theocratic constitution of the Islamic Republic, which in practice ran counter to his support for civil society and the rule of law. In fact, Khatami's emphasis on the rule of law without constitutional change served to reinforce the writ of the theocratic constitution. As such, Khatami's rhetoric went no further than advocating limited civil liberties and better management of government—more pragmatism. He justified his stance by arguing that at its core, Iranian identity is Islamic, and hence Islam cannot be separated from Iranian politics. Pluralism and civil society must find expression within the context of this reality. Khatami's capitulations to Khamenei attested to his reluctance to step beyond the bounds of the constitution of the Islamic Republic. This in turn limited his ability to continue to lead the popular demand for democracy that his own electoral success had been an expression of.[33]

Khatami's dilemma, however, had a cathartic effect on reformist debates. It pushed the debate clearly past Islamic reform and accommodating pluralism within the constitutional framework of the Islamic Republic to demanding democracy under a new constitutional order that would separate religion from politics. By failing to reconcile the demands for change with the existing framework of the Islamic Republic, Khatami's authority as the highest officeholder of the reformist forces diminished and was lost to voices outside the regime.

Khatami's presidency was significant in that it changed the rules of the game in Iranian politics. By emphasizing accountability and "legality" (*qanoun-mandi*), written into legislations by reformists in the parliament between 2000 and 2004, Khatami reduced arbitrary use of power by political leaders and state institutions, and he bound the state to the rule of law. These gains, however, did not sustain reforms or produce a democratic state in Iran. For although the ruling circle would continue to behave in authoritarian ways, they would now do so increasingly within the bounds of the law, using constitutional mechanisms and legal forums.

Khatami sought to integrate the middle class, social aspirations for democracy, and his civil society base of support into the fabric of the Islamic Republic at a time when the leadership of the state regarded such initiatives as detrimental to its interests; thus it became determined to monopolize power by various means, including a well-displayed adherence to the early values of the revolution. With the guardians of the revolution reluctant to change the state to accommodate the demands of the middle class, Khatami's plan of creating a middle-class-based and politically democratic Islamic Republic proved to be an untenable proposition. As a result, Khatami had to choose to act either as the face of the revolution and the Islamic Republic or the leader of the opposition to such tendencies in the society. He reluctantly chose the former, and, with that, the much-vaunted experiment in a democratizing state came to a halt. In the words of one observer, "Khatami did not provide leadership for the reformists—he was more like a spokesman, and no one else had the authority or the mandate to lead."[34] Reformist forces became increasingly alienated from Khatami and lost hope that the Islamic Republic could be changed from within and through participation. The Khatami years were therefore marked by the unraveling rather than strengthening of the momentary marriage of state and democracy in 1997.

By the end of Khatami's first term as president, it was clear that the reform movement had lost its momentum and that conservatives had successfully used state institutions to resist thoroughgoing change. The frustration with the pace of change and Khatami's reluctance to lead the charge against the conservative leadership was reflected in the fact that although Khatami received 78 percent of the votes in the 2001 presidential elections and easily overcame his conservative challenger, Ahmad Tavakoli, voter turnout for the election declined.

Khatami's second term as president was marked by an unimpeded conservative consolidation of power, confirming reformists' thinking that reform could produce meaningful change only if based on changes to the constitution. Erstwhile revolutionaries such as Akbar Ganji and Abbas Abdi also called for constitutional reform. In a letter that he wrote from prison (titled *Republican Man-*

ifesto), Ganji conceded that clerical rule has ingrained totalitarian tendencies. He wrote that the Islamic Republic cannot be meaningfully reformed without fundamental change and the separation of religion from politics. This line of argument echoed secular critiques of the role of Islam in politics by such intellectuals as Javad Tabatabai, who have for some time questioned the promise of Islamic reform as a path to democracy.[35] The secular voices also argue for vesting sovereignty in the people rather than in God or divine law. Almost a century ago, the Constitutional Revolution transformed Iranians from "subjects" to "citizens." The constitution of the Islamic Republic, by placing the notion of "guardianship" over civil society, in effect reversed those gains. The call for reform now aimed to restore sovereignty to the people and hold government accountable to them as citizens. This is a very different paradigm of politics, and it breaks with the reform initiatives that had their roots in and remained conceptually bound to the Islamic Republic. It is a demand to replace rather than reform the Islamic Republic by changing its founding constitutional assumptions.

The conservative drive for power reached its apogee in 2004, when conservatives regained control of parliament by using the Guardian Council to disqualify most reformist candidates. The council disqualified 3,600 reformist candidates—including eighty incumbents—for the 2004 parliamentary elections. The council's verdict was meant to help engineer a conservative takeover of the parliament to further constrict reformist forces. More important, it also sought to give coherence to the conservative political platform under the newly formed Abadgaran faction (E'telaf-e Abadgaran-e Iran-e Islami [The Alliance of the Developers of Islamic Iran]) and erase gray areas between conservatives and reformists.

The "parliamentary coup"—using the Guardian Council to dislodge reformists from parliament—precipitated a political crisis. Arguments by Khatami and even reformist ulama regarding a more tolerant and open Islamic Republic now appeared arcane and of merely marginal value.[36] This not only reinvigorated the call for reform but made presidential election of 2005 important to its realization.

Student activists who had gathered around the Daftar-e Tahkim-e Vahdat (The Office for Strengthening of Unity) to create a unified platform threatened to boycott the presidential elections of 2005, but many students and civil society activists soon became engaged in the election campaign. What followed the 2004 elections was a lively intellectual and political debate that took the Islamic Republic to task and raised the issue of how to democratize the state. Democracy would now have to be debated more vigorously, albeit in the shadow of an ever more dominant conservative political control.

Emergence of a New Conservatism

In many ways, the Khatami period, in spite of all efforts to advocate and exercise democracy, was marked by conservative consolidation of power. During the Khatami years, Iranian society was more engaged in debates on democracy than at any other time in the country's history, but the quest for democracy was eclipsed by the fact that power remained in the hands of an increasingly authoritarian clerical leadership that streamlined its hold over organizational and decision-making apparatuses exactly at the time when the Iranian society showed greater signs of moving toward democracy.[37] The conservative consolidation went beyond just resisting reform. It amounted to the construction of a power structure that was based on a new conception of the relationship of the clerical leadership to the society and economy that was based on a pragmatic political program, espoused by a new breed of conservative intellectuals.[38] Conservative consolidation eschewed ideological posturing of the kind that had currency in the 1980s, and it did not advocate return to rigid conceptions of theocracy. Compelled to compete with Khatami and reformists for legitimacy and popular support in elections, conservatives adapted their views to address social demands. This led to the rise of a pragmatic authoritarianism that entailed a new interpretation of the relation of state and society in the Islamic Republic.

This pragmatic authoritarianism relied on new relationships of economic patronage for social control. The new order combined concentration of power in the office of the Supreme Leader and greater coherence in relations between conservative clerics and the military wing of the regime with a more broad-based and economically motivated relationship with society. Conservative consolidation therefore did not produce monolithic rule or ideologically based totalitarianism but rather a kind of patrimonial authoritarianism that has been evident in other developing countries.

At the heart of this new approach is an alternate vision of reform that is less concerned with culture and politics and more with state-building and development. Given Khatami's focus on culture, this left an opening for conservatives to appeal to public support. By the end of Khatami's first term as president in 2001, it was evident that he was not going to initiate a new program to address economic issues and that he could not deliver on promises of cultural change. The conservatives now had an opportunity to put forth a new political position in place of asserting the ideological values of the Islamic Republic— promising state-building and development. The lacuna in Khatami's program was thus turned into a political advantage for conservatives.

After 2001, conservatives put forth a discourse on development that promised strong government, end to political gridlock, improved management of the economy and social services, and greater prosperity. The discourse appealed to Iranian nationalism, depicting development as a fulfillment of national aspirations. In the 2004 parliamentary elections, the platform of Abadgaran faction was singularly focused on the issue of development. In fact, its choice of name, "Abadgaran" (meaning "developers") reflected that focus. It was coined to both highlight the new conservative discourse and to present conservatives as rivals to reformist managers associated with Rafsanjani's economic policies and Khatami's rise to power, who gathered around Karbaschi's "Kargozaran-e Sazandegi" ("Implementers of Development"). As will be discussed later, the emphasis on development would only increase during the presidential campaign of 2005.

It is important to also note that in the February 2004 municipal elections, which were overseen by the Ministry of Interior, no reformists were barred from running. Still, in those elections reformist candidates were routed by conservatives who ran on a platform that combined demand for effective government with promises on development and better social services. This showed that specific local issues and demand for development mattered more than broader themes and that the conservatives could win on local concerns, avoiding entanglement with broader debates over democracy. The demand for democracy could now be resisted with emphasis on good government and development.[39]

The discourse drew on the example of reformers during the Reza Shah period—who viewed the give-and-take of democracy as a distraction from development—and veiled references to Reza Shah became ubiquitous in these debates. Positing Reza Shah as a model was also designed to draw on his growing popularity. Some twenty-seven years after militant revolutionaries demolished his mausoleum south of Tehran, he was widely idolized by many Iranians as a symbol of nationalism, unwavering commitment to developing the country, and maintenance of territorial integrity. Reza Shah, however, was not a democrat, and his definition of reform was limited to restoring or creating state institutions to provide effective governance and management of the economy. Iran's conservatives also looked to define reform as improving government rather than opening up the political system. Interestingly, the use of the Reza Shah model was particularly evident in the Revolutionary Guard, who perhaps more closely identified with the notion of a military savior for Iran's problems that is so captured in Reza Shah.[40]

To give substance to their developmentalist approach, conservatives looked to the East for a model. Whereas Khatami's approach to reform drew on the experiences of Eastern Europe and Latin America with political change, the conservatives preferred the East Asia model, with its combination of authoritarianism, economic progress, and emphasis on indigenous Asian values. Conservative leaders often talked of their vision to turn Iran into an "Islamic Japan," and they referred to the "China model" as the preferred development path for Iran.[41] This meant economic reforms without commensurate political change, and the generation of prosperity and order to support stable authoritarianism. The China model purports to be a development path that precludes democracy and is based on a social contract wherein prosperity is predicated on and supports authoritarianism.[42] The Asian models held attraction for Iran's leaders because they allowed talking about economic growth through close business–government partnerships with only limited market reforms.

This discourse on development was also influenced by closer economic ties between the clerical leadership and various social groups. These ties had created relationships of patronage that provided a far broader base of support and stability to the ruling conservatives than did their ideological appeal. The growth in the size of the private sector and increase in the price of oil between 2001 and 2005 had expanded the scope of government-business relations and, with it, the ruling regime's political control.[43] The private sector had benefited from foreign multinational activity in Iran that grew after Khatami's election in 1997. The rise in the price of oil had increased the number and size of government contracts, as had growing direct investment in the private sector by large government pension funds such as the Oil Industry Pension Fund or the clergy's pension fund, which is managed by the office of the Supreme Leader. By the end of the Khatami period, the private sector that was a component of the reform movement in 1997–2001 was no longer firmly tied to that movement. Instead, it had grown closer to the conservative power structure.[44]

The private sector's growth in importance since 1997 was a consequence of the relaxation of Western pressure on Iran after Khatami's election, the rising price of oil, and greater economic activity in the middle classes. Its dynamism owed to both new investment and growing consumerism, producing a notable social force in Iran during the Khatami period that did not go unnoticed by the ruling circle.[45]

These developments suggest that, overall, the Khatami presidency was a period of flux for both reformists and conservatives. Both sought to adapt to social changes that had transformed Iran's politics, challenged state power, and provided an opening for democracy. During this period, the social base for both reformism and conservative rule had changed drastically. This in turn transformed the context for state-society relations and for debates over Iran's trajectory of development. The conservatives proved capable of surviving these changes and emerged from the Khatami years as more powerful and with greater control over politics. The growth of the middle class and the private sector had promoted the reformist surge, but did not spell the end of conservative power. The ability of the Islamic Republic to adapt to social change was an important development in this period, and, as the presidential election of 2005 showed, this will likely continue to account for the resilience of conservative rule. However, although ascendant, conservatives were not impervious to change in their own ideas. As conservatives grappled with the changing social scene in Iran, they experimented with anchoring their authority in different state-building models and support of different social strata. Pragmatic conservatives competed with reformists for the support of the middle class and the private sector. This fueled competition in conservative ranks, so that although they were ascendant at the end of the Khatami period, they were by no means monolithic. In fact, the intensity of the competition among conservatives would make the 2005 presidential election significant for no reason other than determining the direction of conservative politics and its prospects of developing a popular base of power. Whether progress toward reform would continue would depend on how the new sociopolitical context would decide the outcome of the 2005 election.

6

Epilogue

Prospects for a Democratic State

The Khatami years brought to the fore major divisions in Iranian society and politics. Hence, as Iran prepared to choose his successor, the country once again found itself confronted with those themes that had early on shaped the trajectory of state formation and political development. The struggles that dominated the 1997–2005 years anchored Iran's politics in the fundamental concern with balancing the needs of state-building and development with the quest for democracy. As a result, a number of central issues were debated as Iranians took stock of the Khatami years and geared up for the 2005 presidential election: the relative powers of the state, social forces, and civil society institutions; the scope of social freedoms and individual rights; the role of religion in politics; oscillation between populist policies and the mercantile economy; and the centrality of nationalism and discourse on culture to political change.

Thus a century after the Constitutional Revolution set the stage for the evolution of Iranian politics, Iranians are once again debating the same core issues that faced state-building and democracy-building at the time. This is not to suggest that Iranian politics has not fundamentally changed but that the central axis of debate and the main dialectic of historical change has remained the same. As was the case almost a century ago, in today's Iran the main thread of Iranian politics is the struggle to build a democratic state—which means a balanced approach to state-building and democracy-building. Grappling with this issue has shaped Iranian political history and will continue to do so until democratic aspirations have been realized.

The context for the democracy debate in Iran and the drive for democracy's realization have been strengthened by demographic changes; decentralization of authority in the form of increased importance of municipal and provincial constituencies; and the decade-long experience with civil society activism, voting, and mobilization of the population during electoral campaigns. However, it is also clear that Iranian politics has not as yet removed the main obstacles to democratization and that state-building and the quest for social and individual freedoms have not converged in a linear process of political change. In the absence of a framework that would bind democracy to state-building, the goals of the latter have impeded the development of the former. The struggle between the two will shape state and society and will determine the pace and direction of Iran's progress toward the goal of a democratic state. The 2005 election proved to be an important turning point in this process.

Choosing Khatami's Successor

In June 2005, Iranians went to the polls in the country's ninth presidential election and chose Mahmoud Ahmadinejad (mayor of Tehran and former Revolutionary Guard and Basij commander) as the country's sixth president and the first who didn't hail from the rank of the clergy since 1981. The election marked the third transfer of the presidency in the post-Khomeini period. It proved to be the most intensely contested election since the 1979 revolution and the first to go to a second round of voting. Close to 30 million people (62 percent of the electorate of 47 million) voted in the first round on June 17, and more than 27 million (60 percent of the electorate) voted in the second round on June 24.

The election produced dramatic results. It brought to power a hard-line conservative populist whose election confirmed the conservative consolidation of power and stood in marked contrast to the popular choice in the 1997. The election also marked a transition of power to the postrevolution, and even the post-Khomeini generation, whose values had come to define the tenor of politics, and a shift away from the middle class and its youth culture to the lower class and its grievances. The presidential campaign was one of the most dynamic and innovative in Iran's history. It brought to the fore intense debates over various conceptions of government and social organization, economic development, and foreign policy. The campaign witnessed experimentation with new language and styles of politics. Some methods that were openly borrowed from campaigns in the West—the use of focus groups, targeted advertising, image management, and sound bites—became a staple of the Iranian political process. The election result, however, opened new fissures in Iranian politics and raised new questions about the prospects of democracy.

Khamenei's drive to consolidate his own power had met with resistance from powerful conservatives associated with the Coalition of Islamic Associations (Hey'at-ha-ye Mo'talefeh-ye Eslami), known in short as the Mo'talefeh; this coalition included senior clerics such as ayatollahs Mahdavi-Kani, Meshkini, and Nateq-Nouri, as well as senior lay politicians such as Habibollah Asgarowladi. The Mo'talefeh was also unhappy with the outcome of the 2004 parliamentary elections, which, despite the conservative victory, had reduced their presence in the parliament in favor of candidates from the Revolutionary Guard and the Abadgaran faction that Khamenei had put together. As a result, the Mo'talefeh looked for as a way to prevent Khamenei from gaining direct control of the presidency. During the election, Ahmadinejad promised to end the monopoly of the bazaar, which is close to the Mo'talefeh, over foreign trade; after the election, his supporters launched a public attack against senior clerics with ties to the bazaar.[1]

The 2005 election campaign thus arrayed those forces that supported Khamenei's greater prominence against those who resisted it. It was for this reason that many, including some in the conservative camp, welcomed the candidacy of Rafsanjani, who was seen as the only leader capable of resisting both personalization of power and the militarization of Iranian politics.

Throughout the Khatami period, municipal and provincial elections had become highly contested grounds between various political factions. Elections were no longer won and lost in Tehran, and broad national issues had to compete with local concerns at the ballot box. This placed greater emphasis on economic issues and patronage in elections, and it made campaigns that had national reach decisive to electoral outcomes. This trend was evident shortly after the 2004 parliamentary elections, when conservative candidates swept municipal elections with well-managed campaigns that had focused on economic issues, a lesson that was not lost on the hard-line conservatives' campaign.

These developments shaped both the context for the presidential election and its significance for the future of Iranian politics.

The Significance of the Election Campaign

The election was unique in that the issues that dominated the campaign were ultimately not the ones that decided the election, and hence the winner was not the one who defined the race. Much of the campaign was dominated by discussion of reform and the demands of the middle class and youths. However, the outcome of the first round quickly shifted the debate to class issues and socioeconomic grievances of the lower classes and disadvantaged provinces. The effects of privatization and the extent of private sector growth in Iran had largely been absent in political discussions. However, in Iran as was also the case in Eastern Europe or Latin America, privatization had led to economic disparities that translated into support for populist platforms at the polls. In 2005, the demand for reform was upstaged by a lower class revolt at the ballot box.

The Guardian Council selected six candidates from a record list of 1,014 to run in the presidential election. The six consisted of Khamenei's protégés Ali Larijani (former head of the Islamic Republic of Iran Broadcasting) and Mahmoud Ahmadinejad; the pragmatic conservative former president Rafsanjani (head of the Expediency Council); two former Revolutionary Guard commanders, Mohsen Rezai (who, although influential in shaping the campaign, withdrew on the eve of the vote) and Mohammad-Baqer Qalibaf; and the moderately pro-reform cleric Mehdi Karroubi (former Speaker of the parliament, member of the Expediency Council and an advisor to the Supreme Leader). The Guardian Council initially disqualified the reformist candidates Mostafa Moin (former minister of science and technology) and Mohsen Mehralizadeh (Khatami's vice president) only to reverse that decision at the behest of the Supreme Leader. However, it was clear from the outset that the election was largely a contest between hard-line and moderate conservatives, and inclusion of reformists was intended to merely ensure a respectable turnout on the election day.

In the campaign, the hard-line candidates adopted a populist platform directed at the urban poor and disadvantaged areas of the country, breaking with focus on the middle class and the private sector that had dominated politics since 1997. They also mobilized their hard-core supporters and the regime's network of security, economic, and religious institutions. The populist rhetoric was not a dominant feature in public debates early on in the campaign. In fact, hard-line conservatives were initially expected to do poorly in the election. Ahmadinejad's surprisingly strong showing in the first round of voting owed to a combination of interference in the election and support from the hard-line conservative vote, which by most estimates had consistently accounted for 18 percent to 20 percent of the electoral vote.[2]

The reformist platform continued where Khatami had left off, promising political change, cultural freedoms, civil society activism, and improvement in women's status. It argued that participation in the elections was the only way to prevent reversal of gains made during the Khatami period and sustaining the momentum for reform. Reformist candidates did not, however, provide a compelling argument that they would fare better than Khatami in achieving these goals, in particular because conservatives were now far more powerful and better organized than they had been in 1997. As such, reformist candidates found it difficult to attract disillusioned pro-democracy forces, which had called for a boycott of the elections, to join the process.

After holding intense debates, building alliances with dissidents such as the Liberation Movement of Iran (which had earlier supported the boycott), and reaching out to marginal groups such as the country's Sunni population, reformist candidates were able to expand their base and mobilize some pro-reform voters and civil society organizations, but they remained vulnerable to threats of boycott. Dissident intellectuals such as Akbar Ganji, along with dissident groups abroad, continued to argue for the boycott. Ganji argued that boycotting the elections was the only way the cause of reform could be advanced, for it would deny the ruling regime legitimacy and would end the impasse that confronted reform.[3]

In addition, the Do-e Khordad Movement had since 1997 fractured and would do so further during the presidential campaign. Moin represented more liberal reformists; Karroubi, the pro-reform elements of the political establishment. Whereas the two factions had converged under Khatami, now each had its own candidate. Although Karroubi did not initially generate much enthusiasm, he eventually gained the support of many in the pro-reform camp, including some intellectual voices such as Abdol-Karim Soroush,[4] and in the end it was Karroubi rather than Moin who emerged as the leading reformist contender.

Moin, who represented Khatami's core constituency, was hard-pressed to retain the allegiance of the reformist political machine—associated with the Kargozaran and Mojahedin-e Enqelab-e Eslami (Mojahedin of the Islamic Revolution)—that had been close to Karroubi and Rafsanjani in the 1990s. That group saw Rafsanjani as the pragmatic choice to strengthen the presidency and limit the powers of the Supreme Leader. The reformist platform proved ill-equipped to address the new context for conservative-reformist competition for power and the change in conservatives' political position, which will be discussed below. The political scene in Iran on the eve of the elections was no longer limited to hard-line conservatives and pro-democracy forces, but included new political voices that defined reform in different terms and promised either populism or a pragmatic alternative to confrontation with the conservative power structure. As a result, reformists were early on compelled to compete for their own constituency. The reformist campaign targeted the urban middle class, virtually ignoring the poor.

Candidates against whom the reformists had originally arrayed themselves, the hard-line conservative Larijani and Ahmadinejad, were not prominent during much of the election campaign and did not define the themes that formed the debates. Far more important were the moderate and pragmatic conservatives—Rafsanjani, Rezai, and Qalibaf—who to varying degrees straddled the boundaries between reformism and conservatism, and who put forward new political programs that confounded the reformist platform.

The pragmatic conservatives were the product of changes within the conservative camp after the parliamentary elections of 2004. The expectation that the presidential election was likely to have a low turnout led to the belief that a conservative candidate would win the presidency, thus intensifying competition among conservatives. That competition led conservative presidential contenders—hailing from various conservative factions and Revolutionary Guard—to differentiate their positions and to broaden their appeal to conservatives and other voters. Various clerical and Islamic associations, such as the Society of the Teachers of the Seminary Center of Qom or the Mo'talefeh, joined the fray to either foster unity or to arbiter the competition, at times conflicting with the Supreme Leader. The paradox of the conservative consolidation of 2001–2005 is that in seeking to limit democratic practices, it actually intensified competition for power in its own ranks, which would have to be settled in national elections. Whereas in 1997 it was reformists who engaged the electoral process, in 2005 it was conservatives who embraced it wholeheartedly.

The competition in the conservative camp led to divergent political paths. Whereas hard-liners turned to the poor for support, pragmatic conservatives looked to the middle class. The hard-liners were initially slow to define their platform. Meanwhile, pragmatic conservatives who targeted the reformist constituency captured most attention early on and looked most promising in the opinion polls. Among the three presidential candidates that represented pragmatic conservatism, Rafsanjani was closest to reformists, and Qalibaf to the conservatives. Rafsanjani's campaign had the support of the Qom establishment and the Implementers of Development, whereas Qalibaf had support from the Supreme Leader and the conservative Abadgaran. Still, despite their differences, these candidates contributed to a new political position that departed from hard-line conservatism in order to compete with reformists for defining the "strategic middle" in Iranian politics. The outcome of the election would show that that middle is ideologically to the right and economically to the left of where pragmatic conservatives and reformists believed it was.

Conservative pragmatists presented new ideas, and, more significant, it introduced a new style to politics, one that used secular and youthful themes, pop music, stylish dress, and colorful advertising. This reflected both the intensity of competition for public support and a purported change in the country's political culture.

The pragmatists did not reject reform but rather redefined it. They did not advocate return to theocracy, revolutionary values, or militant foreign policy; in fact, their campaigns were largely secular in tone and notably silent on Islamic issues. Rather, they focused on pragmatic domestic and foreign policies that, although lacking democratic intent, nevertheless promised change. The new breed of conservatives fashioned themselves as "reformist fundamentalists" (osoulgarayan-e eslah-talab), committed to the Islamic Republic and yet willing to embrace aspects of Khatami's reformist agenda.

Pragmatic conservatives combined promise of economic growth, better living standards, accountable and strong government, and engagement with the outside world with a strong appeal to Iranian nationalism. The central theme in pragmatists' arguments was the promise of a "strong government" (hokumat-e moqtader) that would solve social problems, bring about development, and maintain order. Strong government was defined in terms of competence and the capability to get things done. More important, it meant a government that would be able to work with the Supreme Leader and hence avoid the kind of gridlock that characterized the standoff between Khatami's reformist administration and the conservative leadership. This was an argument that also favored Ahmadinejad, who was expected to fare well with the hard-line conservative parliament. The pragmatic conservatives in effect promised government reform rather than political reform, arguing that this approach would more quickly and directly address economic problems.

The conservative message included the promise of accountability and transparency in government and more aggressive development. Rezai, for instance, was particularly vocal in this regard, promising to shatter the "mafia of rent-seekers (rant-kharan)."[5] This argument would later be adopted by Ahmadinejad's populist platform in the second round. Pragmatic conservative candidates attacked the Khatami government's economic performance and pointed to accomplishments made by conservatives—most notably the development of a nuclear program despite international economic sanctions—as evidence of their ability to do better. The promise of development was couched in nationalist language—as realizing Iran's national aspirations and in terms of the country's demand to be recognized as a "great power." Rezai spoke of Iran's regional influence, while Qalibaf promised to bestow on the country the international status that it deserves and the public demands. The nationalist language used by pragmatic conservatives was reminiscent of the nationalist discourse of the Pahlavi era.

Finally, the pragmatic conservative message included discussion of generational change, not in terms of actual leaders but clearly in terms of political culture and ideas. The election campaign was defined by values of youths, a group that had grown from 25 percent of the population in 1997 to 30 percent in 2004[6]—the generation born after the revolution and even after Khomeini's passage from the scene. This replaced the outlook, values, and ideas of the generation that carried out the revolution. Even leaders such as Rafsanjani, who belonged to that earlier generation, adapted his image and program to the new political climate and saw this election as an opportunity to organize the youths' political power into a formal political structure. The new face of conservative politics in Iran was therefore not defined by ideology but by nationalism, development, and state-building. The intense rivalry of conservatives showed that despite their opposition to reform, they nevertheless looked to public opinion and elections to settle struggles of power.

In the first round, the pragmatic conservative Rafsanjani won 21.2 percent of the vote, followed by hard-line conservative Ahmadinejad with 19.2 percent, reformist Karroubi with 18.7 percent, pragmatic conservative Qalibaf with 13.9 percent, reformist Moin with 13.6 percent, hard-line conservative Larijani with 5.9 percent, and the reformist Mehralizadeh with 4.4 percent. The popularity of the candidates varied widely by region and social group. Every candidate won at least one province; Karroubi, who came in third, won the most, ten. The top vote-getter, Rafsanjani, won only two, but he came in second in nineteen provinces. Mehralizadeh, who finished last, won five provinces, including a sweep of the Azeri northwest.

There were three surprises in this result. First, hard-line conservatives were able to win 25.1 percent of the votes. Karroubi, who trailed Ahmadinejad by 600,000 votes in the final tally, accused the Supreme Leader's son, Guardian Council, and the security forces of interference in the election to ensure Ahmadinejad's second-place finish. Rafsanjani accused hard-liners of breaking the law by engaging in negative campaigning against him, and he threatened to withdraw from the race. However, all this did not obfuscate the fact that hard-line conservatives, who were consistently at the bottom of opinion polls, had done sufficiently well to be able to push their way into the second round. They did this by exploiting socioeconomic grievances that were largely overlooked by others in the campaign. Whereas most candidates had used colorful advertising that targeted the middle class, Ahmadinejad's Spartan campaign, his humble image, and promises of distribution of wealth and continuation of state subsidies—all of which were throwbacks to the Jacobin policies of early years of the revolution—appealed to the lower classes.

Class also played an important role in the second surprise, which was that no reformist candidate made it to the second round, and that among reformists, Karroubi did better than Moin. This can be attributed to Karroubi's direct appeal to the poor by promising to give every Iranian over the age of eighteen the equivalent of $60 every month. In many regards, class and economic issues played a role equally as important as demand for political reform in the election outcome.

The third surprise was the degree of acrimony that emerged between Karroubi and the Supreme Leader over charges of vote gathering, campaign irregularities, and influence peddling by Khamenei's son and the security forces—which included allegations of speeches by military commanders and a fatwa by Ayatollah Mesbah-Yazdi ordering the Guard and the Basij vigilante forces that are attached to it to campaign and vote for Ahmadinejad. The rare caustic public exchange between Karroubi and Khamenei after the first round of voting, Karroubi's resignation as advisor to the Supreme Leader and from the Expediency Council (which were not accepted) and open threats by security forces against him opened a divide in the clerical leadership. This was followed, after Ahmadinejad's victory, by open attack by hard-line activists on senior conservative clerics and the Mo'talefeh, chastising them for supporting Larijani or Rafsanjani and for their role in corruption and monopoly control of the economy.[7] This suggests that the election opened a breach in the ranks of the ulama over the extent of the Supreme Leader's powers and the future of Iran's economy, and it led to a revolt among the conservative base of support against the wealth and power of the senior clerics.

Karroubi's strong performance also attested to the fact that a major failure of the reformists was that they did not create a united front that would bring together the various wings of reformism as had Khatami's campaigns in 1997 and 2001. Moreover, it showed that establishment reformists—who favored political change but remained tied to the existing political system and had not supported cultural change on the scope demanded by liberal reformists—form a large component of the reform movement.

Given the popularity of reform, which was expected to manifest itself in the event of a high turnout, it is important to ask where the reformist vote went if it did not propel a reformist candidate into the second round. The answer perhaps lies in the success of pragmatic conservatives. Rafsanjani and Qalibaf garnered some conservative votes, but they took many more away from reformists. The election results showed that their pragmatic approach to reform had resonated with voters and that their aggressive courting of the private sector, youths, and the middle class had paid dividends. The election showed that reformism is popular but isn't controlled by any one political leader or camp. The failure of Khatami to encapsulate reformism in a single political movement or party had opened the door to various political leaders' laying claim to its values and constituency. This had encouraged conservatives such as Rafsanjani, Rezai, and Qalibaf to move in the direction of reformism, but it had disfavored reformist candidates. Reformism had indeed proved strong—accounting for as much as 16 million of the 29 million votes cast in the first round[8]—but reformists appeared weak, and the main beneficiaries of reformism were pragmatic conservatives. Following the first round of voting, the boundary lines between hard-line and pragmatic conservatives became sharper, and those between pragmatic conservatives and reformists became blurry. Rafsanjani became the candidate of reformists of all shades in the second round of the election as pragmatic conservatives in effect broke completely with hard-line conservatives to become the inheritors of Khatami's mantle.[9]

The Conservative Surge Second Round

The outcome of the first round quickly changed the tenor of the campaign and its central issues. Rafsanjani's campaign continued to reflect middle-class demands for cultural opening and political reform. He was endorsed by reformist intellectuals and politicians in an effort to prevent an Ahmadinejad victory, which they saw as a return to the militancy of early years of the revolution—characterized by reformists as the "Talibanization" of Iran. They also feared that a victory by Ahmadinejad would bring a reversal of economic reforms, which since 1989 had restructured the economy but had benefited the private sector and the middle class. Shocked by the emergence of class politics, the reformist-pragmatic conservative alliance put forth a defensive campaign, hoping to rally the middle class to stop Ahmadinejad. The dilemma facing reformists and pragmatic conservatives was that in an election now focused on socioeconomic grievances, their candidate epitomized the wealth and corruption that the lower class was mobilizing against.

Ahmadinejad's stealth campaign quickly came into the open. Posing as an outsider and a man of the people, one of the *mostaz'afan* (the downtrodden) that the revolution had promised to empower, he promised to fight corruption and the political and economic domination of the first generation of the revolution—and to redistribute wealth to the poor. He touted his record as mayor of Tehran, promising effective, accountable, and transparent government. To his detractors, he promised a future that was modeled after Iran's past: militant Islamic socialism and a Third Worldist foreign policy. His platform appealed to the urban poor and the disadvantaged provinces, who had gained little from privatization strategies and who looked nostalgically to state control of the economy in the 1980s. He subsumed his hard-line ideological position under a populist platform and created a popular base of support for conservative rule. He responded to queries about his ideological agenda by saying, "People think a return to revolutionary values is only a matter of wearing the headscarf. The country's true problem is employment and housing, not what to wear."[10] Of course Ahmadinejad very much cared about what people wear, but he knew that focusing on that would not get him elected.

Although close to two million fewer people voted in the second round, Ahmadinejad won twelve million more votes in this round, winning with a wide margin of 62 percent versus 35 percent for Rafsanjani. That a hard-line conservative won in a high-turnout election showed the extent to which populism resonated with the masses, and it showed that economic issues had trumped reform as the main concern of Iranian politics. By redefining the main divide in Iranian politics, the 2005 election is as significant as the 1997 election.

The Implications for Future Developments

The 2005 presidential elections reconfirmed certain realities and introduced new ideas and practices to Iranian politics that will bear on long-run prospects for democracy in Iran. First, the election process was just as important as the result. The campaign itself led to a cultural opening, engaging the public and breaking political taboos by using music and festivities—which itself marks a milestone in Iranian politics.

Second, the elections entrenched competitive politics in conservative ranks and compelled them to fight for control of the middle in Iranian politics. These were the most closely fought presidential elections in Iran's history, and they were taken particularly seriously by conservatives and their constituency. These were also the first presidential elections in which the candidates' image and message were shaped by the need to garner votes and the realization that to do so, politicians must reflect the demands of their constituencies. This will in the coming years deepen the chasm between the elected and unelected elements in Iran's power structure, intensifying tensions that will push for change. It is now evident that despite all their limitations, elections in Iran matter. Their frequency has affected popular political culture, society, politics, and, even more important, the dynamics of Iran's leadership as well.

Third, the election confirmed the continued popularity of reformism, but it also showed the growing importance of socioeconomic issues. These issues divided the electorate along ideological and class lines and also brought home the complex question concerning the role of elections—as reflectors of socioeconomic demands—in promotion of democracy. The conservatives themselves became divided over these issues, as was evident in the turn of some to populist politics and others to pragmatism and reformism.

Fourth, the electoral campaign and the pattern of voting underscored the growing decentralization of Iranian politics, wherein local issues and patterns of political participation determine electoral outcomes. The two dark horses in the election, Karroubi and Ahmadinejad, did well owing to votes from small towns and poorer provinces as they promised to defend state subsidies before economic reform.[11]

Finally, the outcome compelled reformists to regroup and reformulate their position to reflect changes that the election has brought about. The inclusive nature of the reformist campaign and its willingness to build alliances with pragmatic conservatives in the second round could serve the long-term interests of democracy. The reformists were slow to take stock of the rise of pragmatic conservatives, and they were blindsided by the depth of socioeconomic disgruntlements. Divided over boycott or participation and lacking a united platform or a strong candidate, they failed to mount an effective campaign and to adequately organize the electorate. They mobilized too late to dominate this election but remained important players in the political process. They predicted that a high turnout would favor them, but the election denied them that advantage. In this election, in the words of one prominent reformist editor, "reformism lost to democracy."[12] The challenge before democracy now in Iran is to build a cohesive movement and relate the demand for change to socioeconomic grievances; the challenge, in other words, is to build bridges between the middle and lower classes.

These issues became even more important after Ahmadinejad took over the presidency. His populist approach to the management of the economy and militant foreign policy created tensions among the conservative forces. Disagreements will continue to play themselves out in the governing circles and, ultimately, in future elections. Far from diminishing the importance of competitive politics, public debates, and elections, the conservative victory in 2005 appears to have made them all the more important to the future development of Iranian politics.

A century after the Constitutional Revolution of 1906, Iran is still grappling with how to achieve a democratic state. It is open to question whether Iran is any closer to that goal today than it has been at any other time in the past century. The verdict of the 2005 election was to once again strengthen the state. This outcome does not easily lead to reconciling the long-running conflict between state-building and democracy-building, but it will intensify the competition between the two and make the imperative of that reconciliation the focus of Iranian politics.

Notes

PREFACE

1. John Daniszewski, "Hard-Liner Wins Decisively in Iran Presidential Election," *Los Angeles Times*, June 25, 2005, Web edition, available at http://www.latimes.com/news/nationworld/world/la-fg-iranelect25jun25,0,2087142.story?coll=la-home-headlines

INTRODUCTION

1. On state formation in Europe, see Charles Tilly, ed., *The Formation of National States in Western Europe* (Princeton, N.J.: Princeton University Press, 1975); and Martin Van Creveld, *The Rise and Decline of the State* (New York: Cambridge University Press, 1999). On colonial state formation, see Joel S. Migdal, *Strong Societies and Weak States: State-Society Relations and State Capabilities in the Third World* (Princeton, N.J.: Princeton University Press, 1988); Crawford Young, *The African Colonial State in Comparative Perspective* (New Haven, Conn.: Yale University Press, 1994); and Vali Nasr, "European Colonialism and the Emergence of Modern Muslim States," in *The Oxford History of Islam*, ed. John L. Esposito (New York: Oxford University Press, 1999), 549–99.

2. Francis Fukuyama, " 'Stateness' First," *Journal of Democracy* 16:1 (January 2005): 88.

3. On the Constitution of the Islamic Republic, see Asghar Schirazi, *The Constitution of Iran: Politics and the State in the Islamic Republic* (London: I. B. Tauris, 1997).

4. For general discussions of the idea of democracy and its meaning, see Robert Dahl, *On Democracy* (New Haven, Conn.: Yale University Press,

2000); Robert Dahl, *Democracy and Its Critics* (New Haven, Conn.: Yale University Press, 1991); and Frank Cunningham, *Theories of Democracy: A Critical Introduction* (London: Routledge, 2002).

5. Afshin Molavi, "In Iran: Daring to Dream of Democracy," *Washington Post,* March 7, 2004.

6. On the Constitutional Revolution, see Edward G. Browne, *Persian Revolution of 1905–09* (Cambridge: Cambridge University Press, 1910); Vanessa Martin, *Islam and Modernism: The Iranian Revolution of 1906* (Syracuse, N.Y.: Syracuse University Press, 1989); and Janet Afary, *The Iranian Constitutional Revolution* (New York: Columbia University Press, 1996).

7. David Blackbourn and Geoff Eley, *The Peculiarities of German History: Bourgeois Society and Politics in Nineteenth-Century Germany* (New York: Oxford University Press, 1984), 12.

8. On the importance of state-building, see Eric Nordlinger, "Taking the State Seriously," in *Understanding Political Development,* ed. Samuel P. Huntington and Myron Weiner (New York: HarperCollins, 1987), 353–90.

9. Ellen Trimberger, *Revolution from Above: Military Bureaucrats and Development in Japan, Turkey, Egypt, and Peru* (New Brunswick, N.J.: Transaction Books, 1978).

10. Margaret Levi, *Of Rule and Revenue* (Berkeley: University of California Press, 1988); Thomas Ertman, *Birth of Leviathan: Building States and Regimes in Medieval and Early Modern Europe* (New York: Cambridge University Press, 1997), 317–20; and Tilly, *Formation of National States.*

11. Georg Sorensen, "War and Security-Making: Why Doesn't It Work in the Third World," *Security Dialogue,* 32:3 (2001): 341–54; Francis Fukuyama, *State-Building: Governance and World Order in the Twenty-First Century* (Ithaca, N.Y.: Cornell University Press, 2004).

12. Atul Kohli, *The State and Poverty in India: The Politics of Reform* (New York: Cambridge University Press, 1987), 15–50; and Joel S. Migdal, "Strong States, Weak States: Power and Accommodation," in *Understanding Political Development,* ed. Samuel P. Huntington and Myron Weiner (New York: HarperCollins, 1987), 391–434.

13. Otto Hintze, *The Historical Essays of Otto Hintze,* ed. Felix Gilbert and Robert M. Berdahl (New York: Oxford University Press, 1975); Charles Tilly, *Formation of National States*; and Theda Skocpol, *States and Social Revolutions: A Comparative Analysis of France, Russia, and China* (New York: Cambridge University Press, 1979).

14. Ziya Önis, "The Logic of the Developmental State," *Comparative Politics,* 24:1 (October 1991): 109–26; Chalmers Johnson, "The Developmental State: Odyssey of a Concept," in *The Developmental State,* ed. Meredith Woo-Cumings (Cornell: Cornell University Press, 1999), 32–60; Peter Evans, *Embedded Autonomy: States and Industrial Transformation* (Princeton, N.J.: Princeton University Press, 1995); Alfred Stepan, *The State and Society: Peru in Comparative Perspective* (Princeton, N.J.: Princeton University Press, 1978), 40–45; Timothy Mitchell, "The Limits of the State: Beyond Statist Approaches and Their Critics," *American Political Science Review,* 85:1 (March 1991): 77–96; Joel S. Migdal, "The State in Society: An Approach to Struggles of Domination," in *State Power and Social Forces : Domination and Transformation in the Third World,* ed.

Joel S. Migdal, Atul Kohli, and Vivienne Shue (New York: Cambridge University Press, 1994), 8.

15. Fukuyama, *State-Building*, 6–20.

16. Young, *African Colonial State*, 35–40.

17. Samuel P. Huntington, *Political Order in Changing Societies* (New Haven, Conn.: Yale University Press, 1969), 264–343.

18. Theda Skocpol, *Social Revolutions in the Modern World* (New York: Cambridge University Press, 1994); and the various essays in John Foran, ed., *Theorizing Revolutions: New Approaches from across the Disciplines* (New York: Routledge, 1997).

19. Ted R. Gurr, *Why Men Rebel* (Princeton, N.J.: Princeton University Press, 1969).

20. On the importance of ideology, see Karl Mannheim, *Ideology and Utopia: An Introduction to Sociology of Knowledge*, reprint (London: Routledge & Kegan Paul, 1968). On organization in revolutionary activism, see Tony Smith, *Thinking Like a Communist: State and Legitimacy in the Soviet Union, China, and Cuba* (New York: W. W. Norton, 1987).

21. See, for example, Tim McDaniel, *Autocracy, Modernization, and Revolution in Russia and Iran* (Princeton, N.J.: Princeton University Press, 1991); Theda Skocpol, "Rentier State and Shi'a Islam in the Iranian Revolution," *Theory and Society*, 11:3 (May 1982): 265–83; and various essays in Nikki Keddie, *Debating Revolutions* (New York: New York University Press, 1995).

22. Jeff Goodwin, *No Other Way Out: States and Revolutionary Movements, 1945–1991* (New York: Cambridge University Press, 2001); and Jack Gladstone, *Revolutions: Theoretical, Comparative, and Historical Studies* (San Diego, Calif.: Harcourt Brace Jovanovich, 1986).

23. Daryush Shayegan, *Qu'est-ce qu'une révolution religieuse?* (What Is a Religious Revolution?) (Paris: Albin Michel, 1991).

24. Barrington Moore Jr., *Social Origins of Dictatorship and Democracy: Lord and Peasant in the Making of the Modern World* (Boston: Beacon Press, 1966).

25. See, for instance, Alfred Stepan, *Arguing Comparative Politics* (New York: Oxford University Press, 2001), 109–253; and Juan Linz and Alfred Stepan, *Problems of Democratic Transition and Consolidation* (Baltimore, Md.: Johns Hopkins University Press, 1996), 3–15; and Stephan Haggard and Robert Kaufman, *The Political Economy of Democratic Transitions* (Princeton, N.J.: Princeton University Press, 1995).

26. Adam Przeworski, *Democracy and the Market: Political and Economic Reforms in Eastern Europe and Latin America* (New York: Cambridge University Press, 1991), and Adam Przeworski, *Sustainable Democracy* (New York: Cambridge University Press, 1995).

27. Larry Diamond and Marc Plattner, eds., *The Global Resurgence of Democracy* (Baltimore, Md.: Johns Hopkins University Press, 1993); and Lisa Anderson, *Transitions to Democracy* (New York: Columbia University Press, 1999).

28. Samuel P. Huntington, *The Third Wave: Democratization in the Late Twentieth Century* (Norman: University of Oklahoma Press, 1991).

29. See various articles in Doug McAdam, John McCarthy, Mayer Zald, eds., *Comparative Perspectives on Social Movements* (New York: Cambridge University Press,

1996); Sidney Tarrow, *Power in Movement: Social Movements and Contentious Politics* (New York: Cambridge University Press, 1998); Doug McAdam, Sidney Tarrow, and Charles Tilly, *The Dynamics of Contention* (New York: Cambridge University Press, 2001); and Quintan Wiktorowicz, ed., *Islamic Activism: A Social Movement Theory Approach* (Bloomington: Indiana University Press, 2003).

30. John Keane, *Democracy and Civil Society* (New York: Verso, 1988); and Augustus Richard Norton, *Civil Society in the Middle East*, 2 vols. (Leiden: E. J. Brill, 1996).

31. Samuel P. Huntington, *The Clash Of Civilizations and the Remaking of World Order* (New York: Touchstone Books, 1998); Bernard Lewis, *What Went Wrong? The Clash between Islam and Modernity in the Middle East* (New York: Oxford University Press, 2003).

32. Abdol-Karim Soroush, *Reason, Freedom, and Democracy in Islam*, ed. and trans. Mahmoud Sadri and Ahmad Sadri (New York: Oxford University Press, 2000); Abdulaziz Sachedina, *Islamic Roots of Democratic Pluralism* (New York: Oxford University Press, 2001); Khaled Abou El Fadl, *Islam and the Challenge of Democracy* (Princeton, N.J.: Princeton University Press, 2004).

33. Dale Eickelman and James Piscatori, *Muslim Politics* (Princeton, N.J.: Princeton University Press, 1996).

34. John L. Esposito and John O. Voll, *Islam and Democracy* (New York: Oxford University Press, 1996); also see Seyyed Vali Reza Nasr, "Democracy and Islamic Revivalism," *Political Science Quarterly* 110:2 (Summer 1995): 261–85, and Vali Nasr, "The Rise of 'Muslim Democracy,' " *Journal of Democracy* 16:2 (April 2005): 13–27.

35. Robert W. Hefner, *Civil Islam: Muslims and Democratization in Indonesia* (Princeton, N.J.: Princeton University Press, 2000); Eva Bellin, "Robustness of Authoritarianism in the Middle East: Exceptionalism in Comparative Perspective," *Comparative Politics* 36:2 (January 2004): 139–58; Daniel Brumberg, "The Trap of Liberalized Autocracy," in *Islam and Democracy in the Middle East*, ed. Larry Diamond, Marc Plattner, and Daniel Brumberg (Baltimore, Md.: Johns Hopkins University Press, 2003), 35–47; and Vali Nasr, "Military Rule, Islamism, and Democracy in Pakistan" *Middle East Journal* 58:2 (Spring 2004): 195–209.

36. Said A. Arjomand, *The Turban for the Crown* (New York: Oxford University Press, 1988); and Ervand Abrahamian, *Khomeinism: Essays on the Islamic Republic* (Berkeley: University of California Press, 1993).

CHAPTER 1

1. Ann K. S. Lambton, "The Qajar Dynasty," and "Persian Society under the Qajars," both in Ann K. S. Lambton, *Qajar Persia: Eleven Studies* (Austin: University of Texas Press, 1988), 1–32, and 108–39, respectively.

2. Abbas Amanat, *Pivot of the Universe: Naser al-Din Shah Qajar and the Iranian Monarchy, 1831–1896* (Berkeley: University of California Press, 1997).

3. Nikki R. Keddie, *Religion and Rebellion in Iran: The Iranian Tobacco Protest of 1891–1892* (London: Frank Cass, 1966); Fereydoun Adamiyat, *Shouresh bar Emtiaz-Nameh-ye Reji: Tahlil-e Siasi* (Protest against Régie Concession: A Political Analysis) (Tehran: Payam, 1360/1981).

4. On relations between ulama and bazaar merchants, see Abbas Amanat, "In Between the Madrasa and the Marketplace: The Designation of Clerical Leadership in Modern Shi'ism," in *Authority and Political Culture in Shi'ism,* ed. Said A. Arjomand (Albany: SUNY Press, 1988), 98–132.

5. Nikki R. Keddie, *An Islamic Response to Imperialism* (Berkeley: University of California Press, 1983).

6. Homa Katouzian, *State and Society in Iran: The Eclipse of the Qajars and the Emergence of Pahlavis* (London: I. B. Tauris, 2001).

7. Mehdi Malikzadeh, *Tarikh-e Enqelab-e Mashroutiyat-e Iran* (A History of the Iranian Constitutional Revolution) (Tehran: n.p., 1351/1972–73). For the role of political societies in the Iranian Constitutional Revolution, see also Ann K. S. Lambton, "Secret Societies and the Persian Revolution of 1905–6," in *Qajar Persia,* 301–18, and "Persian Political Societies 1906–11," in *St. Antony's Papers* 16:3 (London, 1963): 41–89.

8. Fereydoun Adamiyat, *Fekr-e Azadi va Moqaddameh-ye Nehzat-e Mashroutiyat-e Iran* (The Idea of Liberty and the Beginning of the Iranian Constitutional Movement) (Tehran: n.p., 1340/1961–62); Fereydoun Adamiyat, *Ide'oloji-ye Nehzat-e Mashroutiyat-e Iran* (The Ideology of the Iranian Constitutional Movement), Vol. 1 (Tehran: Payam, 2535 [1355]/1976); and Fereydoun Adamiyat, *Ide'oloji-ye Nehzat-e Mashroutiyat-e Iran: Jeld-e Dovvom: Majles-e Avval va Bohran-e Azadi* (Ideology of the Iranian Constitutional Movement: Vol. 2: The First Majles and the Crisis of Democracy) (Tehran: Rowshangaram, n.d.).

9. Hamid Algar, *Mirza Malkum Khan: A Biographical Study in Iranian Modernism* (Berkeley: University of California Press, 1973).

10. Ahmad Kasravi, *Tarikh-e Mashrouteh-ye Iran* (A History of the Iranian Constitutional Movement), 13th ed. (Tehran: Amir-Kahir, 2536 [1356]/1978). For a discussion of these perspectives, see also Ali Gheissari, *Iranian Intellectuals in the Twentieth Century* (Austin: University of Texas Press, 1998), 26.

11. Browne, *Persian Revolution of 1905–09.*

12. Abdul-Hadi Hairi, *Shi'ism and Constitutionalism in Iran: A Study of the Role Played by the Persian Residents of Iraq in Iranian Politics* (Leiden: E. J. Brill, 1977); and Hamid Enayat, *Modern Islamic Political Thought* (Austin: University of Texas Press, 1982), 164–75.

13. Gheissari, *Iranian Intellectuals,* 24–25.

14. Said A. Arjomand, *The Shadow of God and the Hidden Imam: Religion, Political Order, and Societal Change in Shi'ite Iran from the Beginning to 1890* (Chicago: University of Chicago Press, 1984).

15. Vanessa Martin, "Shaikh Fazlallah Nuri and the Iranian Revolution of 1905–9," *Middle Eastern Studies* 23:1 (January 1987): 41–53; Shaykh Fadl Allah Nuri, "Book of Admonition to the Heedless and Guidance for the Ignorant" (*Kitab Tadhikart al-Ghafil va Irshad al-Jahil*), ed. and trans. Hamid Dabasi, in *Authority and Political Culture in Shi'ism,* ed. Said A. Arjomand (Albany: SUNY Press, 1988), 354–70.

16. On the Constitutional Revolution, see Browne, *Persian Revolution of 1905–09;* Martin, *Islam and Modernism;* Mangol Bayat, *Iran's First Revolution: Shi'ism and the Constitutional Revolution of 1905–1909* (New York: Oxford University Press, 1991); and Afary, *Iranian Constitutional Revolution.*

17. Mansoureh Ettehadieh, *Majles va Entekhabat: Az Mashrouteh ta Payan-e Qajari-yeh* (Majles and Elections: From the Constitutional Revolution until the End of Qajar Dynasty) (Tehran: Nashr-e Tarikh-e Iran, 1375/1997); Fereydoun Adamiyat, "Barkhord-e Afkar va Takamol-e Parlemani dar Majles-e Avval" (Exchange of Ideas and Parliamentary Development in the First Majles), in Fereydoun Adamiyat, *Maqalat-e Tarikhi* (Historical Essays) (Tehran, 1352/1975), 109–18; *Mozakerat-e Majles dar Dowreh-ye Avval-e Taqniniyeh-ye Majles-e Showra-ye Melli* (Proceedings of the First Majles), with an introduction by Said Nafisi (Tehran: Ketab Khaneh-ye Ibn Sina, 1334/1966).

18. Firoozeh Kashani-Sabet, *Frontier Frictions: Shaping the Iranian Nation, 1804–1946* (Princeton, N.J.: Princeton University Press, 1999).

19. Touraj Atabaki, *Iran and the First World War* (London: I. B. Tauris, 2005).

20. Katouzian, *State and Society*, 88–120; also see Rouhollah K. Ramazani, *The Foreign Policy of Iran, 1500–1941: A Developing Nation in World Affairs* (Charlottesville: University of Virginia Press, 1966), 139–67.

21. For a general treatment of Vosouq's politics and its implications for state formation, see Katouzian, *State and Society*, 120–63. See also Oliver Bast, "Putting the Record Straight: Vosuq al-Dowleh's Foreign Policy in 1918/19," in *Men of Order: Authoritarian Modernization under Ataturk and Reza Shah*, ed. Touraj Atabaki and Erik J. Zurcher (London: I. B. Tauris, 2004), 260–81.

22. On Reza Shah's rise to power, see Cyrus Ghani, *Iran and the Rise of Reza Shah: From Qajar Collapse to Pahlavi Power* (London: I. B. Tauris, 1998); and Stephanie Cronin, *The Army and the Creation of the Pahlavi State in Iran, 1910–1926* (London: Tauris Academic Press, 1997).

23. On the Reza Shah period, see Donald Wilber, *Riza Shah Pahlavi: The Resurrection and Reconstruction of Iran* (Hicksville, N.Y.: Exposition Press, 1975); Amin Banani, *The Modernization of Iran, 1921–41* (Stanford, Calif.: Stanford University Press, 1961); Stephanie Cronin, ed., *The Making of Modern Iran: State and Society under Riza Shah, 1921–1941* (London: Curzon Press, 2003); and Touraj Atabaki and Erik J. Zurcher, *Men of Order: Authoritarian Modernization under Ata Turk and Reza Shah* (London: I. B. Tauris, 2004), 13–43 and 65–97.

24. Cronin, *The Army and the Creation of Pahlavi State*.

25. Kamran Dadkhah, "Roshanfekran-e Irani va Andisheh-e Eqtesadi" (Iranian Intellectuals and Economic Thought), *Iran Nameh* 21:3 (Fall 1382/2003): 285–300.

26. For a study of ulama-state relations, see Shahrough Akhavi, *Religion and Politics in Contemporary Iran: Clergy-State Relations in the Pahlavi Period* (Albany: SUNY Press, 1980); Arang Keshavarzian, "Turban or Hat, Seminarian or Soldier: State Building and Clergy Building in Reza Shah's Iran," *Journal of Church and State* 45:1 (Winter 2003): 81–112; Hamid Basiratmanesh, *Ulama va Regime-e Reza Shah* (Ulama and Reza Shah's Regime) (Tehran: Nashr-e Uruj, 1998).

27. Mohammad Faghfoory, "The Ulama-State Relations in Iran: 1921–41," *International Journal of Middle East Studies* 19:4 (November 1987): 413–32.

28. Arjomand, *Turban for the Crown*, 59–74; W. Floor, *Industrialization in Iran, 1900–1941* (Durham, England: University of Durham Press, 1984); and Massoud Karshenas, *Oil, State, and Industrialization in Iran* (New York: Cambridge University Press, 1990), 64–87.

29. Michael Zirinsky, "Imperial Power and Dictatorship: Britain and the Rise of Reza Shah, 1921–1926," *International Journal of Middle East Studies* 24:4 (November 1992): 639–63. Astonishingly, the author chastises Reza Shah for preventing the separation of Khuzestan.

30. Levi, *Of Rule and Revenue*, 1–10; Joel Migdal, *Strong Societies and Weak States*; Charles Tilly, *Formation of National States*; and Michael Mann, "The Autonomous Power of the State: Its Origins, Mechanisms, and Results," *Archives Européennes de Sociologie* 25:2 (1984): 185–213.

31. H. E. Chehabi, "Staging the Emperor's New Clothes: Dress Codes and Nation-Building under Reza Shah," *Iranian Studies* 26:3–4 (Summer/Fall 1993): 209–29.

32. Mohammad H. Faghfoory, "The Impact of Modernization on the Ulama in Iran, 1925–1941," *Iranian Studies* 26:3–4 (Summer/Fall 1993): 277–312.

CHAPTER 2

1. On this period, see Ervand Abrahamian, *Iran between Two Revolutions* (Princeton, N.J.: Princeton University Press, 1982), 169–280; and Fakhreddin Azimi, *Iran: The Crisis of Democracy* (New York: St. Martin's Press, 1989).

2. Ali Gheissari, "Persia," in *Oxford Companion to the Second World War*, ed. I. C. B. Dear and M. R. D. Foot (Oxford: Oxford University Press, 1995), 874.

3. On this party, see Abrahamian, *Iran between Two Revolutions*, 281–415; and Sepehr Zabih, *The Communist Movement in Iran* (Berkeley: University of California Press, 1966).

4. It is argued that many who experienced their initial political socialization through the Tudeh Party during this period would later join the Pahlavi regime, thus replacing one cult of personality with another. Their "totalitarian addiction" would help mold the structure of authority in the Pahlavi state. See Gholam R. Afkhami, *The Iranian Revolution: Thanatos on a National Scale* (Washington, D.C.: Middle East Institute, 1985), 51–52.

5. Louise Fawcett, *Iran and the Cold War: The Azarbayjan Crisis of 1946* (Cambridge: Cambridge University Press, 1992); Touraj Atabaki, *Azerbaijan: Ethnicity and the Struggle for Power in Iran* (London: I. B. Tauris, 2000), 129–78.

6. Homa Katouzian, "The Strange Politics of Khalil Maleki," in *Reformers and Revolutionaries in Modern Iran*, ed. Stephanie Cronin (London: RoutledgeCurzon, 2004), 165–88.

7. See Richard W. Cottam, *Nationalism in Iran*, 2nd ed. (Pittsburgh: University of Pittsburgh Press, 1979); J. A. Bill and William Roger Louis, eds., *Musaddiq, Iranian Nationalism, and Oil* (Austin: University of Texas Press, 1988); Zabih, *The Communist Movement in Iran*.

8. Homa Katouzian, *Musaddiq and the Struggle for Power in Iran* (London: I. B. Tauris, 1990).

9. Seyyed Vali Reza Nasr, "Religious Modernism in the Arab World, India, and Iran: The Perils and Prospects of a Discourse," *Muslim World* 83:1 (January 1993): 20–47.

10. H. E. Chehabi, *Iranian Politics and Religious Modernism: The Liberation Movement of Iran under the Shah and Khomeini* (Ithaca, N.Y.: Cornell University Press, 1990).

11. Yann Richard, "Shari'at Sangalaji: A Reformist Theologian of the Rida Shah Period), *Authority and Political Culture in Shi'ism,* ed. Said Amir Arjomand (Albany, N.Y.: SUNY Press, 1988), 159–77.

12. For a thorough account of Bazargan's ideas, see Chehabi, *Iranian Politics.*

13. Ibid., 46–50. Also see Mehdi Bazargan, *Gomrahan; Sayr-e Tahavvul-e Qur'an* (The Deceived: The Path of Development of the Qur'an), 2 vols. (Tehran, 1362/1984–85); and Mehdi Bazargan, *Bazgasht be Qur'an* (Return to the Qur'an) (Tehran 1361/1983–84). Also see Ann Lambton, "A Reconsideration of the Position of *Marja'-i Taqlid,*" in *Studia Islamica* 10 (1964): 124–25.

14. Murtaza Mutahhari, *Fundamentals of Islamic Thought: God, Man, and the Universe,* translated from the Persian by R. Campbell, with annotations and an introduction by Hamid Algar (Berkeley, Calif.: Mizan Press, 1985).

15. Richard Campbell, trans. and ed., *Society and Economics in Islam: Writings and Declarations of Ayatollah Sayyid Mahmud Taleqani* (Berkeley, Calif.: Mizan Press, 1982); Ayatollah Sayyid Mahmud Taleqani, *Jahad va Shahadat* (Jihad and Martyrdom) (Tehran, n.d.); Ayatollah Sayyid Mahmud Taleqani, *Az azadi ta shahadat* (From Freedom to Martyrdom) (Tehran, n.d.).

16. Seyyed Mahmood Taleqani, *Islam and Ownership,* trans. Ahmad Jabbari and Farhang Rajaee (Lexington, Ky.: Mazda, 1983), 34–88.

17. Ahmad Rezai, *Nehzat-e Hosseini* (Hossein's Movement) (Tehran: Sazman-e Mojehadin-e Khalq-e Iran, 1976).

18. See Hamid Dabashi, "Ali Shariati's Islam: Revolutionary Uses of Faith in a Post-Traditional Society," *Islamic Quarterly* 27:4 (fourth quarter, 1983): 203–22. Also see Said Amir Arjomand, "Á la Recherche de lá Conscience Collective: Durkheim's Ideological Impact in Turkey and Iran," *American Sociologist* 27 (May 1982): 94–102; and Ali Shariati, *Man and Islam,* trans. Fatollah Marjani (Houston, Tex.: FILINC, n.d.), 82–120; and Ali Rahnema, *An Islamic Utopian: A Political Biography of Ali Shariati* (London: I. B. Tauris, 2000).

19. Shahrough Akhavi, "The Role of the Clergy in Iranian Politics, 1949–1954," in *Musaddiq, Iranian Nationalism, and Oil,* ed. James A. Bill and William Roger Louis (Austin: University of Texas Press, 1988), 91–117; Yann Richard, "Ayatollah Kashani: Precursor of the Islamic Republic?" *Religion and Politics in Iran: Shi'ism from Quietism to Revolution,* ed. Nikki Keddie (New Haven, Conn.: Yale University Press, 1983), 121–24.

20. On Khomeini's life and thought, see Baqer Moin, *Khomeini: Life of the Ayatollah* (London: I. B. Tauris, 1999).

21. See, for instance, the arguments of the fundamentalist activist Nematollah Salehi Najafabadi, in his *Tote'eh-ye Shah bar Zedd-e Imam Khomeini* (Shah's Conspiracy against Imam Khomeini) (Tehran: Moassesse-ye Khadamat-e Farhangi-ye Rasa, 1361/1984).

22. Yann Richard, "L'Organization des Feda'iyan-e eslam, mouvement integriste musulman en Iran (1945–1956), in *Radicalismes islamiques,* ed. O. Carre and P. Dumont, Vol. 1 (Paris: L'Harmattan, 1985), 23–82; and Farhad Kazemi, "Fada'iyan-e Islam: Fanaticism, Politics, and Terror," in *From Nationalism to Revolutionary Islam,* ed. Said A Arjomand (Albany: SUNY Press, 1984), 158–76.

23. Fawcett, *Iran and the Cold War;* Stephen L. McFarland, "A Peripheral View of

the Origins of the Cold War: The Crisis in Iran, 1941–1947," *Diplomatic History* 4 (Fall 1980): 333–51.

24. William Eagleton, *The Kurdish Republic of 1946* (London: Oxford University Press, 1963); and Atabaki, *Azerbaijan: Ethnicity and the Struggle for Power in Iran.*

25. Bill and Louis, *Musaddiq, Iranian Nationalism, and Oil;* Mark Gasiorowski and Malcolm Byrne, eds., *Mohammad Mosaddeq and the 1953 Coup in Iran* (Syracuse, N.Y.: Syracuse University Press, 2004); Mostafa Elm, *Oil, Power, and Principle: Iran's Oil Nationalization and Its Aftermath* (Syracuse, N.Y.: Syracuse University Press, 1992); and Mary Ann Heiss, *Empire and Nationhood: The United States, Great Britain, and Iranian Oil, 1950–1954* (New York: Columbia University Press, 1997).

26. Sepehr Zabih, *The Mossadegh Era* (Chicago: Lake View Press, 1982); Kermit Roosevelt, *Countercoup* (New York: McGraw-Hill, 1979).

27. Mark Gasiorowski, "The 1953 Coup d'Etat in Iran," *International Journal of Middle East Studies* 19:4 (August 1987): 261–86. On the CIA's own role in accusing Mosaddeq of communist leaning, see Stephen Kinzer, *All the Shah's Men: An American Coup and the Roots of Middle East Terror* (New York: Wiley, 2003), 6.

28. See further Gasiorowski, "The 1953 Coup d'Etat"; Donald N. Wilber, "Clandestine Service History: Overthrow of Premier Mossadeq of Iran, November 1952–August 1953," National Security Archive, Electronic Briefing Book, No. 28 http://www.gwu.edu/nsarchiv/NSAEBB/NSAEBB28/#documents; Stephen Dorril, *MI6: Inside the Covert World of Her Majesty's Secret Intelligence Service* (New York: Free Press, 2000), 558–99.

29. Fakhreddin Azimi, "Unseating Mosaddeq: The Configuration and Role of Domestic Forces," in *Mohammad Mosaddeq and the 1953 Coup in Iran,* ed. Mark J. Gasiorowski and Malcolm Byrne (Syracuse, N.Y.: Syracuse University Press, 2004), 27–101.

30. Maziar Behrooz, *Rebels with a Cause: The Failure of the Left in Iran* (London: I. B. Tauris, 1999).

31. Mark Gasiorowski, *U.S. Foreign Policy and the Shah: Building a Client State in Iran* (Ithaca, N.Y.: Cornell University Press, 1991).

32. For examples of these clashes, see Frances Bostock and Geoffrey Jones, *Planning and Power in Iran: Ebtehaj and Economic Development under the Shah* (London: Frank Cass, 1989), 5–8; Vali Nasr, "Politics within the Late-Pahlavi State: The Ministry of Economy and Industrial Policy, 1963–1969," *International Journal of Middle East Studies* 32, 1 (February 2000): 97–122; interviews with Reza Niazmand in the Oral History of Iran Collection of Foundation for Iranian Studies; and Khodadad Farmanfarmaian in the Iranian Oral History Collection of Harvard University.

33. Quoted in Huntington, *Political Order in Changing Societies,* 179.

34. Abbas Milani, *The Persian Sphinx: Amir Abbas Hoveyda and the Riddle of the Iranian Revolution* (Washington, D.C.: Mage Publishers, 2003). Also see Asadollah Alam, *The Shah and I: The Confidential Diary of Iran's Royal Court, 1969–1977,* ed. Alinaqi Alikhani (New York: St. Martin's Press, 1992); and the interviews of Mohammad Baheri, Aqa Khan Bakhtiar, Ahmad Qoreishi, Abdol-Majid Majidi, and Parviz Raji in the Oral History of Iran Collection of Foundation for Iranian Studies.

35. Gholam Reza Afkhami, ed., *Barnamehrizi-ye Umrani va Tasmim Giri-e Siyasi* (Ideology, Process and Politics in Iran's Development Planning). *Interviews with Manu-*

chehr Gudarzi, Khodadad Farmanfarmaian, and Abdol-Majid Majidi (Washington, D.C.: Foundation for Iranian Studies, 1999).

36. See the interview of Manouchehr Goudarzi in the Oral History of Iran Collection of Foundation for Iranian Studies.

37. David Menashri, *Education and the Making of Modern Iran* (Ithaca, N.Y.: Cornell University Press, 1992).

38. Gasiorowski, *U.S. Foreign Policy and the Shah;* Ken Pollock, *The Persian Puzzle: The Conflict between Iran and America* (New York: Random House, 2004).

39. See the interviews of Armin Meyer and Richard Helms, former U.S. ambassadors to Iran, and of Gratian Yatsevitch, former CIA station chief in Iran, in the Oral History of Iran Collection of Foundation for Iranian Studies.

40. Mark J. Gasiorowski, "The Qarani Affair and Iranian Politics," *International Journal of Middle East Studies* 25:4 (November 1993): 625–44.

41. April R. Summitt, "For a White Revolution: John F. Kennedy and the Shah of Iran," *Middle East Journal* 58:4 (Autumn 2004): 560–75.

42. Nasr, "Politics within the Late-Pahlavi State," 97–122.

43. Charles Issawi, "The Iranian Economy 1925–1975: Fifty Years of Economic Development," in *Iran under the Pahlavis,* ed. George Lenczowski (Stanford, Calif.: Hoover Institution, 1978), 129–33; and Massoud Karshenas, *Oil, State, and Industrialization,* 110.

44. Bostock and Jones, *Planning and Power in Iran;* and the interviews of Abol-Hasan Ebtehaj and Khodadad Farmanfarmaian in the Iranian Oral History Collection of Harvard University, and Reza Niazmand in the Oral History of Iran Collection of Foundation for Iranian Studies.

45. On land reform, see Ann Lambton, *The Persian Land Reform: 1962–66* (Oxford: Clarendon Press, 1969); and Afsaneh Najmabadi, *Land Reform and Social Change in Iran* (Salt Lake City: University of Utah Press, 1987). Also see Habib Ladjevardi, ed., *Memoires of Ali Amini* (Boston: Iranian Oral History Project, Harvard University, 1995), 96–103.

46. Nasr, "Politics within the Late-Pahlavi State," 97–122.

47. Shaul Bakhash, *The Reign of the Ayatollahs: Iran and the Islamic Revolution* (New York: Basic Books, 1984).

48. Habib Ladjevardi, ed., *Memoires of Mehdi Haeri-Yazdi* (Boston: Iranian Oral History Project, Harvard University, 2001), 45–50.

49. Bakhash, *Reign of the Ayatollahs,* 33–35.

50. On intellectual developments during this period, see Hamid Dabashi, *Theology of Discontent: The Ideological Foundation of the Islamic Revolution in Iran* (New York: New York University Press, 1993); and Gheissari, *Iranian Intellectuals,* 74–108.

51. Maziar Behrooz, "The Iranian Revolution and the Legacy of the Guerrilla Movement," in *Reformers and Revolutionaries in Modern Iran,* ed. Stephanie Cronin (London: RoutledgeCurzon, 2004), 189–205.

52. Gholam Reza Afkhami, ed., *Siasat va Siyasatguzari-e Eqtesdi dar Iran, 1340–1350* (Ideology, Politics, and Process in Iran's Economic Development, 1960–1970). *Interview with Alinaghi Alikhani* (Washington, D.C.: Foundation for Iranian Studies, 2001).

53. Issawi, "Iranian Economy," 142–43, 150.

54. See Gholam Reza Afkhami's collection of interviews with key figures in Iran's Economic and Social Development, 1941–1978, especially *San'at-e Petroshimi-e Iran: az Aghaz ta Astane-e Enqelab* (The Evolution of Iran's Petrochemical Industry); *Interview with Baqer Mostowfi* (Washington, D.C.: Foundation for Iran Studies, 2001); and *Jame'e, Dowlat, va Jonbesh-e Zanen-e Iran, 1320–1357* (Women, State, and Society in Iran, 1941–1978). *Interview with Mehrangiz Dowlatshahi* (Washington, D.C.: 2002). Also see Habib Lajevardi, ed., *Memoires of Abdolmadjid Madjidi* (Boston: Iranian Oral History Project, Harvard University, 1998).

55. Borrowed from Anthony Parsons, *The Pride and the Fall: Iran, 1974–1979* (London: Jonathan Cape, 1984), 25.

56. On the Women's Organization of Iran, see Afkhami, *Jame'e, Dowlat, va Jonbesh-e Zanan-e Iran, 1342–1357*. On the Shiraz Art Festival, see interviews of Farrokh Ghaffari, Reza Qotbi, Arbi Ovanessian, and Seyyed Hossein Nasr in the Oral History of Iran Collection of Foundation for Iranian Studies.

57. See the interview of Reza Niazmand in the Oral History of Iran Collection of Foundation for Iranian Studies; and interviews of Mohammad Yeganeh and Abol-Qasem Kheradjou in the Iranian Oral History Collection of Harvard University.

58. On problems facing the Iranian economy during this period, see Jahangir Amuzegar, *The Dynamics of the Iranian Revolution: The Pahlavi's Triumph and Tragedy* (Albany: SUNY Press, 1991), esp. 181–82; Robert Looney, *Economic Origins of the Iranian Revolution* (New York: Pergamon Press, 1982); or M. H. Pesaran, "Economic Planning and Revolutionary Upheavals in Iran," in *Iran: A Revolution in Turmoil*, ed. Haleh Afshar (Albany: SUNY Press, 1985), 18. On criticisms of income inequality, see John Foran, *Fragile Resistance: Social Transformation in Iran from 1500 to the Revolution* (Boulder, Colo.: Westview Press, 1993), 309–58; Fred Halliday, *Iran: Dictatorship and Development* (London: Penguin Press, 1979); and Homa Katouzian, *The Political Economy of Modern Iran, 1926–79* (New York: New York University Press, 1981). On income inequality, see Asef Bayat, *Street Politics* (New York: Columbia University Press, 1997); and Farhad Kazemi, "Urban Migrants and the Revolution," *Iranian Studies* 13:1–4 (1980): 257–78.

59. Halliday, *Iran*, 138–72; Katouzian, *Political Economy*, 234–94.

60. McDaniel, *Autocracy, Modernization, and Revolution*.

61. See H. Mahdavy, "The Patterns and Problems of Economic Development in Rentier States: The Case of Iran," in *Studies in the Economic History of the Middle East: From the Rise of Islam to the Present Day*, ed. M. A. Cook (London: Oxford University Press, 1970), 428–67; Afsaneh Najmabadi, "Depoliticization of a Rentier State: The Case of Pahlavi Iran," in *The Rentier State*, ed. Hazem Beblawi and Giacomo Luciani (London: Croom Helm, 1987), 211–27; Theda Skocpol, "Rentier State and Shi'a Islam in the Iranian Revolution," *Theory and Society* 2:3 (May 1982): 265–83; Shahrough Akhavi, "Shi'ism, Corporatism, and Rentierism in the Iranian Revolution," in *Comparing Muslim Societies: Knowledge and the State in a World Civilization*, ed. Juan R. I. Cole (Ann Arbor: University of Michigan Press, 1992), 261–93.

62. Khosrow Fatemi, "Leadership by Distrust: The Shah's Modus Operandi," *Middle East Journal* 36:1 (Winter 1982): 49; and Alinaqi Alikhani, introduction to *The Shah*

and I: The Confidential Diary of Iran's Royal Court, Asadollah Alam, ed. Alinaqi Alikhani (New York: St. Martin's Press, 1991), 7–22.

63. This is seen by some analysts as a primary explanation of the revolution; see, for instance, Misagh Parsa, *Social Origins of the Iranian Revolution* (New Brunswick, N.J.: Rutgers University Press, 1989).

64. For these debates, see Donella H. Meadows et al., *The Limits to Growth: A Report for the Club of Rome's Project on the Predicament of Mankind* (New York: Universe Books, 1972); Ivan Illich, *Deschooling Society: Social Questions* (New York: Penguin Education, 1973); and Bryan S. Turner, ed., *The Talcott Parsons Reader* (Boston: Blackwell, 1999); and Huntington, *Political Order in Changing Societies*.

65. On the project to introduce democracy to the village of Alashtar in the Lorestan province, see the interviews of Majid Rahnema and Juni Farmanfarmaian in the Oral History of Iran Collection of Foundation for Iranian Studies.

66. Parvin Amini, "A Single Party State in Iran, 1975–78: The Rastakhiz Party—the Final Attempt by the Shah to Consolidate His Political Base," *Middle Eastern Studies*, 38: 1 (January 2002): 131–68. See interviews of Gholam Reza Afkhami, Mohammad Baheri, Ahmad Bani-Ahmad, and Ahmad Qoreishi in the Oral History of Iran Collection of Foundation for Iranian Studies.

67. Jerrold Green, *Revolution in Iran: The Politics of Countermobilization* (New York: Praeger, 1982).

68. James A. Bill, *The Eagle and the Lion: The Tragedy of American-Iranian Relations* (New Haven, Conn.: Yale University Press, 1988), 216–60.

69. Shahram Chubin, "Leftist Forces in Iran," *Problems of Communism* (September 1980): 1–25; Naqi Hamidian, *Safar ba Balha-ye Arezou: Sheklgiri-ye Jonbesh-e Cheriki-ye Fadaiyan-e Khalq* (Flight on the Wings of Hope: Formation of the Fadiyan-e Khalq Movement) (Stockholm: Arash Förlag, 2004).

70. Mansoor Moaddel, *Class, Politics, and Ideology in the Iranian Revolution* (New York: Columbia University Press, 1993).

71. Arjomand, *Turban for the Crown*; and Michael M. J. Fischer, *Iran, from Religious Dispute to Revolution* (Cambridge: Harvard University Press, 1980).

72. Hamid Dabashi, "The Poetics of Politics: Commitment in Modern Persian Literature," *Iranian Studies* 18:2–4 (Spring–Autumn 1985): 147–88.

73. Ahmad Karimi-Hakkak, "Protest and Perish: A History of the Writers' Association of Iran," *Iranian Studies* 18:2–4 (Spring–Autumn 1985): 189–229; Gheissari, *Iranian Intellectuals*, 109–11.

74. For more on this topic, see Gheissari, *Iranian Intellectuals*, 111–13; and Ali Gheissari, "Naqd-e Adab-e Ide'olojik: Morouri bar Adabiyat-e Rowshanfekri va Maktabi-ye Iran" (Critique of Ideological Literature: A Review of Intellectual and Doctrinaire Writings in Iran), *Iran Nameh* 12:2 (Spring 1994): 233–58.

75. For instance, in 1979 Iran had close to 50,000 students in the United States alone. On education and student politics, see Menashri, *Education and Development*; and interviews of Faraj Ardalan, Ali Shakeri, Farah Ebrahimi, Mansour Farhang, and Amir Hossein Ganjbakhsh in the Oral History of Iran Collection of Foundation for Iranian Studies.

76. Interviews of Hasan Nazih and Abdol-Karim Lahiji in the Iranian Oral History Project of Harvard University.

77. Benjamin Smith, "Collective Action With or Without Islam: Mobilizing the Bazaar in Iran," in Quintan Wicktorowicz, *Islamic Activism: A Social Movement Theory Approach* (Bloomington: Indiana University Press, 2004), 185–204.

78. Gheissari, *Iranian Intellectuals*, 115–19; and Ali Mirsepassi, *Intellectual Discourse and the Politics of Modernization: Negotiating Modernity in Iran* (New York: Cambridge University Press, 2000).

79. Afshin Matin-Asgari, *Iranian Student Opposition to the Shah* (Costa Mesa, Calif.: Mazda, 2001); Bizhan Jazani, *Armed Struggle in Iran* (n.p., 1973); and *Jongi darbareh-ye Zendegi va Asar-e Bijan Jazani: Majmoue'eh-e Maqalat* (A Compendium on Bijan Jazani's Life and Works: Collection of Essays) (Paris: Editions Khavaran, 1999).

80. See Azar Salamat, "Of Chance and Choice," in *Women in Exile*, ed. Mahnaz Afkhami (Charlottesville: University of Virginia Press, 1994), 85–86; Shahrough Akhavi, "Ideology and the Iranian Revolution," introduction to *Iran since the Revolution: Internal Dynamics, Regional Conflicts and the Superpowers*, ed. Barry M. Rosen (New York: Columbia University Press, 1985), xviii.

81. Hamid Algar, *Islam and Revolution: Writings and Declarations of Imam Khomeini (1941–1980)* (Berkeley, Calif.: Mizan Press, 1981); Moin, *Khomeini*; Vanessa Martin, *Creating an Islamic State: Khomeini and the Making of a New Iran* (London: I. B. Tauris, 2003); Abdulaziz Sachedina, *The Just Ruler (Al-Sultan Al-Adil) in Shi'ite Islam: The Comprehensive Authority of the Jurist in Imamite Jurisprudence* (New York: Oxford University Press, 1988); and Dabashi, *Theology of Discontent*, 409–84.

82. See Said Amir Arjomand, "Ideological Revolution in Shi'ism," in *Authority and Political Culture*, 178–209; see also the interview of Mehdi Haeri-Yazdi in the Oral History of Iran Collection of Foundation for Iranian Studies; and Seyyed Mehdi Haeri-Yazdi, *Hekmat va Hokoumat* (Reason and Governance) (London, 1995).

83. Abdulaziz Sachedina, *Islamic Messianism: The Idea of the Mahdi in Twelver Shi'ism* (Albany: SUNY Press, 1981).

84. On traditional or quietist Shi'ism, see Ann Lambton, *State and Government in Medieval Islam: An Introduction to the Study of Islamic Political Theory of the Jurists* (London: Oxford University Press, 1981), 220–41; Enayat, *Modern Islamic Political Thought*, 160–94; W. M. Floor, "The Revolutionary Character of the Ulama: Wishful Thinking or Reality?" in *Religion and Politics in Iran*, ed. Nikki Keddie (New Haven, Conn.: Yale University Press, 1983), 73–97; and Said Amir Arjomand, "Religion, Political Action, and Legitimate Domination in Shi'ite Iran: Fourteenth to Eighteenth Centuries A.D." *Archives Europeenes De Sociologie* 20:1 (1979): 59–109.

85. Arjomand, "Ideological Revolution in Shi'ism," 178–209; and David Menashri, "Shi'ite Leadership: In the Shadow of Conflicting Ideologies," *Iranian Studies* 13:1–4 (1980): 119–46.

86. Ali Rahnema, *An Islamic Utopian: A Political Biography of Ali Shariati* (London: I.B. Tauris, 1998), 88–130; see Dabashi, *Theology of Discontent*, 61–108, and Gheissari, *Iranian Intellectuals*, 97–107.

87. Enayat, *Modern Islamic Political Thought*, 53–59.

88. Ali Shariati, *Shia* (Shi'ism) (London: MAS, 1979); and Ali Shariati, *Red Shi'ism* (London: n.p., 1979). Also see Gheissari, *Iranian Intellectuals*, 101–5.

89. Ervand Abrahamian, *Radical Islam: The Iranian Mojahedin* (New Haven, Conn.: Yale University Press, 1989).

90. Kamran Scot Aghaie, *The Martyrs of Karbala: Shi'i Symbols and Rituals in Modern Iran* (Seattle: University of Washington Press, 2004), 93–100. See further Ahmad Kazemi Moussavi, "A New Interpretation of the Theory of *Vilayet-i Faqih*," in *Middle Eastern Studies* 28:1 (January 1992): 101.

91. Vali Nasr's interview with Ayatollah Seyyed Mehdi Haeri-Yazdi, who mentioned that many senior ulama were unhappy with Beheshti and Mofatteh's roles in the Revolutionary Council after the revolution, Washington, D.C., October 1989.

92. For details of the revolution, see Charles Kurzman, *The Unthinkable Revolution in Iran* (Cambridge: Harvard University Press, 2004).

93. Interview of Daryush Homayoun in the Oral History of Iran Program of Foundation for Iranian Studies.

94. Charles Kurzman, "The Qum Protests and the Coming of the Iranian Revolution, 1975 and 1978," *Social Science History* 27:3 (September 2003): 287–325.

95. Interview of General Hasan Toufanian in the Oral History of Iran Program of Foundation for Iranian Studies.

96. Interview of Shapur Bakhtiar with the Iranian Oral History Project of Harvard University.

97. Robert E. Huyser, *Mission to Tehran* (New York: HarperCollins, 1987).

98. Bellin, "Robustness of Authoritarianism"; Brumberg, "The Trap of Liberalized Autocracy," 35–47.

99. See the interviews of Generals Hasan Toufanian, Mohsen Hashemi-Nejad, Abdol-Majid Masoumi-Na'ini, Mansour Qadar, and Ahmad-Ali Mohaqqeqi in the Oral History of Iran Collection of Foundation for Iranian Studies; and Admiral Kamal Habibollahi with the Iranian Oral History Collection of Harvard University.

100. Marvin Zonis, *Majestic Failure: The Fall of the Shah* (Chicago: University of Chicago Press, 1991); and H. E. Chehabi, "The Provisional Government and the Transition from Monarchy to Islamic Republic in Iran," in *Between States: Interim Governments and Democratic Transitions*, ed. Yossi Shain and Juan Linz (New York: Cambridge University Press, 1995), 127–43.

101. Sir Denis Wright, *Britain and Iran, 1790–1980: Collected Essays of Sir Denis Wright* (London: Iran Society, 2003), 155. See also Zonis, *Majestic Failure*; and Chehabi, "Provisional Government and the Transition from Monarchy to Islamic Republic in Iran."

CHAPTER 3

1. For "war communism," see Sheila Fitzpatrick, *The Russian Revolution* (New York: Oxford University Press, 1982), 78–82; Alec Nove, "War Communism," in *The Blackwell Encyclopedia of the Russian Revolution*, 2nd ed., ed. Harold Shukman, (Oxford: Blackwell, 1994), 148–50. For a fuller treatment of this topic, see Edward Hallett Carr, *A History of Soviet Russia: The Bolshevik Revolution (1917–1923)*, Vol. 2 (New York: W. W. Norton, 1985), 147–268.

2. R. K. Ramazani, *Revolutionary Iran: Challenge and Response in the Middle East* (Baltimore: Johns Hopkins University Press, 1988).

3. John L. Esposito, ed., *The Iranian Revolution: Its Global Impact* (Gainesville: University Press of Florida, 1990); and Nikki Keddie and Rudi Mathee, eds., *Iran and the Surrounding World: Interactions in Culture and Cultural Politics* (Seattle: University of Washington Press, 2002).

4. Mehdi Mozaffari, *Fatwa: Violence and Discourtesy* (Aarhus: Aarhus University Press, 1998).

5. Karim Sanjabi, *Omidha va Na-Omidiha: Khaterat-e Siyasi Doktor Karim Sanjabi* (Hopes and Disappointments: The Political Memoirs of Dr. Karim Sanjabi) (London: n.p., 1989); and the interviews of Karim Sanjabi in the Iranian Oral History Project of Harvard University, and of Ali Shakeri in the Oral History of Iran Program of Foundation for Iranian Studies.

6. Shahram Chubin, "Leftist Forces in Iran," *Problems of Communism* (September 1980): 1–24.

7. On urban guerrilla movements, see Ervand Abrahamian, "The Guerrilla Movements in Iran, 1963–1977," *MERIP* 86 (March–April 1980): 3–15.

8. Interview of Mehdi Khanbaba-Tehrani in Iranian Oral History Project of Harvard University; Siavosh Bashiri, *Qesseh-ye Savak* (The Story of SAVAK) (Paris: n.p., 1991).

9. See Moaddel, *Class, Politics, and Ideology.*

10. Hamid Dabashi, " 'Islamic Ideology': The Perils and Promises of a Neologism," in *Post-Revolutionary Iran,* ed. Hooshang Amirahmadi and Manouchehr Parvin (Boulder, Colo.: Westview, 1988), 11–21.

11. Fischer, *Iran, from Religious Dispute to Revolution*; Michael M. J. Fischer, "Becoming Mollah: Reflections on Iranian Clerics in a Revolutionary Age," *Iranian Studies* 13: 1–4 (1980): 83–118; and Roy Mottahedeh, *Mantle of the Prophet: Religion and Politics in Iran* (New York: Simon & Schuster, 1985). Also see Ali-Akbar Hashemi-Rafsanjani, *Dowran-e Mobarezeh* (Period of Struggle), ed. Mohsen Hashemi (Tehran: n.p., 1997).

12. Mangol Bayat, "Mahmud Taleqani and the Iranian Revolution," in *Shi'ism, Resistance and Revolution,* ed. Martin Kramer (Boulder, Colo.: Westview Press, 1987), 67–94.

13. Hamid Dabashi, *Theology of Discontent,* 216–72; Sayyid Mahmud Taleqani, *Islam and Ownership,* trans. Ahmad Jabbari and Farhang Rajaee (Lexington, Ky.: Mazda, 1983).

14. On Khomeini's life and thought, see Moin, *Khomeini.*

15. Ervand Abrahamian, *Khomeinism: Essays on the Islamic Republic* (Berkeley: University of California Press, 1993).

16. Many of these pictures were later published in a book with an anonymous author titled *Mofsedin-e fi al-Arz* (Polluters of the Earth) (Tehran: n.p., n.d.).

17. For a discussion on the implications of this attitude in economic planning, see Jahangir Amuzegar, *Iran's Economy under the Islamic Republic* (London: I. B. Tauris, 1993).

18. On Khomeini's views, see Algar, *Islam and Revolution*; also see Abol-Hasan Bani Sadr, *The Fundamental Principles and Precepts of Islamic Government,* trans. Mo-

hammad R. Ghanoonparvar (Lexington, Ky.: Mazda, 1981); Dabashi, *Theology of Discontent*, 409–84; Moin, *Khomeini*; Vanessa Martin, *Creating an Islamic State*; Hamid Mavani, "Analysis of Khomeini's Proofs for al-Wilaya al-Mutlaqa (Comprehensive Authority) of the Jurist," in *The Most Learned of the Shi'a: The Institution of Marja' Taqlid*, ed. Linda S. Walbridge (New York: Oxford University Press, 2001), 183–201.

19. See, in this regard, Ishtiaq Ahmed, *The Concept of an Islamic State: An Analysis of the Ideological Controversy in Pakistan* (New York: St. Martin's Press, 1987); L. Carl Brown, *Religion and State: The Muslim Approach to Politics* (New York: Columbia University Press, 2000); Seyyed Vali Reza Nasr, "Ideology and Institutions in Islamist Approaches to Public Policy," *International Review of Comparative Public Policy* 9 (1997): 41–67.

20. On Mawdudi, see Seyyed Vali Reza Nasr, *Mawdudi and the Making of Islamic Revivalism* (New York: Oxford University Press, 1996).

21. Hamid Enayat, "Iran: Khumayni's Concept of the 'Guardianship of the Jurisconsult,'" in *Islam in the Political Process*, ed. James Piscatori (New York: Cambridge University Press, 1983), 160–80.

22. Dabashi, *Theology of Discontent*, 409–84; and Daniel Brumberg, "Khomeini's Legacy: Islamic Rule and Islamic Social Justice," in *Spokesmen for the Despised*, ed. R. Scott Appleby (Chicago: University of Chicago Press, 1997), 16–82.

23. Arjomand, *Shadow of God*; Said A. Arjomand, "The State and Khomeini's Islamic Order," *Iranian Studies* 13:1–4 (1980): 147–64.

24. For a discussion of its effects on the Iranian revolution, see, for example, Yann Richard, *Shi'ite Islam* (Cambridge, Mass.: Blackwell, 1995), 27–32.

25. See the various essays in Peter J. Chelkowski, ed., *Taziyeh: Ritual and Drama in Iran* (New York: New York University Press, 1979).

26. For further discussion, see Haggay Ram, *Myth and Mobilization in Revolutionary Iran: The Use of The Friday Congregational Sermon* (Washington, D.C.: American University Press, 1994).

27. David Menashri, *Iran: A Decade of War and Revolution* (New York: Holmes & Meier, 1990), 112–15.

28. Kaveh Ehsani, "Prospects for Democratization in Iran," paper delivered at Concordia University, Montreal, November 2004.

29. For a detailed overview of the early years of the revolution, see Shaul Bakhash, *The Reign of the Ayatollahs: Iran and the Islamic Revolution* (New York: Basic Books, 1984). On the revolutionary committees, see 56–59.

30. Ibid, 63; Kenneth Katzman, *The Warriors of Islam: Iran's Revolutionary Guard* (Boulder, Colo.: Westview Press, 1993).

31. Bakhash, *Reign of the Ayatollahs*, 59–63. Also see the memoirs of a notoriously ruthless revolutionary judge, Sadeq Khalkhali, *Ayyam Enzeva: Khaterat Ayatollah Khalkhali* (Days of Seclusion: Memoirs of Ayatollah Khalkhali) (Tehran: 1378/2000).

32. Amuzegar, *Iran's Economy under the Islamic Republic*, 26–39; and Vahid Nowshirvani and Patrick Clawson, "The State and Social Equity in Postrevolutionary Iran," in *The Politics of Social Transformation in Afghanistan, Iran and Pakistan*, ed. Myron Weiner and Ali Banuazizi (Syracuse, N.Y.: Syracuse University Press, 1994), 254–57.

33. Mohammad-Hossein Beheshti, *Eqtesad-e Eslami* (Islamic Economics) (Tehran:

n.p., 1370/1990). For further discussion, see Cyrus Bina and Hamid Zanganeh, *Modern Capitalism and Islamic Ideology in Iran* (New York: St. Martin's Press, 1992).

34. Bakhash, *Reign of the Ayatollahs,* 72–73.

35. Ibid., 75–88.

36. On the constitution, see Schirazi, *The Constitution of Iran.*

37. Shahrough Akhavi, "Iran: Implementation of an Islamic State," in John L. Esposito, ed., *Islam in Asia* (New York: Oxford University Press, 1987), 27–52.

38. Quoted in Bakhash, *Reign of Ayatollahs,* 75.

39. Interview of leftist activist Bahram Khozai, in the Oral Collection of Iran Program of Foundation for Iranian Studies.

40. Sussan Siavoshi, *Liberal Nationalism in Iran: The Failure of a Movement* (Boulder, Colo.: Westview Press, 1990), 129–72.

41. Ervand Abrahamian, *Radical Islam: The Iranian Mojahedin* (New Haven: Yale University Press), 206–23.

42. See Pierre Salinger, *America Held Hostage: The Secret Negotiations* (New York: Doubleday, 1981); Warren Christopher, ed., *American Hostages in Iran* (New Haven, Conn.: Yale University Press, 1985); Amir Taheri, *Nest of Spies: America's Journey to Disaster in Iran* (London: Hutchinson, 1988); Gary Sick, *All Fall Down: America's Tragic Encounter with Iran* (New York: Penguin Books, 1986); David Farber, *Taken Hostage: The Iran Hostage Crisis and America's First Encounter with Radical Islam* (Princeton, N.J.: Princeton University Press, 2004); William O. Beeman, *The "Great Satan" vs. the "Mad Mullahs": How the United States and Iran Demonized Each Other* (Westport, Conn.: Praeger, 2005).

43. For an insider's account see Massoumeh Ebtekar, *Takeover in Tehran: The Inside Story of the 1979 U.S. Embassy Capture* (New York: Talon Books, 2001).

44. Interview of Mansour Farhang with the Oral History Collection of Foundation for Iranian Studies.

45. Ebrahim Yazdi, *Akharin Talash-ha dar Akharin Rouzha* (Last Efforts in the Last Days) (Tehran: Roshdieh, 1987).

46. Rouhollah K. Ramazani, "Iran: The Islamic Cultural Revolution," in *Change and the Muslim World,* ed. Phillip Stoddard, David Cuthell, and Margaret Sullivan (Syracuse, N.Y.: Syracuse University Press, 1981), 40–48.

47. On the scale of the campaign of violence, see Soroush Irfani, *Iran's Islamic Revolution: Popular Liberation or Religious Dictatorship* (London: Zed Books, 1983).

48. Haggay Ram, "Crushing the Opposition: Adversaries of the Islamic Republic of Iran," *Middle East Journal* 46:3 (Summer 1992): 426–39.

49. See Ervand Abrahamian, *Tortured Confessions: Prisons and Public Recantations in Modern Iran* (Berkeley: University of California Press, 1999); Salamat, "Of Chance and Choice," 85–86.

50. Abrahamian, *Tortured Confessions,* 177–208.

51. On the executions, see ibid., 209–28.

52. On the war, see Shahram Chubin and Charles Tripp, *Iran and Iraq at War* (London: I. B. Tauris, 1989); and Efraim Karsh, *The Iran-Iraq War, 1980–1988* (London: Osprey, 2002).

53. Charles Tilly, "War Making and State Making as Organized Crime," in *Bringing the State Back In,* ed. Peter Evans, Dietrich Rueschmeyer, and Theda Skocpol (New

York: Cambridge University Press, 1985), 169–91; Michael Mann, *The Sources of Social Power*, Vol. 1, *A History of Power from the Beginning to A.D. 1760* (Cambridge: Cambridge University Press, 1986).

54. Joel S. Migdal, *Strong Societies and Weak States*.

55. Charles Tilly, "Reflections on the History of European State-Making," in *The Formation of National States in Western Europe*, ed. Charles Tilly (Princeton, N.J.: Princeton University Press, 1975), 42. Also, see Michael N. Barnett, *Confronting the Costs of War: Military Power, State, and Society in Egypt and Israel* (Princeton, N.J.: Princeton University Press, 1992).

56. Farhad Khosrokhavar, *L'islamisme et la mort. Le martyre révolutionnaire en Iran* (Paris: Harmattan, 1995).

57. Menashri, *Iran: Decade of War and Revolution*, 217–361.

58. Arjomand, *Turban for the Crown*, 167–68.

59. H. E. Chehabi, "Religion and Politics in Iran: How Theocratic Is the Islamic Republic?" *Dædalus* 120:3 (Summer 1991): 69–92.

60. Arjomand, *Turban for the Crown*, 169.

61. Ibid.

62. Shahrough Akhavi, "Clerical Politics in Iran Since 1979," in *The Iranian Revolution and the Islamic Republic*, ed. Nikki Keddie and Eric Hooglund (Syracuse, N.Y.: Syracuse University Press, 1986), 57–73.

63. Shahram Chubin, "The Islamic Republic's Foreign Policy in the Gulf," in *Shi'ism, Resistance and Revolution*, ed. Martin Kramer (Boulder, Colo.: Westview Press, 1987), 159–72.

64. Mehdi Moslem, *Factional Politics in Post-Khomeini Iran* (Syracuse, N.Y.: Syracuse University Press, 2002), 62–70.

65. Bahman Bakhtiari. *Parliamentary Politics in Revolutionary Iran: The Institutionalization of Factional Politics* (Gainesville: University of Florida Press, 1996), 99–234.

66. On these debates, see Shaul Bakhash, "Islam and Social Justice in Iran," in *Shi'ism: Resistance and Revolution*, ed. Martin Kramer (Boulder, Colo.: Westview Press, 1987), 95–115; Shaul Bakhash, "The Politics of Land, Law, and Social Justice in Iran," *Middle East Journal* 43:2 (Spring 1989): 186–201; Mansour Moaddel, "Class Struggle in Post-Revolutionary Iran." *International Journal of Middle East Studies* 23:3 (August 1991): 317–43; and Fatemeh Moghadam, "State, Political Stability, and Property Rights," in *Iran after the Revolution: Crisis of an Islamic State*, ed. Saeed Rahnema and Sohrab Behdad (London: I. B. Tauris, 1995), 45–64.

67. Moslem, *Factional Politics*, 47–80.

68. Hooshang Amirahmadi, *Revolution and Economic Transition: The Iranian Experience* (Albany: SUNY Press, 1990); and Sohrab Behdad, "The Post-Revolutionary Economic Crisis," in *Iran After the Revolution*, ed. Saeed Rahnema and Sohrab Behdad (London: I. B. Tauris, 1995), 97–128.

69. Amuzegar, *Iran's Economy under the Islamic Republic*, 269–309.

70. On the Moussavi period, see Anoushiravan Ehteshami, *After Khomeini: The Iranian Second Republic* (New York: Routledge, 1995), 77–99.

71. Jahangir Amuzegar, "The Iranian Economy before and after the Revolution," *Middle East Journal* 46:3 (Summer 1992): 418.

72. Akhavi, "Shi'ism, Corporatism, and Rentierism," 261–93.

73. Amuzegar, "Iranian Economy," 418; also see Nowshirvani and Clawson, "The State and Social Equity," 239–54.

74. Amuzegar, *Iran's Economy under the Islamic Republic,* 64–65.

75. Amuzegar, "Iranian Economy," 418.

76. Ibid., 419.

77. Djavad Salehi-Isfahani, "The Oil Sector after the Revolution," in *Iran after the Revolution: Crisis of an Islamic State,* ed. Saeed Rahnema and Sohrab Behdad (London: I. B. Tauris, 1995), 150–73.

78. Massoud Karshenas and Hassan Hakimian, "Oil, Economic Diversification, and Democratic Process in Iran," *Iranian Studies* 38:1 (March 2005): 68–71.

79. Ibid., 69.

CHAPTER 4

1. On the concept of Thermidor, see Crane Brinton, *The Anatomy of Revolution* (New York: Vintage Books, 1965); on its application to Iran, see Fariba Adelkhah, Jean-François Bayart, and Olivier Roy, *Thermidor en Iran* (Brussels: Complexe, 1993).

2. For discussions of the "developmental state" see Önis, "The Logic of the Developmental State," 109–26; Stephan Haggard, *Pathways from the Periphery: The Politics of Growth in the Newly Industrializing Countries* (Ithaca, N.Y.: Cornell University Press, 1990); and Peter Evans, *Embedded Autonomy.*

3. Saeed Rahnema, "Continuity and Change in Industrial Policy," in *Iran after the Revolution: Crisis of an Islamic State,* ed. Saeed Rahnema and Sohrab Behdad (London: I. B. Tauris, 1995), 129–49; Mansour Bitaraf, "Eslahat-e Eqtesadi Pas az Jang Ejtenabnapazir Boud" (Economic Reforms after the War Were Inevitable), *Iran,* December 3, 2005, available at http://www.iran-newspaper.com/1384/840912/html/iraneconomic.htm#s550905

4. Azadeh Kian-Thiébaut, "Political and Social Transformation in Post-Islamist Iran," *MERIP* 212 (Fall 1999): 12–16.

5. Chehabi, "Religion and Politics in Iran," 69–92.

6. On factionalism during the Rafsanjani period, see David Menashri, *Post-Revolutionary Politics in Iran: Religion, Society, and Power* (London: Frank Cass, 2001), 47–77.

7. See the interview of Eslam Kazemieh in the Oral History of Iran Collection of Foundation for Iranian Studies.

8. Juan Cole, *Sacred Space and Holy War: The Politics, Culture, and History of Shi'ite Islam* (London: I. B Tauris, 2002), 233–47.

9. Farzin Sarabi, "The Post-Khomeini Era in Iran: The Elections of the Fourth Islamic Majles," *Middle East Journal* 48:1 (Winter 1994): 89–107.

10. On supervisory councils, see Wilfried Buchta, *Who Rules Iran? The Structure of Power in the Islamic Republic* (Washington, D.C.: Washington Institute for Near East Policy, 2000), 59–63.

11. Amuzegar, *Iran's Economy under the Islamic Republic,* 48.

12. Mohsen Milani, "The Transformation of Velayet-e Faqih Institution: From Kho-

meini to Khamenei," *Muslim World* 82:2–3 (July–October 1992): 175–90; and Mohsen Milani, "The Evolution of the Iranian Presidency: From Bani Sadr to Rafsanjani," *British Journal of Middle Eastern Studies* 2 (1993): 82–89.

13. Schirazi, *The Constitution of Iran*, 52–55.

14. Kazemi Moussavi, "A New Interpretation of the Theory of Velayat-i Faqih," 101–7.

15. David Menashri, *Post-Revolutionary Politics in Iran: Religion, Society, and Power* (London: Frank Cass, 2001), 64.

16. *Sarab-e Sazandegi: Didgahha-ye Enteqadi Dar Bare-ye Amalkard-e Hasht-Sale-ye Dowlat-e Hashemi Rafsanjani* (The Mirage of Development: Critical Perspectives on the Record of the Eight-Year Government of Hashemi Rafsanjani) (Tehran: Rozname-ye Salaam, 1378/1998).

17. For a critical assessment of Rafsanjani's policies, see Akbar Ganji, *Alijenab-e Sorkhpoush va 'Alijenaban-e Khakestari: Asib-shenasi-ye Gozar be Dowlat-e Demokratik-e Towse'e-gera* (The Red Eminence and the Gray Eminences: Pathology of Transition to the Developmental Democratic State) (Tehran: Tarh-e No, 1378/1998).

18. Habib Davaran and Farhad Behbahani, *Do Khatereh az Zendan: Dar Mehmani-ye Hajji Aqa va Dastan-e Yek E'teraf dar Sal-e 1369* (Two Prison Memoirs: In the Party of Hajj Aqa and the Story of a Confession in 1990) (Tehran: Omid-e Farda, 1382/2003). For the full text of the letter, see 318–25.

19. See the interview of former Foreign Minister Ali-Akbar Velayati with *Baztab*, May 1, 2005, available at http://baztab.com/news/23783.ph

20. Jahangir Amuzegar, "Iran's Economy and the U.S. Sanctions," *Middle East Journal* 51:2 (Spring 1997): 185–99; and Jahangir Amuzegar, "Adjusting to Sanctions," *Foreign Affairs* (May/June 1997): 31–41.

21. Amirahmadi, *Revolution and Economic Transition*, 231–34.

22. Ibid., 294; and Karshenas and Hakimian, "Oil, Economic Diversification and Democratic Process."

23. Amuzegar, *Iran's Economy*, 75.

24. Firouzeh Khalatbari, "A Unique Underground Economy," in *The Economy of Islamic Iran: Between State and Market*, ed. Thierry Coville (Tehran: Institut Français de recherches en Iran, 1994), 113–38.

25. Behdad, "The Post-Revolutionary Economic Crisis," 97–128; and Mohsen M. Milani, *The Making of Iran's Islamic Revolution: From Monarchy to Islamic Republic*, 2nd ed. (Boulder, Colo.: Westview Press, 1994), 219–42.

26. Amirahmadi, *Revolution and Economic Transition*, 235–90.

27. Ehsani, "Prospects for Democracy in Iran."

28. Masserat Amir-Ebrahimi, "L'image socio-géographique de Téhéran en 1986" (A Socio-Geographic Picture of Tehran in 1986), in *Téhéran: Capitale bicentenaire*, ed. Bernard Hourcade and Chahryar Adle (Tehran: The Two-Hundred Year Old Capital) (Paris: Institut français de recherche en Iran, 1992), 267–79; and Farhad Khosrokhavar, "Nouvelle banlieu et marginalité: la cité Taleghani à Khak-e Sefid" (New Suburbs and Marginality: The Taleqani City of Khak-e Sefid), in *Téhéran: Capitale bicentenaire*, ed. Bernard Hourcade and Chahryar Adle (Tehran: The Two-Hundred Year Old Capital) (Paris: Institut français de recherche en Iran, 1992), 307–27.

29. Djavad Salehi-Isfahani, "Human Resources in Iran: Potentials and Challenges," *Iranian Studies* 38:1 (March 2005): 125–30.

30. Ali Rabi'i, *Negah be Jame'e-Shenasi-ye Tahavvolat-e Arzeshi* (An Overview of Sociology of Transformation in Values) (Tehran: Farhang va Andisheh, 1997), 134–49.

31. Ibid.

32. Farhad Khosrokhavar, Shapour Etemad, and Masoud Mehrabi, "Report on Science in Post-Revolutionary Iran," Parts 1 and 2: "Emergence of a Scientific Community?" and "The Scientific Community's Problems of Identity," *Critique: Critical Middle Eastern Studies* 13:2,3 (Summer, Fall 2004): 209–24, 363–382.

33. Gawdat Bahgat, "The New Iran: A Myth or Reality?" *Asian Affairs* 85:2 (June 1998): 143.

34. On Iran's foreign policy during this period, see Mark Gasiorowski and Nikki Keddie, eds., *Neither East nor West: Iran, the Soviet Union, and the United States* (New Haven, Conn.: Yale University Press, 1990); and Mehdi Mozaffari, "Revolutionary, Thermidorian, and Enigmatic Foreign Policy," *International Relations* 14:5 (1999): 9–28.

35. Amuzegar, *Iran's Economy under the Islamic Republic*, 61.

36. On Soroush's works, see Abdol-Karim Soroush, *Bast-e Tajrobeh-ye Nabavi* (Expansion of the Prophetic Experience) (Tehran: Serat, 1999); Soroush, *Reason, Freedom, and Democracy in Islam*; Valla Vakili, "Abdolkarim Soroush and the Critical Discourse in Iran," in *Makers of Contemporary Islam*, ed. John Esposito and John Voll (New York: Oxford University Press, 2001), 150–76; and Mehrzad Boroujerdi, *Iranian Intellectuals and the West: The Tormented Triumph of Nativism* (Syracuse, N.Y.: Syracuse University Press, 1996), 156–75; Farzin Vahdat, *God and Juggernaut: Iran's Intellectual Encounter with Modernity* (Syracuse, N.Y.: Syracuse University Press, 2002), 198–211.

37. See, for instance, Abdol-Karim Soroush, *Modara va Modiriyat* (Tolerance and Administration) (Tehran: Serat, 1997).

38. Ali Gheissasi and Vali Nasr, "The Democracy Debate in Iran," *Middle East Policy Journal* 11:2 (Summer 2004): 94–106.

39. Ibid.

40. Farhad Khosrokhavar, "Neo-Conservative Intellectuals in Iran," *Critique* 19 (Fall 2001): 5–30; Mohammad-Said Bahmanpour, "Jashn-e Khatm-e Din ra Gerefte'id na Khatm-e Nobovvat" (You Are Celebrating the End of Religion, Not the Seal of Prophecy), *Baztab*, September 3, 2005, available at http://www.baztab.com/news/28559.php

41. Amirahmadi, *Revolution and Economic Transition*, 236–59.

42. Amuzegar, *Iran's Economy*, 49–51.

43. Anoushiravan Ehteshami, *After Khomeini: The Iranian Second Republic* (New York: Routledge, 1995), 100.

44. On this period, see, further, Bahman Ahmadi Amouie, *Eqtesad-e Siyasi Jomhouri Eslami* (Political Economy of the Islamic Republic) (Tehran: Gam-e No, 1380/2002).

45. Ali Rahnema and Farhad Nomani, *The Secular Miracle: Religion, Politics, and Economic Policy in Iran* (London: Zed Books, 1990).

46. Kamal Asari, "Eqtesad-e Iran, Goriz az Tangnaha" (Iran's Economy, Escaping Constraints), *Ettela'at-e Siyasi Eqtesadi* 32 (1989): 38–47.

47. H. E. Chehabi, "Ardebil Becomes Province: Center-Periphery Relations in Iran," *International Journal of Middle East Studies* 29:2 (May 1997): 235–53.

48. Sohrab Behdad, "The Political Economy of Islamic Planning in Iran," in *Post-Revolutionary Iran*, ed. Hooshang Amirahmadi and Monouchehr Parvin (Boulder, Colo.: Westview Press, 1988), 107–25.

49. Ehteshami, *After Khomeini*, 103.

50. Firouzeh Khalatbari, "The Tehran Stock Exchange and Privatisation," in *The Economy of the Islamic Iran*, ed. Thierry Coville (Tehran: Institut Français de recherches en Iran, 1994), 177–208; and Ahmad R. Jalali-Naini, "Capital Accumulation and Economic Growth in Iran: Past Experience and Future Prospects," *Iranian Studies* 38:1 (March 2005): 109.

51. Karshenas and Hakimian, "Oil, Economic Diversification and Democratic Process," 77; and Massoud Karshenas and M. Hashem Pesaran, "Exchange Rate Unification, the Role of Markets, and Planning in Iranian Economic Reconstruction," in *The Economy of the Islamic Iran*, ed. Thierry Coville (Tehran: Institut Français de recherches en Iran, 1994), 141–76.

52. Ehteshami, *After Khomeini*, 105–8.

53. Ibid., 112–13.

54. Amuzegar, *Iran's Economy*, 269–326.

55. Ali Rashidi, "The Process of De-Privatisation," in *The Economy of the Islamic Iran*, ed. Thierry Coville (Tehran: Institut Français de recherches en Iran, 1994), 37–68.

56. Bijan Khajehpour, "Domestic Political Reforms and Private Sector Activity in Iran," *Social Research* 67:2 (Summer 2000): 577–98.

57. On the development of the housing sector market, see Kamal Athari, "The Housing Sector in Iran," in *The Economy of the Islamic Iran*, ed. Thierry Coville (Tehran: Institut Français de recherches en Iran, 1994), 253–60.

58. Kaveh Ehsani, "Municipal Matters: The Urbanization of Consciousness and Political Change," *MERIP* 212 (Autumn 1999): 22–27.

59. Ehteshami, *After Khomeini*, 103–4.

60. Suzanne Maloney, "Agents or Obstacles? Parastatal Foundations and Challenges for Iranian Development," in *The Economy of Iran: Dilemmas of an Islamic State* (London: I. B. Tauris, 2001), ed. Parvin Alizadeh, 145–76; Hooshang Amirahmadi, "Bunyad," in *The Encyclopedia of the Modern Islamic World*, ed. John L. Esposito (New York: Oxford University Press), 1, 234–37; "Bonyad-e Shahid," in *Encyclopedia Iranica*, ed. Ehsan Yarshater (Costa Mesa, Calif.: Mazda, 1987), 2, 36–61; and Ahmad Mawlawi, Mohammad T. Mostafawi, and Ali Shahrukhzadeh, "Astan-e Qods-e Razavi," in *Encyclopedia Iranica*, ed. Ehsan Yarshater (Costa Mesa, Calif.: 1987), 2, 826–37.

61. Ali Ansari, *Iran, Islam and Democracy: The Politics of Managing Change* (London: Royal Institute of International Affairs, 2000), 52–81.

62. Ibid, 60.

63. Ibid.

64. Asghar Schirazi, *The Islamic Development Policy: The Agrarian Question in Iran* (Boulder, Colo.: Lynne Rienner, 1993).

65. David Menashri, "Strange Bedfellows: The Khomeini Coalition," *Jerusalem Quarterly* 12 (Summer 1979): 34–48.

66. Farah Azari, "The Post-Revolutionary Women's Movement in Iran," in *Women of Iran: Conflict with Fundamentalism*, ed. Farah Azari (London: Ithaca Press, 1983), 190–225; and Guity Nashat, "Women in the Ideology of the Islamic Republic," in *Women and the Revolution in Iran*, ed. Guity Nashat (Boulder, Colo.: Westview, 1983), 195–216.

67. Ramazani, "Iran: The 'Islamic Cultural Revolution,'" 40–48.

CHAPTER 5

1. See various essays in Akbar Ganji, *Tarik-khaneh-ye Ashbah: Asib-shenasi-ye Gozar be Dowlat-e Demokratik-e Towse'e-gera* (Ghosts' Darkhouse: Pathology of Transition to the Developmental Democratic State) (Tehran: Tarh-e No, 1378/1998), 13–15; and Ganji, *Alijenab-e Sorkhpoush va Alijenaban-e Khakestari*.

2. Ehsani, "Prospects for Democracy in Iran," 5.

3. Numbers are cited by National Youth Organization of Iran. See http://www .nyoir.org/eng/Iranian-Youth-Today-Employment.htm

4. Farhad Khosrokhavar, "Iran's New Intellectuals," *Social Compass* 51:2 (June 2004): 191–202; and Khosrowkhavar, Etemad, and Mehrabi, "Report on Science in Post-Revolutionary Iran."

5. "The Conservatives Misjudged: A Conversation with Ahmad Bourghani," *MERIP* 212:3 (Fall 1999): 36–37.

6. On the election see, Ansari, *Iran, Islam, and Democracy*, 82–109.

7. Seyyed Mohammad Khatami, *Bim-e Mouj* (Fear of Wave) (Tehran: Sazeman-e Chapp va Entesharat-e Vezarat-e Farhang va Ershad-e Eslami, 1372/1993).

8. On the views of Khatami and his supporters, see Mohammad Khatami, *Az Donya-ye Shahr ta Shahr-e Donya* (From the City's World to the World's City) (Tehran: Ney, 1997); Mohammad Khatami, *Eslam, Rouhaniyyat, va Enqelab-e Islami* (Islam, the Ulama, and the Islamic Revolution) (Tehran: Tarh-e Naw, 2000); Fariborz Etemadi, ed., *Doctor Mohajerani, Az Ra'y-e E'temad ta Estizah* (Doctor Mohajerani: From Vote of Confidence to Impeachment) (Tehran: Hezb-e Kargozaran-e Sazandegi, 1999); Akbar Ganji, *Kimiya-ye Azadi: Defa'iyat-e Akhar Ganji dar Dadgah-e Konferans-e Berlin* (Elixir of Freedom: Akbar Ganji's Defense at the Berlin Conference Trial) (Tehran: Tarh-e No, 2001); Geneive Abdo, "Iran's Generation of Outsiders," *Washington Quarterly* 24:4 (Autumn 2001): 163–71.

9. Interestingly, this is the way that hard-line conservatives have interpreted the support of the Radical faction for Khatami; see the comments of the executive secretary of *Ansar-e Hezbollah*, Hossein Allahkaram, at http://www.ansarnews.com/index .php?papu=ews/showmessage&code=2

10. Jonathan Lyons and Geneive Abdo, *Answering Only to God: Faith and Freedom in Twenty-First Century Iran* (New York: Holt & Co., 2003).

11. Ibid. For 1997 developments, see, for example, essays in *MERIP* 212:3 (Fall 1999), special issue, "Pushing the Limits: Iran's Islamic Revolution at Twenty," with guest editor Kaveh Ehsani; note, in particular, Ehsani's paper, "*Do-e Khordad* and the Specter of Democracy," 10–11. Also see Babak Dad, *Sad Rouz ba Khatami* (Hundred Days With Khatami) (Tehran, 1377/1999); the various essays in Haleh Esfandiari and Andrea Bertone, eds., *An Assessment of the Iranian Presidential Elections* (Washington, D.C.: Woodrow Wilson Center for International Scholars, 2002); David Menashri, *Post-*

Revolutionary Politics in Iran: Religion, Society and Power (London: Frank Cass, 2001), 131–62; and Bijan Khajehpour-Khouei, "Iran's Presidential Election: A New Phase in Post-Revolutionary Development," *Muslim Politics Report* 13 (May/June 1997), 1, 6.

12. Ehsani, "Prospects for Democracy in Iran," 5.

13. For 1997 developments, see *MERIP* 212:3 (Fall 1999); Ehsani, *"Do-e Khordad* and the Specter of Democracy," 10–11 and 16.

14. Said A. Arjomand, "Civil Society and the Rule of Law in the Constitutional Politics of Iran under Khatami," *Social Research* 67:2 (Summer 2000): 283–301.

15. Farhang Rajaee, "A Thermidor of 'Islamic Yuppies': Conflict and Compromise in Iran's Politics," *Middle East Journal* 53:2 (Spring 1999): 217–31.

16. For a discussion of Khatami's cultural policies, see Buchta, *Who Rules Iran?* 123–24.

17. See Akbar Ganji's essays on Rafsanjani period in Akbar Ganji, *Alijenab-e Sorkh-poush*.

18. Buchta, *Who Rules Iran?* 124.

19. Kaveh Ehsani, "Prospects for Democratization in Iran."

20. Ibid., 125–28; and Geneive Abdo, "Rethinking the Islamic Republic: A 'Conversation' with Ayatollah Husain 'Ali Montazeri," *Middle East Journal* 55:1 (Winter 2001): 9–24.

21. Farzin Vahdat, "Post-Revolutionary Discourses of Mohammad Mojtahed Shabestari and Mohsen Kadivar," *Critique* 16 (2000): 31–45; and 17 (2000): 135–57; and Mahmoud Sadri, "Sacral Defense of Secularism: the Political Theologies of Soroush, Shabestari, and Kadivar," *International Journal of Politics, Culture, and Society* 15:2 (December 2001): 257–70.

22. Geneive Abdo, "The Fragility of Khatami's Revolution," *Washington Quarterly* 23, 4 (Autumn 2000): 55–62.

23. Fariba Adelkhah, *Being Modern in Iran* (New York: Columbia University Press, 2000).

24. Olivier Roy, "The Crisis of Religious Legitimacy in Iran," *Middle East Journal* 53: 2 (Spring 1999): 201–16.

25. Buchta, *Who Rules Iran?* 122.

26. Lyons and Abdo, *Answering Only to God.*

27. The reformist journalist Mohammad Qouchani has identified this trend as a rising Bonapartism in Iranian politics; see http://www.sharghnewspaper.com/840227/html/index.htm

28. *The Economist,* January 17, 2004, 20.

29. "Text of Confessions of Amir Farshad Ebrahimi," *Mihan.* Available at http://www.mihan.net/59/mihan-59-06-01.htm. Ebrahimi was an intelligence operative who worked for the Ministry of Intelligence. He was closely involved with planning and carrying out attacks on reformists. The text of his "confessions" was viewed as a powerful testament to the conservative plan of action against reformists.

30. Ansari, *Iran, Islam, and Democracy,* 116–18.

31. Hootan Shambayati, "A Tale of Two Mayors: Courts and Politics in Iran and Turkey," *International Journal of Middle East Studies* 36:2 (May 2004): 253–75; and Buchta, *Who Rules Iran?* 140–42.

32. Christopher de Bellaigue, "Iran's Last Chance for Reform," *Washington Quarterly* 24:4 (Autumn 2001): 71–80.

33. Kaveh Ehsani, "Existing Political Vessels Cannot Contain Reform Movement: A Conversation with Sai'id Hajjarian," *MERIP* 212:3 (Fall 1999): 40–43.

34. Nasser Hadian-Jazy, a professor at Tehran University, as quoted in Scott Peterson, "How Iran's Reformers Lost Their Political Way," *Christian Science Monitor*, July 1, 2005. See the Web edition at http://www.csmonitor.com/2005/0701/p04s01-wome.html

35. Milton Viorst, "The Limits of the Revolution: Changing Iran," *Foreign Affairs* 74: 6 (November/December 1995): 63–76.

36. See Shabestari's comments cited in "Intellectually Victorious, but Politically Defeated," in *Qantara.de*, http://www.qantara.de/webcom/show_article.php/_c-476/_nr -317/i.html?PHPSESSID=45ae2c364b42b2fa80a7da7286e95b69. In the same source, he states that youths view reformists as backward.

37. Ray Takeyh and Nikolas K. Gvosdev, "Pragmatism in the Midst of Iranian Turmoil," *Washington Quarterly* (Autumn 2004): 33–56.

38. Farhad Khosrokhavar, "Neo-Conservative Intellectuals in Iran," 5–30.

39. See the interview of Guard commander and Commander of Police Mohammad Baqer Qalibaf: "Dr. Qalibaf: Arse-ye Eqtesad-e Keshvar dar Saliyan-e Gozashteh Dast-e Nirouha-ye Enqelab Naboudeh Ast" ("Dr. Qalibaf: The Country's Economy in Recent Years Has Not Been in the Hands of Revolutionary Forces"), *Khatt-e Nohom*, April 2, 2005: http://www.9line.ir/comments.asp?ide=350. Qalibaf asserted that civilian leaders had proved incapable of effectively managing government affairs and pursuing development, and he suggested that the Guard would be well capable of providing effective government and achieving development.

40. In a telling statement attributed to the Qalibaf, he answered a question about his program as president with the following: "I think the country needs order and stability. There has to be accountability for everything. . . . [P]eople are tired of politicians. Don't you see how people in the street and coffee shops say 'may God bless Reza Khan [Reza Shah]?' What Iran needs is a Reza Khan. I am the Hezbollahi Reza Khan," cited in *Daricheh*, May 11, 2005, Web edition, http://www.daricheh.org/news.php ?newsid=1804 Qalibaf is said to have made the statement at a campaign event on May 8, 2005. Later Qalibaf denied having compared himself with Reza Khan, but the fact that the story rang true of the promises he had been making and was widely reported is of significance. Also see the reformist editor of *Sharq*'s comparison of Revolutionary Guard candidates and Reza Khan, Mohammad Qouchani, "Reqabat-e Farmandehan ba Siyasatmdaran" (Competition of Commanders with Politicians), *Sharq*, May 17, 2005, Web edition, at http://www.sharghnewspaper.com/840227/html/index.htm.

41. Afshin Molavi, "Buying Time in Tehran: Iran and the China Model" *Foreign Affairs* 83:6 (September/October 2004): 9–16. In an interview with Agence France Press, Iran's new Speaker of the parliament promised that the main objective of the conservatives would be to turn Iran into an "Islamic Japan." "Profile of Developers of Islamic Iran Alliance," *Iran* 9:2734 (February 25, 2004): 3–6, available at http://www.netiran .com/?fn=artd(596).

42. On discussions of relations between authoritarianism and development and its manifestation in Asia, see Robert Wade, *Governing the Market: The Theory and the*

Role of Government in East Asian Industrialization (Princeton, N.J.: Princeton University Press, 1990); and Larry Diamond and Marc Plattner, introduction to *Economic Reform and Democracy*, ed. Larry Diamond and Marc Plattner (Baltimore: Johns Hopkins University Press, 1995), ix–xii.

43. Bahman Ahmadi Amouie, *Eqtesad-e Siyasi Jomhouri Eslami* (Political Economy of the Islamic Republic) (Tehran: Gam-e NoNaw, 1380/[2002]).

44. The reformist Said Hajjarian identifies the newly rich private sector as a stumbling block to democracy. See http://www.sharghnewspaper.com/840228/html/index .htm

45. Bijan Khajehpour, "Domestic Political Reforms and Private Sector Activity in Iran," *Social Research* 67:2 (Summer 2000): 577–98.

CHAPTER 6

1. "The Right Wing, Leave Fundamentalists Alone!" see http://www.ansarnews .com/index.php?papu=article/showarticle&code=50.

2. Ehsani, "Prospects for Democratization in Iran," 2–3.

3. Interview of Akbar Ganji with Mina Baharmast in *Radio Farda*, http://www .radiofarda.com/iran_article /2005/6/cb7b464e-82a8-4abb-aafo-b84633907ef6.html

4. Soroush endorsed Karroubi in an interview with Maryam Kashani in *Rouz*, "Moin Will Have the Same Fate as Khatami," at http://roozonline.com/11english/ 007830.shtml.

5. Interview of Mohsen Rezai with *Baztab* (May 2, 2005), at http://baztab.com/ news/23920.php. These views were also echoed by Larijani and the hard-line conservatives. See http://www.farsnews.com/NewsVm.asp?ID=155929.

6. Numbers are cited by the National Youth Organization of Iran. See http://www .nyoir.org/eng/Iranian-Youth-Today-Employment.htm

7. See the criticism of senior conservative clerics in *Ansar News*, the organ of the hard-line group Ansar-e Hezbollah, in an article titled: "The Right Wing, Leave Fundamentalists Alone!" available at http://www.ansarnews.com/index.php?papu=article/ showarticle&code=50.

8. Niloufar Mansourian, "Eslahgarayan Shanzdah Million Ra'i, Osoulgarayan Yazdah Million Ra'i" (Reformists Sixteen Million Votes, Fundamentalists Eleven Million Votes) *Sharq*, June 18, 2005, Web edition, at www.sharghnewspaper.com/840329/html/ index.htm

9. See calls for supporting Rafsanjani in an open letter signed by leading reformist intellectuals and activists in *Debsh*, June 19, 2005, at http://tribune.debsh.com/ archives/sunday%7C2005,jun,19%7C11;17;52.php

10. Cited in Nazila Fathi, "Blacksmith's Son Emphasized His Modest Roots," *New York Times*, June 26, 2005, Web edition, at http://www.nytimes.com/2005/06/26/ international/middleeast/26mayor.html

11. Kaveh Ehsani, "Iran's Presidential Run-Off: the Long View," *Middle East Report Online*, June 24, 2005, www.merip.org

12. Mohammad Qouchani, "Were We Defeated?" *Sharq* June 26, 2005, Web edition, at http://www.sharghnewspaper.com/840405/html/index.htm

Bibliography

ARCHIVAL SOURCES

Oral History of Iran Collection of Foundation for Iranian Studies; interviews of

Gholam-Reza Afkhami
Faraj Ardalan
Mohammad Baheri
Aqa Khan Bakhtiar
Ahmad Baniahmad
Farah Ebrahimi
Mansour Farhang
Juni Farmanfarmaian
Amir-Hossein Ganjbakhsh
Farrokh Ghaffari
Manouchehr Goudarzi
General Mohsen Hasheminejad
Richard Helms
Daryoush Homayoun
Eslam Kazemieh
Bahram Khozai
General Abdol-Majid Ma'soumi-Na'ini
Abdol-Majid Majidi
Armin Meyer
General Ahmad-Ali Mohaqqeqqi
Seyyed Hossein Nasr
Reza Niazmand
Arbi Ovanessian

General Mansour Qadar
Ahmad Qoreishi
Reza Qotbi
Majid Rahnema
Parviz Raji
Ali Shakeri
General Hasan Toufanian
Gratian Yatsevitch

The Iranian Oral History Collection of Harvard University; interviews of

Shapour Bakhtiar
Abol-Hasan Ebtehaj
Khodadad Farmanfarmaian
Admiral Kamal Habibollahi
Mehdi Haeri-Yazdi
Mehdi Khanbaba-Tehrani
Abol-Qasem Kheradjou
Abdol-Karim Lahiji
Hasan Nazih
Karim Sanjabi
Mohammad Yeganeh

PRINT AND ONLINE NEWSPAPERS

Bahmanpour, Mohammad-Said. "Jashn-e Khatm-e Din ra Gerefteh'id na Khatam-e No-
    bovvat" (You Have Celebrated the Seal of Religion, Not the Seal of Prophecy).
    Baztab, September 3, 2005, Web edition, http://www.baztab.com/news/28559.php.
Daniszewski, John. "Hard-Liner Wins Decisively in Iran Presidential Election." *Los An-
    geles Times*, June 25, 2005, Web edition, http://www.latimes.com/news/
    nationworld/world/la-fg-iranelect25jun25,0,2087142.story?coll=la-home-headlines.
Debsh, June 19, 2005, http://tribune.debsh.com/archives/sunday|2005,jun,19|11;17;52
    .php.
Fathi, Nazila. "Blacksmith's Son Emphasized His Modest Roots." *New York Times*, June
    26, 2005, Web edition, http://www.nytimes.com/2005/06/26/international/
    middleeast/26mayor.html.
Interview of Hossein Allahkaram in *Ansar News* http://www.ansarnews.com/index.php
    ?papu=news/showmessage&code=2.
Interview of Mohammad Baqer-Qalibaf in "Dr. Qalibaf: Arseh-ye Eqtesad-e Keshvar dar
    Saliyan-e Gozashteh Dast-e Nirouha-ye Enqelab Naboudeh Ast" ("Dr. Qalibaf: The
    Country's Economy in Recent Years Has Not Been in the Hands of Revolutionary
    Forces"). *Khatt-e Nohom*, April 2, 2005, available at http://www.9line.ir/comments
    .asp?ide=350.
Interview of Akbar Ganji with Mina Baharmast in *Radio Farda*. Available at http://www
    .radiofarda.com/iran_article/2005/6/cb7b464e-82a8–4abb-aafo–b84633907ef6
    .html.

Interview of Ali Larijani. Available at http://www.farsnews.com/NewsVm.asp?ID=155929.

Interview of Mohsen Rezai with *Baztab*, May 2, 2005. Available at http://baztab.com/news/23920.php.

Interview with Mohammad Mojtahed-Shabestari in "Intellectually Victorious, but Politically Defeated." *Qantara.de*. Available at http://www.qantara.de/webcom/show_article.php/_c-476/_nr-317/i.html?PHPSESSID=45ae2c364b42b2fa80a7da7286e95b69.

Interview of Abdol-Karim Soroush with Maryam Kashani in *Rouz*, "Moin Will Have the Same Fate as Khatami." Available at http://roozonline.com/11english/007830.shtml.

Interview of former Foreign Minister Ali-Akbar Velayati with *Baztab*, May 1, 2005. Available at http://baztab.com/news/23783.php.

Khojasteh-Rahimi, Reza, and Sheibani, Maryam. "Gerdehamai Rowshanfekran Bara-ye Demokrasy" (Gathering of Intellectuals for Democracy). *Sharq*, May 18, 2005, Web edition, http://www.sharghnewspaper.com/840228/html/index.htm.

Mansourian, Niloufar. "Eslahgarayan Shanzdah Milyoun Ra'y, Osoulgarayan Yazdah Milyoun Ra'y" (Reformists Sixteen Million Votes, Fundamentalists Eleven Million Votes). *Sharq*, June 18, 2005, Web edition, www.sharghnewspaper.com/840329/html/index.htm.

Molavi, Afshin. "In Iran: Daring to Dream of Democracy." *Washington Post*, March 7, 2004.

Peterson, Scott. "How Iran's Reformers Lost Their Political Way." *Christian Science Monitor*, July 1, 2005. Available at http://www.csmonitor.com/2005/0701/p04s01–wome.html.

"Profile of Developers of Islamic Iran Alliance." *Iran*, 9:2734, February 25, 2004, 3–6. Available at http://www.netiran.com/?fn=artd(596).

Qouchani, Mohammad. "Reqabat-e Farmandehan ba Siyasatmdaran" (Competition of Commanders with Politicians). *Sharq*, May 17, 2005, Web edition, http://www.sharghnewspaper.com/840227/html/index.htm.

———. "Aya ma Shekast-Khordim?" (Were We Defeated?) *Sharq*, June 26, 2005, Web edition, http://www.sharghnewspaper.com/840405/html/index.htm.

"The Right Wing, Leave Fundamentalists Alone!" Available at http://www.ansarnews.com/index.php?papu=article/showarticle&code=50.

"Text of Confessions of Amir Farshad Ebrahimi." *Mihan*. Available at http://www.mihan.net/59/mihan-59–06–01.htm.

BOOKS AND ARTICLES

Abdo, Geneive. "The Fragility of Khatami's Revolution," *Washington Quarterly* 23, 4 (Autumn 2000): 55–62.

———. "Iran's Generation of Outsiders." *Washington Quarterly* 24, 4 (Autumn 2001): 163–71.

———. "Rethinking the Islamic Republic: A 'Conversation' with Ayatollah Husain 'Ali Montazeri." *Middle East Journal* 55, 1 (Winter 2001): 9–24.

Abou El Fadl, Khaled. *Islam and the Challenge of Democracy*. Princeton, N.J.: Princeton University Press, 2004.

Abrahamian, Ervand. "The Guerrilla Movements in Iran 1963–1977." *MERIP* 86 (March–April 1980): 3–15.

———. *Iran between Two Revolutions*. Princeton, N.J.: Princeton University Press, 1982.

———. *Khomeinism: Essays on the Islamic Republic*. Berkeley: University of California Press, 1993.

———. *Radical Islam: The Iranian Mojahedin*. New Haven, Conn.: Yale University Press, 1989.

———. *Tortured Confessions: Prisons and Public Recantations in Modern Iran*. Berkeley: University of California Press, 1999.

Adamiyat, Fereydoun. "Barkhord-e Afkar va Takamol-e Parlemani dar Majles-e Avval" (Exchange of Ideas and Parliamentary Development in the First Majles). In *Maqalat-e Tarikhi* (Historical Essays), 109–18. Tehran: 1352/1975.

———. *Fekr-e Azadi va Moqaddameh-ye Nehzat-e Mashroutiyat-e Iran* (The Idea of Liberty and the Beginning of the Iranian Constitutional Movement). Tehran: 1340/1961–62.

———. *Ide'oloji-ye Nehzat-e Mashroutiyat-e Iran* (The Ideology of the Iranian Constitutional Movement). Vol. 1. Tehran: 2535 [1355]/1976.

———. *Ide'oloji-ye Nehzat-e Mashroutiyat-e Iran: Jeld-e Dovvom: Majles-e Avval va Bohran-e Azadi* (Ideology of the Iranian Constitutional Movement: Vol. 2: The First Majles and the Crisis of Democracy). Tehran: n.d.

———. *Shouresh bar Emtiaz-Nameh-ye Reji: Tahlil-e Siasi* (Protest against Régie Concession: a Political Analysis). Tehran: Payam, 1360/1981.

Adelkhah, Fariba. *Being Modern in Iran*. New York: Columbia University Press, 2000.

Adelkhah, Fariba, Jean-François Bayart, and Olivier Roy. *Thermidor en Iran*. Brussels: Complexe, 1993.

Afary, Janet. *The Iranian Constitutional Revolution*. New York: Columbia University Press, 1996.

Afkhami, Gholam-Reza, ed. *Barnamehrizi-ye Umrani va Tasmim Giri-e Siyasi (Ideology, Process and Politics in Iran's Development Planning)*. Interviews with Manuchehr Gudarzi, Khodadad Farmanfarmaian, and Abdol-Majid Majidi. Washington, D.C.: Foundation for Iranian Studies, 1999.

———. *The Iranian Revolution: Thanatos on a National Scale*. Washington, D.C.: Middle East Institute, 1985.

———. *Jame'h, Dowlat, va Jonbesh-e Zanan-e Iran, 1320–1357 (Women, State, and Society in Iran, 1941–1978)*. Interview with Mehrangiz Dowlatshahi. Washington, D.C.: Foundation for Iranian Studies, 2002.

———. *Jame'h, Dowlat, va Jonbesh-e Zanan-e Iran, 1342–1357 (Women, State, and Society in Iran, 1963–1978)*. Interview with Mahnaz Afkhami. Washington, D.C.: Foundation for Iranian Studies, 2003.

———. *San'at-e Petroshimi-e Iran: az Aghaz ta Astane-e Enqelab (The Evolution of Iran's Petrochemical Industry)*. Interview with Baqer Mostowfi. Washington, D.C.: Foundation for Iran Studies, 2001.

———. *Siasat va Siyasatguzari-e Eqtesdi dar Iran, 1340–1350 (Ideology, Politics, and Pro-*

cess in Iran's Economic Development, 1960–1970). Interview with Alinaghi Alikhani. Washington, D.C.: Foundation for Iranian Studies, 2001.

Aghaie, Kamran Scot. *The Martyrs of Karbala: Shi'i Symbols and Rituals in Modern Iran.* Seattle: University of Washington Press, 2004.

Ahmadi Amouie, Bahman. *Eqtesad-e Siyasi Jomhouri Eslami* (Political Economy of the Islamic Republic). Tehran: Gam-e No, 1380/2002.

Ahmed, Ishtiaq. *The Concept of an Islamic State: An Analysis of the Ideological Controversy in Pakistan.* New York: St. Martin's Press, 1987.

Akhavi, Shahrough. "Clerical Politics in Iran since 1979." In *The Iranian Revolution and the Islamic Republic,* ed. Nikki Keddie and Eric Hooglund, 57–73. Syracuse, N.Y.: Syracuse University Press, 1986.

———. "Ideology and the Iranian Revolution." Introduction to *Iran since the Revolution: Internal Dynamics, Regional Conflicts, and the Superpowers,* ed. Barry M. Rosen, xi–xx. New York: Columbia University Press, 1985.

———. "Iran: Implementation of an Islamic State." In *Islam in Asia,* ed. John L. Esposito, 27–52. New York: Oxford University Press, 1987.

———. *Religion and Politics in Contemporary Iran: Clergy-State Relations in the Pahlavi Period.* Albany: State University of New York Press, 1980.

———. "The Role of the Clergy in Iranian Politics, 1949–1954." In *Musaddiq, Iranian Nationalism, and Oil,* ed. James A. Bill and William Roger Louis, 91–117. Austin: University of Texas Press, 1988.

———. "Shi'ism, Corporatism, and Rentierism in the Iranian Revolution." In *Comparing Muslim Societies: Knowledge and the State in a World Civilization,* ed. Juan R. I. Cole, 261–93. Ann Arbor: University of Michigan Press, 1992.

Alam, Asadollah. *The Shah and I: The Confidential Diary of Iran's Royal Court, 1969–1977,* ed. Alinaqi Alikhani. New York: St. Martin's Press, 1992.

Algar, Hamid. *Islam and Revolution: Writings and Declarations of Imam Khomeini (1941–1980).* Berkeley, Calif.: Mizan Press, 1981.

———. *Mirza Malkum Khan: A Biographical Study in Iranian Modernism.* Berkeley: University of California Press, 1973.

Alikhani, Alinaqi. Introduction to *The Shah and I: The Confidential Diary of Iran's Royal Court, 1969–1977,* Asadollah Alam, ed. Alinaqi Alikhani, 7–22. New York: St. Martin's Press, 1992.

Amanat, Abbas. "In between the Madrasa and the Marketplace: The Designation of Clerical Leadership in Modern Shi'ism." In *Authority and Political Culture in Shi'ism,* ed. Said A. Arjomand, 98–132. Albany: State University of New York Press, 1988.

———. *Pivot of the Universe: Naser al-Din Shah Qajar and the Iranian Monarchy, 1831–1896.* Berkeley: University of California Press, 1997.

Amini, Parvin. "A Single Party State in Iran, 1975–78: The Rastakhiz Party—the Final Attempt by the Shah to Consolidate His Political Base." *Middle Eastern Studies* 38, 1 (January 2002): 131–68.

Amirahmadi, Hooshang. "Bunyad." In *The Encyclopedia of the Modern Islamic World,* Vol. 1, ed. John L. Esposito, 234–37. New York: Oxford University Press, 1995.

———. *Revolution and Economic Transition: The Iranian Experience.* Albany: State University of New York Press, 1990.

Amir-Ebrahimi, Masserat. "L'image socio-géographique de Téhéran en 1986" (A Socio-Geographic Picture of Tehran in 1986). In *Téhéran: Capitale bicentenaire* (Tehran: The Two-Hundred-Year-Old Capital), ed. Bernard Hourcade and Chahryar Adle, 267–79. Paris: Institut français de recherche en Iran, 1992.

Amuzegar, Jahangir. "Adjusting to Sanctions." *Foreign Affairs* (May/June 1997): 31–41.

———. *The Dynamics of the Iranian Revolution: The Pahlavi's Triumph and Tragedy.* Albany: State University of New York Press, 1991.

———. "The Iranian Economy before and after the Revolution." *Middle East Journal* 46, 3 (Summer 1992): 413–25.

———. "Iran's Economy and the U.S. Sanctions." *Middle East Journal* 51, 2 (Spring 1997): 185–99.

———. *Iran's Economy under the Islamic Republic.* London: I. B. Tauris, 1993.

Anderson, Lisa. *Transitions to Democracy.* New York: Columbia University Press, 1999.

Ansari, Ali. *Iran, Islam, and Democracy: The Politics of Managing Change.* London: Royal Institute of International Affairs, 2000.

Arjomand, Said A. "Civil Society and the Rule of Law in the Constitutional Politics of Iran under Khatami." *Social Research* 67, 2 (Summer 2000): 283–301.

———. "Ideological Revolution in Shi'ism." In *Authority and Political Culture in Shi'ism,* ed. Said A. Arjomand, 178–209. Albany: State University of New York Press, 1988.

———. "Á la Recherche de lá Conscience Collective: Durkheim's Ideological Impact in Turkey and Iran." *American Sociologist* 27 (May 1982): 94–102.

———. "Religion, Political Action, and Legitimate Domination in Shi'ite Iran: Fourteenth to Eighteenth Centuries A.D." *Archives Europeenes De Sociologie* 20, 1 (1979): 59–109.

———. *The Shadow of God and the Hidden Imam: Religion, Political Order, and Societal Change in Shi'ite Iran from the Beginning to 1890.* Chicago: University of Chicago Press, 1984.

———. *The Turban for the Crown.* New York: Oxford University Press, 1988.

Asari, Kamal. "Eqtesad-e Iran, Goriz az Tangnaha" (Iran's Economy, Escaping Constraints). *Ettela'at-e Siyasi Eqtesadi* 32 (1989): 38–47.

———. "The Housing Sector in Iran." In *The Economy of Islamic Iran: Between State and Market,* ed. Thierry Coville, 253–60. Tehran: Institut Français de recherches en Iran, 1994.

Atabaki, Touraj. *Azerbaijan: Ethnicity and the Struggle for Power in Iran.* London: I. B. Tauris, 2000.

———. *Iran and the First World War.* London: I. B. Tauris, 2005.

Atabaki, Touraj, and Erik J. Zurcher. *Men of Order: Authoritarian Modernization under Ata Turk and Reza Shah.* London: I. B. Tauris, 2004.

Azari, Farah. "The Post-Revolutionary Women's Movement in Iran." In *Women of Iran: Conflict with Fundamentalism,* ed. Farah Azari, 190–225. London: Ithaca Press, 1983.

Azimi, Fakhreddin. *Iran: The Crisis of Democracy.* New York: St. Martin's Press, 1989.

———. "Unseating Mosaddeq: The Configuration and Role of Domestic Forces." *Mohammad Mosaddeq and the 1953 Coup in Iran,* ed. Mark J. Gasiorowski and Malcolm Byrne, 27–101. Syracuse, N.Y.: Syracuse University Press, 2004.

Bahgat, Gawdat. "The New Iran: A Myth or Reality?" *Asian Affairs*, 85, 2 (June 1998): 141–60.

Bakhash, Shaul. "Islam and Social Justice in Iran." In *Shi'ism: Resistance and Revolution*, ed. Martin Kramer, 95–115. Boulder: Westview Press, 1987.

———. "The Politics of Land, Law, and Social Justice in Iran." *Middle East Journal* 43, 2 (Spring 1989): 186–201.

———. *The Reign of the Ayatollahs: Iran and the Islamic Revolution*. New York: Basic Books, 1984.

Bakhtiari, Bahman. *Parliamentary Politics in Revolutionary Iran: The Institutionalization of Factional Politics*. Gainesville: University Press of Florida, 1996.

Banani, Amin. *The Modernization of Iran, 1921–41*. Stanford, Calif.: Stanford University Press, 1961.

Bani Sadr, Abol-Hasan. *The Fundamental Principles and Precepts of Islamic Government*. Translated by Mohammad R. Ghanoonparvar. Lexington, Ky.: Mazda, 1981.

Barnett, Michael N. *Confronting the Costs of War: Military Power, State, and Society in Egypt and Israel*. Princeton, N.J.: Princeton University Press, 1992.

Bashiri, Siavosh. *Qesseh-ye Savak* (The Story of SAVAK). Paris, 1991.

Basiratmanesh, Hamid. *Ulama va Regime-e Reza Shah* (Ulama and Reza Shah's Regime). Tehran: Nashr-e Uruj, 1998.

Bayat, Asef. *Street Politics*. New York: Columbia University Press, 1997.

Bayat, Mangol. *Iran's First Revolution: Shi'ism and the Constitutional Revolution of 1905–1909*. New York: Oxford University Press, 1991.

———. "Mahmud Taleqani and the Iranian Revolution." In *Shi'ism, Resistance, and Revolution*, ed. Martin Kramer, 67–94. Boulder, Colo.: Westview Press, 1987.

Bazargan, Mehdi. *Bazgasht be Quran* (Return to the Quran). Tehran 1361/1983–84.

———. *The Deceived: Gomrahan; Sayr-e Tahavvul-e Qur'an* (The Path of Development of the Qur'an). 2 vols. Tehran, 1362/1984–85.

Beeman, William O. *The "Great Satan" vs. the "Mad Mullahs": How the United States and Iran Demonized Each Other*. Westport, Conn.: Praeger, 2005.

Behdad, Sohrab. "The Political Economy of Islamic Planning in Iran." In *Post-Revolutionary Iran*, ed. Hooshang Amirahmadi and Monouchehr Parvin, 107–25. Boulder, Colo.: Westview Press, 1988.

———. "The Post-Revolutionary Economic Crisis." In *Iran after the Revolution: Crisis of an Islamic State*, ed. Saeed Rahnema and Sohrab Behdad, 97–128. London: I. B. Tauris, 1995.

Beheshti, Mohammad-Hossein. *Eqtesad-e Eslami* (Islamic Economics). Tehran: n.p., 1370/1990.

Behrooz, Maziar. "The Iranian Revolution and the Legacy of the Guerrilla Movement." In *Reformers and Revolutionaries in Modern Iran*, ed. Stephanie Cronin, 189–205. London: RoutledgeCurzon, 2004.

———. *Rebels with a Cause: The Failure of the Left in Iran*. London: I. B. Tauris, 1999.

Bellin, Eva. "Robustness of Authoritarianism in the Middle East: Exceptionalism in Comparative Perspective." *Comparative Politics* 36, 2 (January 2004): 139–58.

Bill, James A. *The Eagle and the Lion: The Tragedy of American-Iranian Relations*. New Haven, Conn.: Yale University Press, 1988.

Bill, James A., and William Roger Louis, eds. *Musaddiq, Iranian Nationalism, and Oil.* Austin: University of Texas Press, 1988.

Bina, Cyrus, and Hamid Zanganeh. *Modern Capitalism and Islamic Ideology in Iran.* New York: St. Martin's Press, 1992.

Blackbourn, David, and Geoff Eley. *The Peculiarities of German History: Bourgeois Society and Politics in Nineteenth-Century Germany.* New York: Oxford University Press, 1984.

"Bonyad-e Shahid." In *Encyclopedia Iranica,* Vol. 2, ed. Ehsan Yarshater, 36–61. Costa Mesa, Calif.: Mazda, 1987.

Boroujerdi, Mehrzad. *Iranian Intellectuals and the West: The Tormented Triumph of Nativism.* Syracuse, N.Y.: Syracuse University Press, 1996.

Bostock, Frances, and Geoffrey Jones. *Planning and Power in Iran: Ebtehaj and Economic Development under the Shah.* London: Frank Cass, 1989.

Brinton, Crane. *The Anatomy of Revolution.* New York: Vintage Books, 1965.

Brown, L. Carl. *Religion and State: The Muslim Approach to Politics.* New York: Columbia University Press, 2000.

Browne, Edward G. *Persian Revolution of 1905–1909.* Cambridge: Cambridge University Press, 1910.

Brumberg, Daniel. "Khomeini's Legacy: Islamic Rule and Islamic Social Justice." In *Spokesmen for the Despised,* ed. R. Scott Appleby, 16–82. Chicago: University of Chicago Press, 1997.

———. "The Trap of Liberalized Autocracy." In *Islam and Democracy in the Middle East,* ed. Larry Diamond, Marc Plattner, and Daniel Brumberg, 35–47. Baltimore, Md.: Johns Hopkins University Press, 2003.

Buchta, Wilfried. *Who Rules Iran? The Structure of Power in the Islamic Republic.* Washington, D.C.: Washington Institute for Near East Policy, 2000.

Campbell, Richard, trans. and ed. *Society and Economics in Islam: Writings and Declarations of Ayatollah Sayyid Mahmud Taleqani.* Berkeley, Calif.: Mizan Press, 1982.

Carr, Edward Hallett. *A History of Soviet Russia: The Bolshevik Revolution (1917–1923).* Vol. 2. New York: W. W. Norton, 1985.

Chehabi, H. E. "Ardebil Becomes Province: Center-Periphery Relations in Iran." *International Journal of Middle East Studies* 29, 2 (May 1997): 235–53.

———. *Iranian Politics and Religious Modernism: The Liberation Movement of Iran under the Shah and Khomeini.* Ithaca, N.Y.: Cornell University Press, 1990.

———. "The Provisional Government and the Transition from Monarchy to Islamic Republic in Iran." In *Between States: Interim Governments and Democratic Transitions,* ed. Yossi Shain and Juan Linz, 127–43. New York: Cambridge University Press, 1995.

———. "Religion and Politics in Iran: How Theocratic Is the Islamic Republic?" *Dædalus* 120, 3 (Summer 1991): 69–92.

———. "Staging the Emperor's New Clothes: Dress Codes and Nation-Building under Reza Shah." *Iranian Studies* 26, 3–4 (Summer/Fall 1993): 209–29.

Chelkowski, Peter J., ed. *Taziyeh: Ritual and Drama in Iran.* New York: New York University Press, 1979.

Christopher, Warren, ed. *American Hostages in Iran*. New Haven, Conn.: Yale University Press, 1985.

Chubin, Shahram. "The Islamic Republic's Foreign Policy in the Gulf." In *Shi'ism, Resistance, and Revolution*, ed. Martin Kramer, 159–72. Boulder, Colo.: Westview Press, 1987.

———. "Leftist Forces in Iran." *Problems of Communism* (September 1980): 1–25.

Chubin, Shahram, and Charles Tripp. *Iran and Iraq at War*. London: I. B. Tauris, 1989.

Cole, Juan. *Sacred Space and Holy War: The Politics, Culture, and History of Shi'ite Islam*. London: I. B. Tauris, 2002.

Cottam, Richard W. *Nationalism in Iran*. 2nd ed. Pittsburgh: University of Pittsburgh Press, 1979.

Cronin, Stephanie. *The Army and the Creation of the Pahlavi State in Iran, 1910–1926*. London: Tauris Academic Press, 1997.

———. ed. *The Making of Modern Iran: State and Society under Riza Shah, 1921–1941*. London: Curzon Press, 2003.

Cunningham, Frank. *Theories of Democracy: A Critical Introduction*. London: Routledge, 2002.

Dabashi, Hamid. "Ali Shariati's Islam: Revolutionary Uses of Faith in a Post-Traditional Society." *Islamic Quarterly* 27, 4 (fourth quarter, 1983): 203–22.

———. " 'Islamic Ideology': The Perils and Promises of a Neologism." In *Post-Revolutionary Iran*, ed. Hooshang Amirahmadi and Monouchehr Parvin, 11–21. Boulder, Colo.: Westview Press, 1988.

———. "The Poetics of Politics: Commitment in Modern Persian Literature." *Iranian Studies* 18, 2–4 (Spring–Autumn 1985): 147–88.

———. *Theology of Discontent: The Ideological Foundation of the Islamic Revolution in Iran*. New York: New York University Press, 1993.

Dad, Babak. *Sad Rouz ba Khatami* (Hundred Days with Khatami). Tehran: 1377/1999.

Dadkhah, Kamran. "Rowshanfekran-e Irani va Andisheh-ye Eqtesadi" (Iranian Intellectuals and Economic Thought). *Iran Nameh* 21, 3 (Fall 1382/2003): 285–300.

Dahl, Robert. *Democracy and Its Critics* (New Haven, Conn.: Yale University Press, 1991.

———. *On Democracy*. New Haven, Conn.: Yale University Press, 2000.

Daneshvar, Parviz. *Revolution in Iran*. New York: St. Martin's Press, 1996.

Davaran, Habib, and Farhad Behbahani. *Do Khatereh az Zendan: Dar Mehmani-ye Hajji Aqa va Dastan-e Yek E'teraf dar Sal-e 1369* (Two Prison Memoirs: In the Party of Hajj Aqa and the Story of a Confession in 1990). Tehran: Omid-e Farda, 1382/2003.

de Bellaigue, Christopher. "Iran's Last Chance for Reform." *Washington Quarterly* 24, 4 (Autumn 2001): 71–80.

Diamond, Larry, and Marc Plattner, eds. *The Global Resurgence of Democracy*. Baltimore, Md.: Johns Hopkins University Press, 1993.

———. Introduction to *Economic Reform and Democracy*, ed. Larry Diamond and Marc Plattner, ix–xii. Baltimore: Johns Hopkins University Press, 1995.

Dorril, Stephen. *MI6: Inside the Covert World of Her Majesty's Secret Intelligence Service*. New York: Free Press, 2000: 558–99.

Eagleton, William. *The Kurdish Republic of 1946*. London: Oxford University Press, 1963.

Ebtekar, Massoumeh. *Takeover in Tehran: The Inside Story of the 1979 U.S. Embassy Capture*. New York: Talon Books, 2001.

Ehsani, Kaveh. "Existing Political Vessels Cannot Contain Reform Movement: A Conversation with Sai'id Hajjarian." *MERIP* 212, 3 (Fall 1999): 40–43.

———. "Iran's Presidential Run-Off: The Long View." *Middle East Report Online*, June 24, 2005, www.merip.org

———. "Municipal Matters: The Urbanization of Consciousness and Political Change." *MERIP* 212 (Autumn 1999): 22–27.

———. "Prospects for Democratization in Iran." Paper delivered at Concordia University, Montreal, November 2004.

Ehteshami, Anoushiravan. *After Khomeini: the Iranian Second Republic*. New York: Routledge, 1995.

Eickelman, Dale, and James Piscatori. *Muslim Politics*. Princeton, N.J.: Princeton University Press, 1996.

Elm, Mostafa. *Oil, Power, and Principle: Iran's Oil Nationalization and Its Aftermath*. Syracuse, N.Y.: Syracuse University Press, 1992.

Enayat, Hamid. Iran: Khumayni's Concept of the 'Guardianship of the Jurisconsult.' " In *Islam in the Political Process*, ed. James Piscatori, 160–80. New York: Cambridge University Press, 1983.

———. *Modern Islamic Political Thought*. Austin: University of Texas Press, 1982.

Ertman, Thomas. *Birth of Leviathan: Building States and Regimes in Medieval and Early Modern Europe*. New York: Cambridge University Press, 1997.

Esfandiari, Haleh, and Andrea Bertone, eds. *An Assessment of the Iranian Presidential Elections*. Washington, D.C.: Woodrow Wilson Center for International Scholars, 2002.

Esposito, John L., ed. *The Iranian Revolution: Its Global Impact*. Gainesville: University Press of Florida, 1990).

Esposito, John L., and John O. Voll. *Islam and Democracy*. New York: Oxford University Press, 1996.

Etemadi, Fariborz, ed. *Doctor Mohajerani, Az Ra'y-e E'temad ta Estizah* (Doctor Mohajerani: From Vote of Confidence to Impeachment). Tehran: Hezb-e Kargozaran-e Sazandegi, 1999.

Ettehadieh, Mansoureh. *Majles va Entekhabat: Az Mashrouteh ta Payan-e Qajariyeh* (Majles and Elections: From the Constitutional Revolution until End of Qajar Dynasty). Tehran: Nashr-e Tarikh-e Iran, 1375/1997.

Evans, Peter. *Embedded Autonomy: States and Industrial Transformation*. Princeton, N.J.: Princeton University Press, 1995.

Faghfoory, Mohammad H. "The Impact of Modernization on the Ulama in Iran, 1925–1941." *Iranian Studies* 26, 3–4 (Summer/Fall 1993): 277–312.

———. "The Ulama-State Relations in Iran: 1921–41." *International Journal of Middle East Studies* 19, 4 (November 1987): 413–32.

Farber, David. *Taken Hostage: The Iran Hostage Crisis and America's First Encounter with Radical Islam*. Princeton, N.J.: Princeton University Press, 2004.

Fatemi, Khosrow. "Leadership by Distrust: The Shah's Modus Operandi." *Middle East Journal* 36, 1 (Winter 1982): 48–61.

Fawcett, Louise. *Iran and the Cold War: The Azarbayjan Crisis of 1946.* Cambridge: Cambridge University Press, 1992.

Fischer, Michael M. J. "Becoming Mollah: Reflections on Iranian Clerics in a Revolutionary Age." *Iranian Studies* 13, 1–4 (1980): 83–118.

———. *Iran, from Religious Dispute to Revolution.* Cambridge: Harvard University Press, 1980.

Fitzpatrick, Sheila. *The Russian Revolution.* New York: Oxford University Press, 1982.

Floor, Willem. *Industrialization in Iran, 1900–1941.* Durham: University of Durham Press, 1984.

———. "The Revolutionary Character of the Ulama: Wishful Thinking or Reality?" In *Religion and Politics in Iran : Shi'ism from Quietism to Revolution,* ed. Nikki Keddie, 73–97. New Haven, Conn.: Yale University Press, 1983.

Foran, John. *Fragile Resistance: Social Transformation in Iran from 1500 to the Revolution.* Boulder, Colo.: Westview Press, 1993.

———, ed. *Theorizing Revolutions: New Approaches from across the Disciplines.* New York: Routledge, 1997.

Fukuyama, Francis. *State-Building: Governance and World Order in the Twenty-First Century.* Ithaca, N.Y.: Cornell University Press, 2004.

———. " 'Stateness' First." *Journal of Democracy* 16, 1 (January 2005): 84–88.

Ganji, Akbar. *Alijenab-e Sorkhpoush va 'Alijenaban-e Khakestari: Asib-shenasi-ye Gozar be Dowlat-e Demokratik-e Towse'e-gera* (The Red Eminence and the Gray Eminences: Pathology of Transition to the Developmental Democratic State). Tehran: Tarh-e No, 1378/1998.

———. *Kimiya-ye Azadi: Defa'iyat-e Akbar Ganji dar Dadgah-e Konferans-e Berlin* (Elixir of Freedom: Akbar Ganji's Defense at the Berlin Conference Trial). Tehran: Tarh-e No, 2001.

———. *Tarik-khaneh-ye Ashbah: Asib-shenasi-ye Gozar be Dowlat e Demokratik-e Towse'e-gera* (Ghosts' Darkhouse: Pathology of Transition to the Developmental Democratic State). Tehran: Tarh-e No, 1378/1998.

Gasiorowski, Mark J. *U.S. Foreign Policy and the Shah: Building a Client State in Iran.* Ithaca, N.Y.: Cornell University Press, 1991.

Gasiorowski, Mark J., and Malcolm Byrne, eds. *Mohammad Mosaddeq and the 1953 Coup in Iran.* Syracuse, N.Y.: Syracuse University Press, 2004.

Gasiorowski, Mark J., and Nikki Keddie, eds. *Neither East nor West: Iran, the Soviet Union, and the United States.* New Haven, CONN.: Yale University Press, 1990.

———. "The Qarani Affair and Iranian Politics," *International Journal of Middle East Studies,* 25, 4 (November 1993): 625–44.

Ghani, Cyrus. *Iran and the Rise of Reza Shah: From Qajar Collapse to Pahlavi Power.* London: I. B. Tauris, 1998.

Gheissari, Ali. *Iranian Intellectuals in the Twentieth Century.* Austin: University of Texas Press, 1998.

———. "Naqd-e Adab-e Ide'olojik: Morouri bar Adabiyat-e Rowshanfekri va Maktabi-ye

Iran" (Critique of Ideological Literature: A Review of Intellectual and Doctrinaire Writings in Iran). *Iran Nameh* 12, 2 (Spring 1994): 233–58.

———. "Persia." In *The Oxford Companion to the Second World War,* ed. I.C.B. Dear and M.R.D. Foot, 874. Oxford: Oxford University Press, 1995.

Gheissari, Ali, and Vali Nasr. "The Conservative Consolidation in Iran." *Survival* 47, 2 (Summer 2005): 175–90.

———. "The Democracy Debate in Iran." *Middle East Policy Journal* 11, 2 (Summer 2004): 94–106.

Gladstone, Jack. *Revolutions: Theoretical, Comparative, and Historical Studies.* San Diego, Calif.: Harcourt Brace Jovanovich, 1986.

Goodwin, Jeff. *No Other Way Out: States and Revolutionary Movements, 1945–1991.* New York: Cambridge University Press, 2001.

Green, Jerrold. *Revolution in Iran: The Politics of Countermobilization.* New York: Praeger, 1982.

Gurr, Ted R. *Why Men Rebel.* Princeton, N.J.: Princeton University Press, 1969.

Haeri-Yazdi, Sayyed Mehdi. *Hekmat va Hokoumat* (Reason and Governance). London: n.p., 1995.

Haggard, Stephan, and Robert Kaufman. *The Political Economy of Democratic Transitions.* Princeton, N.J.: Princeton University Press, 1995.

Hairi, Abdul-Hadi. *Shi'ism and Constitutionalism in Iran: A Study of the Role Played by the Persian Residents of Iraq in Iranian Politics.* Leiden: E. J. Brill, 1977.

Halliday, Fred. *Iran: Dictatorship and Development.* London: Penguin Press, 1979.

Hamidian, Naqi. *Safar ba Balha-ye Arezou: Sheklgiri-ye Jonbesh-e Cheriki-ye Fadaiyan-e Khalq* (Flight on the Wings of Hope: Formation of the Fadaiyan-e Khalq Movement). Stockholm: Arash Förlag, 2004.

Hashemi-Rafsanjani, Ali-Akbar. *Dowran-e Mobarezeh* (Period of Struggle). Edited by Mohsen Hashemi. Tehran: 1997.

Hefner, Robert W. *Civil Islam: Muslims and Democratization in Indonesia.* Princeton, N.J.: Princeton University Press, 2000.

Heiss, Mary Ann. *Empire and Nationhood: The United States, Great Britain, and Iranian Oil, 1950–1954.* New York: Columbia University Press, 1997.

Hintze, Otto. *The Historical Essays of Otto Hintze.* Edited by Felix Gilbert and Robert M. Berdahl. New York: Oxford University Press, 1975.

Huntington, Samuel P. *Political Order in Changing Societies.* New Haven, Conn.: Yale University Press, 1969.

———. *The Clash of Civilizations and the Remaking of World Order.* New York: Touchstone Books, 1998.

———. *The Third Wave: Democratization in the Late Twentieth Century.* Norman: University of Oklahoma Press, 1991.

Huyser, Robert E. *Mission to Tehran.* New York: HarperCollins, 1987.

Illich, Ivan. *Deschooling Society.* New York: Penguin Education, 1973.

Irfani, Soroush. *Iran's Islamic Revolution: Popular Liberation or Religious Dictatorship.* London: Zed Books, 1983.

Issawi, Charles. "The Iranian Economy 1925–1975: Fifty Years of Economic Development." In *Iran under the Pahlavis,* ed. George Lenczowski, 129–33. Stanford, Calif.: Hoover Institution Press, 1978.

Jalali-Naini, Ahmad R. "Capital Accumulation and Economic Growth in Iran: Past Experience and Future Prospects." *Iranian Studies* 38, 1 (March 2005): 91–116.

Jazani, Bizhan. *Armed Struggle in Iran.* N.p., 1973.

Johnson, Chalmers. "The Developmental State: Odyssey of a Concept." In *The Developmental State,* ed. Meredith Woo-Cumings, 32–60. Cornell: Cornell University Press, 1999.

Jongi darbareh-ye Zendegi va Asar-e Bijan Jazani: Majmoue'eh-e Maqalat (A Compendium on Bijan Jazani's Life and Works: Collection of Essays). Paris: Editions Khavaran, 1999.

Karimi-Hakkak, Ahmad. "Protest and Perish: A History of the Writers' Association of Iran." *Iranian Studies* 18, 2–4 (Spring–Autumn 1985): 189–229.

Karsh, Efraim. *The Iran-Iraq War, 1980–1988.* London: Osprey, 2002.

Karshenas, Massoud. *Oil, State, and Industrialization in Iran.* New York: Cambridge University Press, 1990.

Karshenas, Massoud, and Hassan Hakimian. "Oil, Economic Diversification and Democratic Process ion Iran." *Iranian Studies* 38, 1 (March 2005): 67–90.

Karshenas, Massoud, and M. Hashem Pesaran. "Exchange Rate Unification, the Role of Markets and Planning in Iranian Economic Reconstruction." In *The Economy of Islamic Iran: Between State and Market,* ed. Thierry Coville, 141–76. Tehran: Institut Français de recherches en Iran, 1994.

Kashani-Sabet, Firoozeh. *Frontier Frictions: Shaping the Iranian Nation, 1804–1946.* Princeton, N.J.: Princeton University Press, 1999.

Kasravi, Ahmad. *Tarikh-e Mashrouteh-ye Iran* (A History of the Iranian Constitutional Movement). 13th ed. Tehran: 2536 [1356]/1978.

Katouzian, Homa. *Musaddiq and the Struggle for Power in Iran.* London: I. B. Tauris, 1990.

———. *The Political Economy of Modern Iran, 1926–79.* New York: New York University Press, 1981.

———. *State and Society in Iran: The Eclipse of the Qajars and the Emergence of Pahlavis.* London: I. B. Tauris, 2001.

———. "The Strange Politics of Khalil Maleki." In *Reformers and Revolutionaries in Modern Iran,* ed. Stephanie Cronin, 165–88. London: RoutledgeCurzon, 2004.

Katzman, Kenneth. *The Warriors of Islam: Iran's Revolutionary Guard.* Boulder, Colo.: Westview Press, 1993.

Kazemi, Farhad. "Fada'iyan-e Islam: Fanaticism, Politics and Terror." *From Nationalism to Revolutionary Islam,* ed. Said A Arjomand, 158–76. Albany: State University of New York Press, 1984.

———. "Urban Migrants and the Revolution." *Iranian Studies* 13, 1–4 (1980): 257–78.

Kazemi Moussavi, Ahmad. "A New Interpretation of the Theory of *Vilayet-i Faqih.*" *Middle Eastern Studies* 28, 1 (January 1992): 101–7.

Keane, John. *Democracy and Civil Society.* New York: Verso, 1988.

Keddie, Nikki R. *Debating Revolutions.* New York: New York University Press, 1995.

———. *An Islamic Response to Imperialism.* Berkeley: University of California Press, 1983.

————. *Religion and Rebellion in Iran: The Iranian Tobacco Protest of 1891–1892.* London: Frank Cass, 1966.

Keddie, Nikki R., and Rudi Mathee, eds. *Iran and the Surrounding World: Interactions in Culture and Cultural Politics.* Seattle: University of Washington Press, 2002.

Keshavarzian, Arang. "Turban or Hat, Seminarian or Soldier: State Building and Clergy Building in Reza Shah's Iran." *Journal of Church and State* 45, 1 (Winter 2003): 81–112.

Khajehpour, Bijan. "Domestic Political Reforms and Private Sector Activity in Iran." *Social Research* 67, 2 (Summer 2000): 577–98.

————. "Iran's Presidential Election: A New Phase in Post-Revolutionary Development." *Muslim Politics Report* 13 (May/June 1997): 1, 6.

Khalatbari, Firouzeh. "A Unique Underground Economy." In *The Economy of Islamic Iran: Between State and Market,* ed. Thierry Coville, 113–38. Tehran: Institut Français de recherches en Iran, 1994.

Khalkhali, Sadeq. *Ayyam Enzeva: Khaterat Ayatollah Khalkhali* (Days of Seclusion: Memoirs of Ayatollah Khalkhali). Tehran: 1378/2000.

Khatami, Seyyed Mohammad. *Az Donya-ye Shahr ta Shahr-e Donya* (From the City's World to the World's City). Tehran: Ney, 1997.

————. *Bim-e Mouj* (Fear of Wave). Tehran: Sazeman-e Chapp va Entesharat-e Vezarat-e Farhang va Ershad-e Eslami, 1372/1993.

————. *Eslam, Rouhaniyyat, va Enqelab-e Islami* (Islam, the Ulama, and the Islamic Revolution). Tehran: Tarh-e Naw, 2000.

Khosrokhavar, Farhad. "Iran's New Intellectuals." *Social Compass* 51, 2 (June 2004): 191–202.

————. *L'islamisme et la mort. Le martyre révolutionnaire en Iran.* Paris: Harmattan, 1995.

————. "Neo-Conservative Intellectuals in Iran." *Critique* 19 (Fall 2001): 5–30.

————. "Nouvelle banlieu et marginalité: la cité Taleghani à Khak-e Sefid" (New Suburbs and Marginality: the Taleqani City of Khak-e Sefid). In *Téhéran:capitale bicentenaire* (Tehran: The Two-Hundred-Year-Old Capital), ed. Bernard Hourcade and Chahryar Adle, 307–27. Paris: Institut français de recherche en Iran, 1992.

Khosrokhavar, Farhad, Shapour Etemad, and Masoud Mehrabi. "Report on Science in Post-Revolutionary Iran," Parts 1 and 2: "Emergence of a Scientific Community?" and "The Scientific Community's Problems of Identity." *Critique: Critical Middle Eastern Studies* 13, 2–3 (Summer, Fall 2004): 209–24, 363–82.

Kian-Thiébaut, Azadeh. "Political and Social Transformation in Post-Islamist Iran." *MERIP* 212 (Fall 1999): 12–16.

Kinzer, Stephen. *All the Shah's Men: An American Coup and the Roots of Middle East Terror.* New York: Wiley, 2003.

Kohli, Atul. *The State and Poverty in India: The Politics of Reform.* New York: Cambridge University Press, 1987.

Kurzman, Charles. "The Qum Protests and the Coming of the Iranian Revolution, 1975 and 1978." *Social Science History* 27, 3 (September 2003): 287–325.

————. *The Unthinkable Revolution in Iran.* Cambridge: Harvard University Press, 2004.

Ladjevardi, Habib, ed. *Memoires of Abdolmadjid Madjidi*. Boston: Iranian Oral History Project, Harvard University, 1998.

———, ed. *Memoires of Ali Amini*. Boston: Iranian Oral History Project, Harvard University, 1995.

———, ed. *Memoires of Mehdi Haeri-Yazdi*. Boston: Iranian Oral History Project, Harvard University, 2001.

Lambton, Ann K. S. *The Persian Land Reform: 1962–66*. Oxford: Clarendon Press, 1969.

———. "Persian Political Societies 1906–11." *St. Antony's Papers*, 16, 3 (London, 1963): 41–89.

———. *Qajar Persia: Eleven Studies*. Austin: University of Texas Press, 1988.

———. "A Reconsideration of the Position of *Marja'-i Taqlid*." *Studia Islamica* 10 (1964): 124–25.

———. *State and Government in Medieval Islam: An Introduction to the Study of Islamic Political Theory of the Jurists*. London: Oxford University Press, 1981.

Levi, Margaret. *Of Rule and Revenue*. Berkeley: University of California Press, 1988.

Lewis, Bernard. *What Went Wrong? The Clash between Islam and Modernity in the Middle East*. New York: Oxford University Press, 2003.

Linz, Juan, and Alfred Stepan. *Problems of Democratic Transition and Consolidation*. Baltimore, Md.: John Hopkins University Press, 1996.

Looney, Robert. *Economic Origins of the Iranian Revolution*. New York: Pergamon Press, 1982.

Lyons, Jonathan, and Geneive Abdo. *Answering Only to God: Faith and Freedom in Twenty-First Century Iran*. New York: Holt & Co., 2003.

Mahdavy, H. "The Patterns and Problems of Economic Development in Rentier States: The Case of Iran." In *Studies in the Economic History of the Middle East: From the Rise of Islam to the Present Day*, ed. M. A. Cook, 428–67. London: Oxford University Press, 1970: 428–67.

Malikzadeh, Mehdi. *Tarikh-e Enqelab-e Mashrutiyat-e Iran* (A History of the Iranian Constitutional Revolution). Tehran, 1351/1972–73.

Maloney, Suzanne. "Agents or Obstacles? Parastatal Foundations and Challenges for Iranian Development." In *The Economy of Iran: Dilemmas of an Islamic State*, ed. Parvin Alizadeh, 145–76. London: I. B. Tauris, 2001.

Mann, Michael. "The Autonomous Power of the State: Its Origins, Mechanisms, and Results." *Archives Européennes de Sociologie* 25, 2 (1984): 185–213.

———. *The Sources of Social Power. Vol. 1 of A History of Power from the Beginning to A.D. 1760*. Cambridge: Cambridge University Press, 1986.

Mannheim, Karl. *Ideology and Utopia: An Introduction to Sociology of Knowledge*. London: Routledge & Kegan Paul, 1968.

Martin, Vanessa. *Creating an Islamic State: Khomeini and the Making of a New Iran*. London: I. B. Tauris, 2003.

———. *Islam and Modernism: The Iranian Revolution of 1906*. Syracuse, N.Y.: Syracuse University Press, 1989.

———. "Shaikh Fazlallah Nuri and the Iranian Revolution of 1905–9." *Middle Eastern Studies* 23, 1 (January 1987): 41–53.

Matin-Asgari, Afshin. *Iranian Student Opposition to the Shah*. Costa Mesa, Calif.: Mazda, 2001.

Mavani, Hamid. "Analysis of Khomeini's Proofs for al-Wilaya al-Mutlaqa (Comprehensive Authority) of the Jurist." In *The Most Learned of the Shi'a: The Institution of Marja' Taqlid*, ed. Linda S. Walbridge, 183–201. New York: Oxford University Press, 2001.

Mawlawi, Ahmad, Mohammad T. Mostafawi, and Ali Shahrukhzadeh. "Astan-e Qods-e Razavi." In *Encyclopedia Iranica*, Vol. 2, ed. Ehsan Yarshater, 826–37. Costa Mesa, Calif.: Mazda, 1987).

McAdam, Doug, John McCarthy, and Mayer Zald, eds. *Comparative Perspectives on Social Movements*. New York: Cambridge University Press, 1996.

McAdam, Doug, Sidney Tarrow, and Charles Tilly. *The Dynamics of Contention*. New York: Cambridge University Press, 2001.

McDaniel, Tim. *Autocracy, Modernization, and Revolution in Russia and Iran*. Princeton: Princeton University Press, 1991.

McFarland, Stephen L. "A Peripheral View of the Origins of the Cold War: The Crisis in Iran, 1941–1947." *Diplomatic History* 4 (Fall 1980): 333–51.

Meadows, Donella H., et al. *The Limits to Growth: A Report for the Club of Rome's Project on the Predicament of Mankind*. New York: Universe Books, 1972.

Menashri, David. *Education and the Making of Modern Iran*. Ithaca, N.Y.: Cornell University Press, 1992.

———. *Iran: A Decade of War and Revolution*. New York: Holmes & Meier, 1990.

———. *Post-Revolutionary Politics in Iran: Religion, Society, and Power*. London: Frank Cass, 2001.

———. "Shi'ite Leadership: In the Shadow of Conflicting Ideologies." *Iranian Studies* 13, 1–4 (1980): 119–46.

———. "Strange Bedfellows: The Khomeini Coalition." *Jerusalem Quarterly* 12 (Summer 1979): 34–48.

Migdal, Joel S. "The State in Society: An Approach to Struggles of Domination." *State Power and Social Forces: Domination and Transformation in the Third World*, ed. Joel S. Migdal, Atul Kohli, and Vivienne Shue, 7–35. New York: Cambridge University Press, 1994.

———. *Strong Societies and Weak States: State-Society Relations and State Capabilities in the Third World*. Princeton, N.J.: Princeton University Press, 1988.

———. "Strong States, Weak States: Power and Accommodation." In *Understanding Political Development*, ed. Samuel P. Huntington and Myron Weiner, 391–434. New York: HarperCollins, 1987.

Milani, Abbas. *The Persian Sphinx: Amir Abbas Hoveyda and the Riddle of the Iranian Revolution*. Washington, D.C.: Mage Publishers, 2003.

Milani, Mohsen M. "The Evolution of the Iranian Presidency: From Bani Sadr to Rafsanjani." *British Journal of Middle Eastern Studies* 2 (1993): 82–89.

———. *The Making of Iran's Islamic Revolution: From Monarchy to Islamic Republic*. 2nd ed. Boulder, Colo.: Westview Press, 1994.

———. "The Transformation of Velayet-e Faqih Institution: From Khomeini to Khamenei." *Muslim World* 82, 2–3 (July–October 1992): 175–90.

Mirsepassi, Ali. *Intellectual Discourse and the Politics of Modernization: Negotiating Modernity in Iran.* New York: Cambridge University Press, 2000.

Mitchell, Timothy. "The Limits of the State: Beyond Statist Approaches and Their Critics." *American Political Science Review* 85, 1 (March 1991): 77–96.

Moaddel, Mansoor. *Class, Politics, and Ideology in the Iranian Revolution.* New York: Columbia University Press, 1993.

———. "Class Struggle in Post-Revolutionary Iran." *International Journal of Middle East Studies* 23, 3 (August 1991): 317–43.

Mofsedin-e fi al-Arz (Polluters of the Earth). Tehran: N.d.

Moghadam, Fatemeh. "State, Political Stability and Property Rights." In *Iran after the Revolution: Crisis of an Islamic State,* ed. Saeed Rahnema and Sohrab Behdad, 45–64. London: I. B. Tauris, 1995.

Moin, Baqer. *Khomeini: Life of the Ayatollah.* London: I. B. Tauris, 1999.

Molavi, Afshin. "Buying Time in Tehran: Iran and the China Model." *Foreign Affairs* 83, 6 (September/October 2004): 9–16.

Moore, Barrington, Jr. *Social Origins of Dictatorship and Democracy: Lord and Peasant in the Making of the Modern World.* Boston: Beacon Press, 1966.

Moslem, Mehdi. *Factional Politicds in Post-Khomeini Iran.* Syracuse, N.Y.: Syracuse University Press, 2002.

Mottahedeh, Roy. *Mantle of the Prophet: Religion and Politics in Iran.* New York: Simon & Shuster, 1985.

Mozaffari, Mehdi. *Fatwa: Violence and Discourtesy.* Aarhus: Aarhus University Press, 1998.

———. "Revolutionary, Thermidorian, and Enigmatic Foreign Policy." *International Relations* 14, 5 (1999): 9–28.

Mozakerat-e Majles dar Dowreh-ye Avval-e Taqniniyeh-ye Majles-e Showra-ye Melli (Proceedings of the First Majles). Introduction by Said Nafisi., Tehran: Ketab Khaneh-ye Ibn Sina, 1334/1966.

Mutahhari, Murtaza. *Fundamentals of Islamic Thought: God, Man, and the Universe.* Translated from the Persian by R. Campbell, with annotations and an introduction by Hamid Algar. Berkeley, Calif.: Mizan Press, 1985.

Najmabadi, Afsaneh. "Depoliticization of a Rentier State: The Case of Pahlavi Iran." *The Rentier State,* ed. Hazem Beblawi and Giacorno Luciani, 211–27. London: Croom Helm, 1987.

———. *Land Reform and Social Change in Iran.* Salt Lake City: University of Utah Press, 1987.

Nashat, Guity. "Women in the Ideology of the Islamic Republic." In *Women and the Revolution in Iran,* ed. Guity Nashat, 195–216. Boulder, Colo.: Westview, 1983.

Nasr, Seyyed Vali Reza. "Democracy and Islamic Revivalism." *Political Science Quarterly* 110, 2 (Summer 1995): 261–85.

———. "European Colonialism and the Emergence of Modern Muslim States." In *The Oxford History of Islam,* ed. John L. Esposito, 549–99. New York: Oxford University Press, 1999.

———. "Ideology and Institutions in Islamist Approaches to Public Policy." *International Review of Comparative Public Policy* 9 (1997): 41–67.

————. *Mawdudi and the Making of Islamic Revivalism.* New York: Oxford University Press, 1996.

————. "Military Rule, Islamism, and Democracy in Pakistan." *Middle East Journal* 58, 2 (Spring 2004): 195–209.

————. "Politics within the Late-Pahlavi State: The Ministry of Economy and Industrial Policy, 1963–1969." *International Journal of Middle East Studies* 32, 1 (February 2000): 97–122.

————. "Religious Modernism in the Arab World, India, and Iran: The Perils and Prospects of a Discourse." *Muslim World* 83, 1 (January 1993): 20–47.

————. "The Rise of 'Muslim Democracy.' " *Journal of Democracy* 16, 2 (April 2005): 13–27.

Nordlinger, Eric. "Taking the State Seriously." In *Understanding Political Development*, ed. Samuel P. Huntington and Myron Weiner, 353–90. New York: HarperCollins, 1987.

Norton, Augustus Richard. *Civil Society in the Middle East.* 2 vols. Leiden: E. J. Brill, 1996.

Nove, Alec. "War Communism." In *The Blackwell Encyclopedia of the Russian Revolution*, 2nd ed., ed. Harold Shukman, 148–150. Oxford: Blackwell, 1994.

Nowshirvani, Vahid, and Patrick Clawson. "The State and Social Equity in Postrevolutionary Iran." *The Politics of Social transformation in Afghanistan, Iran and Pakistan,* ed. Myron Weiner and Ali Banuazizi, 228–69. Syracuse, N.Y.: Syracuse University Press, 1994.

Nuri, Shaykh Fadl Allah. "Book of Admonition to the Heedless and Guidance for the Ignorant" (*Kitab Tadhikart al-Ghafil va Irshad al-Jahil*). Translated and edited by Hamid Dabasi. In *Authority and Political Culture in Shi'ism,* ed. Said A. Arjomand, 354–70. Albany: State University of New York Press, 1988.

Önis, Ziya. "The Logic of the Developmental State." *Comparative Politics* 24, 1 (October 1991): 109–26.

Parsa, Misagh. *Social Origins of the Iranian Revolution.* New Brunswick, N.J.: Rutgers University Press, 1989.

Parsons, Anthony. *The Pride and the Fall: Iran, 1974–1979.* London: Jonathan Cape, 1984.

Pesaran, H. "Economic Planning and Revolutionary Upheavals in Iran." In *Iran: A Revolution in Turmoil,* ed. Haleh Afshar, 15–50. Albany: State University of New York Press, 1985.

Przeworski, Adam. *Democracy and the Market: Political and Economic Reforms in Eastern Europe and Latin America.* New York: Cambridge University Press, 1991.

————. *Sustainable Democracy.* New York: Cambridge University Press, 1995.

Rabi'i, Ali. *Negah be Jame'e-Shenasi-ye Tahavvolat-e Arzeshi* (An Overview of Sociology of Transformation in Values). Tehran: Farhang va Andisheh, 1997.

Rahnema, Ali. *An Islamic Utopian: A Political Biography of Ali Shariati.* London: I. B. Tauris, 2000.

Rahnema, Ali, and Farhad Nomani. *The Secular Miracle: Religion, Politics, and Economic Policy in Iran.* London: Zed Books, 1990.

Rahnema, Saeed. "Continuity and Change in Industrial Policy." In *Iran after the Revolution: Crisis of An Islamic State,* ed. Saeed Rahnema and Sohrab Behdad, 129–49. London: I. B. Tauris, 1995.

Rajaee, Farhang. "A Thermidor of 'Islamic Yuppies': Conflict and Compromise in Iran's Politics." *Middle East Journal* 53, 2 (Spring 1999): 217–31.

Ram, Haggay. "Crushing the Opposition: Adversaries of the Islamic Republic of Iran." *Middle East Journal* 46, 3 (Summer 1992): 426–39.

———. *Myth and Mobilization in Revolutionary Iran: The Use of the Friday Congregational Sermon.* Washington, D.C.: American University Press, 1994.

Ramazani, Rouhollah K. *The Foreign Policy of Iran, 1500–1941: A Developing Nation in World Affairs.* Charlottesville: University of Virginia Press, 1966.

———. "Iran: The 'Islamic Cultural Revolution.'" In *Change and the Muslim World,* ed. Phillip Stoddard, David Cuthell, and Margaret Sullivan, 40–48. Syracuse, N.Y.: Syracuse University Press, 1981.

———. *Revolutionary Iran: Challenge and Response in the Middle East.* Baltimore: Johns Hopkins University Press, 1988.

Rashidi, Ali. "The Process of De-Privatisation." In *The Economy of Islamic Iran: Between State and Market,* ed. Thierry Coville, 37–68. Tehran: Institut Français de recherches en Iran, 1994.

Rezai, Ahmad. *Nehzat-e Hosseini* (Hossein's Movement). Tehran: Sazman-e Mojehadin-e Khalq-e Iran, 1976.

Richard, Yann. "Ayatollah Kashani: Precursor of the Islamic Republic?" In *Religion and Politics in Iran: Shi'ism from Quietism to Revolution,* ed. Nikki Keddie, 121–24. New Haven, Conn.: Yale University Press, 1983.

———. "L'Organization des Feda'iyan-e eslam, mouvement integriste musulman en Iran (1945–1956). In *Radicalismes islamiques,* Vol. 1, ed. O. Carre and P. Dumont, 23–82. Paris: L'Harmattan, 1985.

———. "Shari'at Sangalaji: A Reformist Theologian of the Rida Shah Period. In *Authority and Political Culture in Shi'ism,* ed. Said Amir Arjomand, 159–77. Albany: State University of New York Press, 1988.

———. *Shi'ite Islam.* Cambridge: Blackwell, 1995.

Roosevelt, Kermit. *Countercoup.* New York: McGraw-Hill, 1979.

Roy, Olivier. "The Crisis of Religious Legitimacy in Iran." *Middle East Journal* 53, 2 (Spring 1999): 201–16.

Sachedina, Abdulaziz. *Islamic Messianism: The Idea of the Mahdi in Twelver Shi'ism.* Albany: State University of New York Press, 1981.

———. *Islamic Roots of Democratic Pluralism.* New York: Oxford University Press, 2001.

———. *The Just Ruler (Al-Sultan Al-Adil) in Shi'ite Islam: The Comprehensive Authority of the Jurist in Imamite Jurisprudence.* New York: Oxford University Press, 1988.

Sadri, Mahmoud. "Sacral Defense of Secularism: The Political Theologies of Soroush, Shabestari, and Kadivar." *International Journal of Politics, Culture, and Society* 15, 2 (December 2001): 257–70.

Salamat, Azar. "Of Chance and Choice." In *Women in Exile,* ed. Mahnaz Afkhami, 78–99. Charlottesville: University of Virginia Press, 1994.

Salehi-Isfahani, Djavad. "Human Resources in Iran: Potentials and Challenges." *Iranian Studies* 38, 1 (March 2005): 117–47.

———. "The Oil Sector after the Revolution." In *Iran after the Revolution: Crisis of an Islamic State,* ed. Saeed Rahnema and Sohrab Behdad, 150–73. London: I. B. Tauris, 1995.

Salehi Najafabadi, Nematollah. *Tote'eh-ye Shah bar Zedd-e Imam Khomeini* (Shah's Conspiracy against Imam Khomeini). Tehran: Moassesse-ye Khadamat-e Farhangi-ye Rasa, 1361/1984.

Salinger, Pierre. *America Held Hostage: The Secret Negotiations.* New York: Doubleday, 1981.

Sanjabi, Karim. *Omidha va Na-Omidiha: Khaterat-e Siyasi Doktor Karim Sanjabi* (Hopes and Disappointments: The Political Memoirs of Dr. Karim Sanjabi). London: n.p., 1989.

Sarab-e Sazandegi: Didgahha-ye Enteqadi Dar Bare-ye Amalkard-e Hasht-Sale-ye Dowlat-e Hashemi Rafsanjani (The Mirage of Development: Critical Perspectives on the Record of the Eight Year Government of Hashemi Rafsanjani). Tehran: Rozname-ye Salaam, 1378/1998.

Sarabi, Farzin. "The Post-Khomeini Era in Iran: The Elections of the Fourth Islamic Majles." *Middle East Journal* 48, 1 (Winter 1994): 89–107.

Schirazi, Asghar. *The Constitution of Iran: Politics and the State in the Islamic Republic.* London: I. B. Tauris, 1997.

———. *The Islamic Development Policy: The Agrarian Question in Iran.* Boulder, Colo.: Lynne Reinner, 1993.

Shambayati, Hootan. "A Tale of Two Mayors: Courts and Politics in Iran and Turkey." *International Journal of Middle East Studies* 36, 2 (May 2004): 253–75.

Shariati, Ali. *Man and Islam.* Translated by Fatollah Marjani. Houston, Tex: FILINC, n.d.

———. *Red Shi'ism.* London: n.p., 1979.

———. *Shia* (Shi'ism). London: MAS, 1979.

Shayegan, Daryush. *Qu'est-ce qu'une révolution religieuse?* (What Is a Religious Revolution?) Paris: Albin Michel, 1991.

Siavoshi, Sussan. *Liberal Nationalism in Iran: The Failure of a Movement.* Boulder, Colo.: Westview Press, 1990.

Sick, Gary. *All Fall Down: America's Tragic Encounter with Iran.* New York: Penguin Books, 1986.

Skocpol, Theda. "Rentier State and Shi'a Islam in the Iranian Revolution." *Theory and Society* 11, 3 (May 1982): 265–83.

———. *States and Social Revolutions: A Comparative Analysis of France, Russia, and China.* New York: Cambridge University Press, 1979.

Smith, Benjamin. "Collective Action with or without Islam: Mobilizing the Bazaar in Iran." In *Islamic Activism: A Social Movement Theory Approach,* ed. Quintan Wicktorowicz, 185–204. Bloomington: Indiana University Press, 2004.

Smith, Tony. *Thinking Like a Communist: State and Legitimacy in the Soviet Union, China, and Cuba.* New York: W. W. Norton, 1987.

Sorensen, Georg. "War and Security-Making: Why Doesn't It Work in the Third World." *Security Dialogue* 32, 3 (2001): 341–54.

Soroush, Abdol-Karim. *Modara va Modiriyat* (Tolerance and Administration). Tehran: Serat, 1997.

————. *Reason, Freedom, and Democracy in Islam*. Edited and translated by Mahmoud Sadri and Ahmad Sadri. New York: Oxford University Press, 2000.

Stepan, Alfred. *Arguing Comparative Politics*. New York: Oxford University Press, 2001.

————. *The State and Society: Peru in Comparative Perspective*. Princeton, N.J.: Princeton University Press, 1978.

Summitt, April R. "For a White Revolution: John F. Kennedy and the Shah of Iran." *Middle East Journal* 58, 4 (Autumn 2004): 560–75.

Taheri, Amir. *Nest of Spies: America's Journey to Disaster in Iran*. London: Hutchinson, 1988.

Takeyh, Ray, and Nikolas K. Gvosdev. "Pragmatism in the Midst of Iranian Turmoil." *Washington Quarterly* (Autumn 2004): 33–56.

Taleqani, Seyyed Mahmoud. *Az azadi ta shahadat* (From Freedom to Martyrdom). Tehran, n.d.

————. *Islam and Ownership*. Translated by Ahmad Jabbari and Farhang Rajaee. Lexington, Ky.: Mazda, 1983.

————. *Jahad va Shahadat* (Jihad and Martyrdom). Tehran: n.d.

Tarrow, Sidney. *Power in Movement: Social Movements and Contentious Politics*. New York: Cambridge University Press, 1998.

Tilly, Charles. "Reflections on the History of European State-Making." *The Formation of National States in Western Europe*, ed. Charles Tilly, 3–84. Princeton, N.J.: Princeton University Press, 1975.

————. "War Making and State Making as Organized Crime." In *Bringing the State back In*, ed. Peter Evans, Dietrich Rueschmeyer, and Theda Skocpol, 169–91. New York: Cambridge University Press, 1985.

Trimberger, Ellen. *Revolution from Above: Military Bureaucrats and Development in Japan, Turkey, Egypt, and Peru*. New Brunswick, N.J.: Transaction Books, 1978.

Turner, Bryan S. *The Talcott Parsons Reader*. Boston: Blackwell, 1999.

Vahdat, Farzin. *God and Juggernaut: Iran's Intellectual Encounter with Modernity*. Syracuse, N.Y.: Syracuse University Press, 2002.

————. "Post-Revolutionary Discourses of Mohammad Mojtahed Shabestari and Mohsen Kadivar." *Critique* 16 (2000): 31–45; and 17 (2000): 135–57.

Vakili, Valla. "Abdolkarim Soroush and the Critical Discourse in Iran." In *Makers of Contemporary Islam*, ed. John Esposito and John Voll, 150–76. New York: Oxford University Press, 2001.

Van Creveld, Martin. *The Rise and Decline of the State*. New York: Cambridge University Press, 1999.

Viorst, Milton. "The Limits of the Revolution: Changing Iran." *Foreign Affairs* 74, 6 (November/December 1995): 63–76.

Wade, Robert. *Governing the Market: The Theory and the Role of Government in East Asian Industrialization*. Princeton, N.J.: Princeton University Press, 1990.

Wilber, Donald. "Clandestine Service History: Overthrow of Premier Mossadeq of Iran, November 1952–August 1953." National Security Archive, Electronic Briefling Book, No. 28. Available at http://www.gwu.edu/~nsarchiv/NSAEBB/NSAEBB28/#documents.

———. *Riza Shah Pahlavi: The Resurrection and Reconstruction of Iran.* Hicksville, N.Y.: Exposition Press, 1975.

Wright, Sir Denis. *Britain and Iran, 1790–1980: Collected Essays of Sir Denis Wright.* London: Iran Society, 2003.

Yazdi, Ebrahim. *Akharin Talash-ha dar Akharin Rouzha* (Last Efforts in the Last Days). Tehran: Roshdieh, 1987.

Young, Crawford. *The African Colonial State in Comparative Perspective.* New Haven, Conn.: Yale University Press, 1994.

Zabih, Sepehr. *The Communist Movement in Iran.* Berkeley: University of California Press, 1966.

———. *The Mossadegh Era.* Chicago: Lake View Press, 1982.

Zirinsky, Michael. "Imperial Power and Dictatorship: Britain and the Rise of Reza Shah, 1921–1926." *International Journal of Middle East Studies* 24, 4 (November 1992): 639–63.

Zonis, Marvin. *Majestic Failure: The Fall of the Shah.* Chicago: University of Chicago Press, 1991.

Index